THE
ENLIGHTENED
MOM

Also by Terri Amos-Britt

Books

Message Sent: Retrieving the Gift of Love

Audio

The Enlightened Mom Meditations

Message Sent: Meditations for Retrieving the Gift of Love

All products are available at www.TheEnlightenedMom.com.

THE ENLIGHTENED MOM

A Mother's Guide for Bringing
Peace, Love & Light to Your Family's Life

Terri Amos-Britt

WorldofLite Publishing

Grateful acknowledgement is made to the following for permission to reprint previously published material: Arthur Samuel Joseph for *Vocal Power: Harnessing the Power Within*. Copyright 2001. * Beyond Words Publishing, Inc. for *Raising Everyday Heroes: Parenting Children to be Self-Reliant* by Dr. Elisa Medhus. Copyright 2004. * Brown Books Publishing Group for *Row, Row, Row Your Boat: A Guide for Living Life in the Divine Flow* by Steven Lane Taylor. Copyright 2004. * Centerpointe Research Institute for *Thresholds of the Mind: Your Personal Roadmap to Success, Happiness and Contentment* by Bill Harris. Copyright 2002. * Hay House Inc. for *Ask and It Is Given: Learning to Manifest Your Desires (The Teachings of Abraham)* by Jerry and Esther Hicks. Copyright 2004. * Hay House Inc. for *Power vs. Force: The Hidden Determinants of Human Behavior* by Dr. David R. Hawkins. Copyright 2002. * Hay House, Inc. for *You Can Heal Your Life* by Louise L. Hay. Copyright 1999. * Hazelden Foundation for *Beyond Co-dependency: And Getting Better All the Time* by Melody Beattie. Copyright 1989. * Heartways Press, Inc. for *Love Without Conditions: Reflections of the Christ Mind* by Paul Ferrini. Copyright 1995. * Llewellyn Worldwide, Ltd for *Animal Speak: The Spiritual & Magical Powers of Creatures Great and Small* by Ted Andrews. Copyright 2002. * New World Library for *Creating True Prosperity* by Shakti Gawain. Copyright 1997. * New World Library for *The Life You Were Born to Live: A Guide to Finding Your Life Purpose* by Dan Millman. Copyright 1993. * Scriptures taken from the *HOLY BIBLE, NEW INTERNATIONAL VERSION*. Copyright 1973, 1978, 1984, by International Bible Society. Used by permission of Zondervan Publishing House. All rights reserved. * The Career Press, Inc. for *The Power of Your Other Hand: A Course in Channeling the Inner Wisdom of the Right Brain* by Lucia Capacchione, Ph.D. Copyright 2001.

The stories that appear in this book are true. Permission has been generously granted for stories to be published. The names of all Enlightened Mom students and clients have been changed to protect privacy, as well as some of the friends' names mentioned.

Published by WorldofLite Publishing
A division of Enlightened Family Institute, Inc.
Destin, FL

For information about bulk book sales, contact:
sales@TheEnlightenedMom.com

Library of Congress Control Number: 2011926740

Library of Congress Cataloguing-in-Publication-Data
The Enlightened Mom:
A Mother's Guide for Bringing Peace, Love & Light to Your Family's Life

ISBN 0-9719694-3-4

www.TheEnlightenedMom.com

*This book is dedicated with gratitude
and love to my mom, Lee Utley,
and to the many moms who
have touched my life.*

CONTENTS

FOREWORD
by Marci Shimoff

*T*here is nothing more important in the world of motherhood than the example you set for your children. And the most valuable example you can set is that of love and inner happiness.

Congratulations! You're taking an extraordinary step towards helping your children by reading *The Enlightened Mom*. In this book, Terri Amos-Britt shows you how to heal your life, helping you become a more joyful, loving mom. I've personally experienced Terri's work and it is absolutely life-transforming!

Over the last 20 years, I've spoken in front of hundreds of thousands about my books, *Happy for No Reason, Love for No Reason*, and the *Chicken Soup for the Mother's Soul* series. Through this work, I've seen how people's lives change for the better when they make a decision to heal. In *The Enlightened Mom*, Terri offers you a breakthrough approach to healing that will enable you to become a role model of happiness and love for your children.

It's clear—your children pick up your habits. If you have a habit of denying yourself, of giving to others and not giving to yourself, then your children are unconsciously learning this from you. But if you have habits that are supportive of happiness and self-love, your kids will learn those. You can't teach your children habits that you don't have.

While most teachings about motherhood focus on the behaviors of the children and how to handle those behaviors, Terri's approach to motherhood is different. She knows that what's primary to being a great mom is your relationship with yourself. In this book, Terri focuses on where the real power lies: your ability to heal yourself and create a wonderful relationship within. This approach is unique and spot on.

Terri has both the wisdom and the experience to be your guide. This comes from a deep knowingness, her own experiences of motherhood, and the results of The Enlightened Mom classes she's been teaching over the past decade. Along with offering profound concepts of healing, Terri provides the most effective tools and techniques available. With these, any mother can create fast and lasting changes in her life and home. I believe in Terri's processes 100%. I've seen miracles happen with her work.

I often hear moms ask, "Am I being selfish to want to take care of myself?" In fact, it's the least selfish thing you can do. Because when you take care of yourself, when you heal yourself and are whole inside, you are influencing your family, your community and ultimately the world. This Chinese Proverb says it best:

When there is light in the soul, there will be beauty in the person.
When there is beauty in the person, there will be harmony in the house.
When there is harmony in the house, there will be order in the nation.
When there is order in the nation, there will be peace in the world.

~~~~~

A MESSAGE
FROM TERRI...

elcome to *The Enlightened Mom*! You are about to embark on a journey that will not only heal your life, but will set the tone for your family to heal, too. As you absorb the information that I'm about to share with you, and do the exercises and meditations given, you will see that you, Mom, have the power to create a life of peace, abundance and joy. This is the greatest gift you will ever give your family. But it starts with you claiming that power! You are making that choice today by stepping onto the path of The Enlightened Mom.

The Enlightened Mom is a book that provides information and tools to heal and transform your life. I have also recorded *The Enlightened Mom Meditations*, a powerful series of 25 guided meditations that work hand-in-hand with the information in each chapter of this book. These meditations allow you to quickly and easily move past the negative programming of your mind, to access the wisdom and love of your heart.

Throughout this book, I will explain the different meditations and how they are done. Simply follow the book and, when prompted, go to the specific CD mentioned to deepen your healing. The first meditation, as seen in Chapter 1, is *Set an Intention*. This meditation is available for free as my special "thank you" for stepping onto this path. Visit www.TheEnlightenedMom.com/freemeditation to download it now. You will also find a link there to purchase the entire series of meditations.

I would also like to invite you to join us in The Enlightened Mom global community, a healing space created to celebrate and support you. Connect with me personally, as well as with moms from around the world, who are taking a stand for healing. Our community is free to join and members receive 25% off of many Enlightened Mom products. And while there, check out The Enlightened Mom Book Club. Be a part of our online club or see how to create your own. Go to www.TheEnlightenedMom.com/global-community to learn more about the many benefits of being an Enlightened Mom!

Thank you for being here, Mom, because when you heal, your family heals…the world heals!

With love and light!

~Terri Amos-Britt
Destin, FL

Love is the answer.
It is always the key.
It breaks down the walls
Between you and me.

Love is abundant.
It's not far from sight.
Ask to receive it
And you'll be led to the light.

For the light is within
Both you and me.
It tells the truth
Of who we can be.

It's ours to remember.
It's why we're here.
Turn to love
And there is no fear.

For God has not given us the spirit of fear,
but of power, love and a sound mind.

II TIMOTHY 1:7

INTRODUCTION

Stepping onto the Path

om, I know you want the best for your family. I get how much you love them. I am a mom like you. I understand what it's like to love your family so much that you'll do just about anything for them. I also know that in your effort to be the best mom you can be, you deny your needs.

You've probably picked up this book believing there is something else you "must do" for your family to make them happy. Wrong! The only thing I'm inviting you to do is to create a connection to your heart, finally loving, honoring and embracing the way God made you. And as you do, you become a more loving mom.

You are of value. You are special and unique. If you don't know this, it's because you are living from false beliefs that say you're not good enough simply for being you. You don't have to be the best mom. This drive is what makes you so frustrated with your life. All you have to do is embrace the unique lovable you and allow that love to overflow to your family. This is the greatest gift you can give your loved ones: setting an example of peace, light and love for everyone! Most of us don't know this truth, so we continue to deny how we were created, shutting down our hearts, our passions and our dreams. And as a result, we slowly die within.

~~~~~~

"Debbie has been in a terrible car accident. She's in the hospital and they don't believe she'll make it through the night."

I'll never forget the night I received that call. My best friend from my old high school days was about to die.

"Why, God? Why did this happen to Deb?" I prayed. "I don't get it. She's a mom with three kids, trying so hard to make life work. She's had a rough time over the years and now life has been pretty good for her. Why?"

I didn't get an answer immediately. I waited thousands of miles away for any news that might tell me something.

"She was out looking for one of her kids, Terri." Another old friend shared this message with me over the phone. "She was concerned about him and was sitting at a stop sign about to pull out when she picked up her cell phone. She wasn't watching. She pulled out and didn't see the truck coming over the hill. It T-boned her on her driver's side door. They had to cut her out of the car."

Would Debbie make it? I was scared to death for her. I was scared for me, too. I couldn't stop crying.

I flashed back to a few years prior to Debbie's accident. I spent some time in Arkansas and, as a result, got to see Debbie. Deb was doing well then. She was fairly content. She had a terrific job. And she was doing well financially. The only problem she struggled with was trying to do everything "right" for her kids.

Deb never felt truly loved and accepted growing up. She didn't believe she was good enough to be loved. That's why she worked so hard as a mother. She wanted to make sure her kids were happier than she had been. She ran herself ragged filled with guilt, trying to make everything perfect for her family. She believed that by giving herself up, they would feel loved and, thus, would be saved from the past pain she had experienced.

The night Debbie had her car wreck, she was scattered. She was worried and alone, and if I were to guess, felt quite out of control. Trying to save one of her children is what almost killed Debbie that night. Thankfully, she lived.

Debbie's accident is a mirror for what we do as mothers. We try to create perfect lives for our kids, believing this will bring them happiness. We give ourselves up to the point of losing ourselves, believing this will make them feel loved. I believe that's why I cried so much the night of Debbie's accident. Of course, I was sad and terribly worried for her. But I knew in my heart there was more. I was crying for my own life. I was crying for all of the times I had let myself down out of a need to "save" my family from possible pain. I knew that by doing everything for them, I was slowly dying within. Debbie did the same.

Debbie's accident reflected how she lived her life. In her zest to be a good mom, she almost lost herself. She lived in fear. Her concerns were about making money, getting her kids to classes, and making sure that they had all of the opportunities she didn't.

Just like Debbie, we mommas want the best for our kids. But for most of us, this desire is based in the subconscious societal belief that says abundance comes from the things you own, the accomplishments you achieve, how you look, whether you're good or bad, or the amount of money you have. This belief says that life is a competition and we must perform to get ahead. So we mommas perform for our families, trying to do everything "right," hoping they might experience more abundance than we had. True abundance, however, doesn't come from other people's approval, accomplishments or material things. It comes when you say "YES!" to your heart and open up to the love within.

Mom, you create real abundance when you get completely connected to who you are and the way you were created. You do this by taking responsibility for your own happiness, accepting and loving yourself, and letting go of past beliefs that say you aren't good enough just for being you. You release the need to have others' approval. You value the real you.

True abundance is when you trust yourself enough to release the controls of your life and surrender to the messages in your heart, creating a connection to God. It is in this connection that you discover the love you've always wanted. And as you do this for yourself, you become an example for everyone else.

God created each and every one of us as unique beings. Each of us has a purpose. That purpose is to be an expression of love and to share that gift with the world around us. THIS is abundance. But when we live by the belief that says we must deny ourselves to be good mothers, we lose our connections. We deny ourselves believing this is the best gift we can give our families. This is a lie. The best gift you will ever give your loved ones is to go within and find your heart. This is where God lives. This is where peace, abundance and love reside.

I went into the American Automobile Association one day to get my car registration. As I walked up to the counter a young woman stood before me to take care of my paperwork. I asked her how she was doing. This was her response, "I'm exhausted and counting the minutes until five o'clock."

"Oh, have you had a bad day?" I asked.

"I'm just tired," she said. "I'm the mother of four kids and they are wearing me down. There are so many things to take care of. Whew! I'm really tired."

"Hmmm," I said. "May I give you a little advice? I'm a spiritual coach and I just happen to be writing a book about this."

As she nodded her head yes, I shared with her this simple truth, "You cannot make your kids happy. People have to choose to do this for themselves. If you live your life running on empty doing everything for everyone else, you will take out your resentments on them whether you want to or not. Your anger and sadness will overflow to everyone you love. Your life will be filled with knee-jerk reactions causing you great guilt and shame. When you give up your own happiness, you are an example for your kids to grow up and do the same. However, when you take care of your needs first and fill your cup up with love, that love will overflow to everyone else. Your life will be an example for your kids to grow up and love themselves. Your family will get the very best of love when you first find it within yourself."

"Wow!" she said. "Why hasn't anyone ever told me that before? It makes a lot of sense."

"Well," I responded, "you probably didn't have a good role model to learn from. Most moms don't live by this belief."

"You're right. My mom was an alcoholic," she added. "I grew up having to take care of her and the rest of my family. I'm not the way my mom was, but I'm still struggling. I don't do anything for myself."

I understood her thinking completely. No matter what your childhood was like, whether or not you had a mom, if your main caregiver didn't take care of his or her own needs then you are most likely not taking care of your needs. Your parent's or caretaker's example has been handed down to you and, thus, you remain disconnected from your heart. You've been ingrained with the belief that says to take time for yourself is selfish. True selfishness, however, is when you don't love and honor the way you were created. Take the time to get to know yourself and follow your heart. Living from your heart creates a connection and puts God first.

When you take time to love and honor the way you were created, you put God first.

God speaks to you via the messages in your heart. These messages guide you and help you create the abundant life you crave. But to listen to those messages, you must slow down and get to know who you really are. We mommas don't tend to do this. Instead, we continue to deny ourselves, shutting down to God's guidance and love. When you finally love yourself enough to open up and receive this kind of abundance, you will become a light for all those you love.

My paperwork was done with the young woman, as well as my mission. I knew God had put me before her to help her heal. She said her good-byes and added, "I'm so glad I called your name today."

"Me, too," I said, and then added one last thought, "The key is for you to give yourself PERMISSION to love yourself, creating a connection to God in your heart. You are the creator of your life. This is your choice and the greatest gift you will ever give your children." And with that, she smiled, stepping onto the path of The Enlightened Mom.

The path of The Enlightened Mom is an adventure to your heart. It takes you straight to God. It doesn't matter what your religious beliefs are, what color you are, or where you're from, this path will teach you how to open up and connect to God's love. Our egos tell us lies of how we "must be" to experience love. Our hearts tell us the truth: the love has always been there. It's inside of you.

All throughout this book I will talk about God. I believe our ultimate goal as humans is to move out of ego and reconnect to God. This is why we are here. I am a Christian by faith. However, what I was told as a child is different from what I believe now. I grew up believing that God's kingdom is somewhere outside of us and that we have to perform to get there. "The Kingdom of God is within you." (Luke 17:21) This is what Christ told us and why I believe he was sent here. He exemplified union with God. Christ showed us how to find that connection to God within ourselves. When you connect to your heart, you live as Christ did. You become an example of kindness, compassion, forgiveness and love.

The path of The Enlightened Mom moves you out of ego where there is always fear and a need to control. It guides you to trust, resting in the knowingness that you are not alone. The path of The Enlightened Mom is one filled with miracles and abundance. As you read through this book, you will see miracle after miracle that happened in my life. Some were small; some will make your jaw drop. This is what happens when you align your head with your heart and allow God to be the guide. You realize that God truly IS your protector and provider.

If you're ready to create this kind of life, Mom, I invite you to dive within. Do all of the exercises in this book. And when guided, go to The Enlightened Mom Meditation CDs to deepen your healing. Allow yourself to open up to the love within. Your life is going to change and so will your family's. You will be amazed at what you discover!

If you really want to have fun on this journey, do it with a friend or a small group of women that you care about and love. Create a book club and at your gatherings, go over what you've learned from each chapter. Share, laugh, and cry. Open up your hearts. Be intimate with one another.

I have five close friends with whom I've shared my journey. They are my spiritual buddies. We each do it a little differently, but nonetheless we all live our lives creating a connection to God. To be able to learn from one another and celebrate each other's miracles together has been one of the greatest gifts of my life. This is what is so special about this path: you no longer feel the need to compete with others, seeing who is best. When you live from the belief that each of us is perfect just the way we were created and that we all are traveling our own unique paths then there is no need to compete. Instead, you love and celebrate one another.

The tools in this book will change your life forever. Barb, one of my oldest friends, told me one day that my life had changed so much over the years that people I know now wouldn't recognize me if they had a glimpse of my life back then. It was filled with anger, resentment and blame when we first met. Of course there was a loving, kind side to me, but the pain sat right beneath the surface. It made me somewhat hot-headed and a control freak. My pain stemmed from a lack of loving myself.

Most people would never imagine that I disliked myself back then. My life was filled with accomplishments and success. I even won the title of Miss USA in 1982. But in that moment of winning, there was only emptiness. I was driven by a deep desire to experience love and acceptance, but didn't find it there. I continued my search as a host in the television industry. My search failed. That's when I let my career go and made a choice to become a mom. What I soon discovered, however, is that my need for love was still there. I had a standard in my mind of what a good mom should be. I wanted the best for my family so they would be happy. But deep down, I wanted to do things right so they would love and accept me. I lived by a set of rules that controlled my life and told me how I "must be" to receive love. I was miserable. I truly believed that love was a reward you received by doing things right or by being best. These rules not only affected my life, but also made me want to control everything around me, especially my kids.

I took a good look at my family dynamics and realized that I was putting the same negative beliefs on my kids as I put on myself. Each rooted in the false societal belief that says love comes from the outside world, not from within.

Then it hit me. I thought I was protecting my family by impressing my beliefs on them of how you "must be" to receive love. I truly believed this equated to being a great mom. But instead of protecting them, I now knew I was handing my pain down to my kids. That's when I made a decision to go within and heal.

Thankfully, my life changed when I got to know who I really am. I quit performing for love and released the rules and negative beliefs that drove me and kept me from being the loving, dynamic person God created me to be. As I let go, I found my heart and created a connection to God. Finally, I discovered the love I had been searching for my whole life.

Mom, you are about to learn the tools that I used to rid the negative programming from my life. I am not the same person I used to be. As I have walked this path and used the tools that I'm about to share with you, I have healed. And, as a result, my family has healed. Our communication has grown. And where there was once judgment, blame and a need to control, there is now abundance and love. So whether you want to travel this journey by yourself or with a friend, it doesn't matter. What does matter is that you open up and celebrate who you are! It's time to create a connection to your heart and step onto the path of The Enlightened Mom.

~~~~~

Enlightened:
Having knowledge and spiritual insight;
freed from illusion

PART I

Create A Connection

CHAPTER 1

Open Up to Receive Love

om, what's your life like right now? Do you feel joyous and alive? Do you get up each day filled with passion and purpose, and a smile on your face? Or do you wake up feeling tired and overwhelmed as if it's time to hit the floor racing again? My guess is that if you're picking up this book, your answer is closer to the latter one. Have you ever asked yourself why you constantly feel as if you're racing?

Maybe your issue isn't about racing, but rather about feeling angry or frustrated with your family situation. Why do you feel this way? I have an answer for you. You feel this way because you're not listening to your heart; you've disconnected from God.

As mothers, our greatest desire is for our children to grow up and have abundant lives. We want them to have an abundance of love, an abundance of success, an abundance of peace and happiness. We do everything for our kids, believing that the more we do for them and the more we teach them that they will have these things. As a result, we deny ourselves. We become rundown, angry, resentful, or frustrated and often take out our pain on them. Don't you hate it when you lash out and get angry with your kids, especially when you have knee-jerk reactions and don't know why?

Are you married? What's happening with that relationship? Is it happy and alive? Or do you feel some underlying resentment and think about running for the hills? Are you speaking your feelings and saying what you need? Or do you stuff everything in out of an old belief that says, "If I say what I feel, I might be rejected and lose my spouse's love?"

If any of these issues resonate with you, you may be living from a belief that says, "It is my responsibility to make my family feel happy and loved. Therefore, I must deny my thoughts and feelings to be a good wife and mother."

I know you want to be the best you can be for your family, and I know that you believe your actions are loving, but in truth, they aren't. When you don't say what you need, when you don't set boundaries, or when you don't respect and love yourself and follow the passion in your heart, your actions send a message to your loved ones that says, "You must perform to be loved. You must deny who you are and how you were created to make others happy. And by making others happy, only then will you receive love."

We have been ingrained with the belief that says love comes from the outside world. This is why we're all performing, trying to be "the best" or do things right, because of this deep-seated belief telling us this is how we "must be" to receive love. But this isn't love. This is survival. Survival comes from the head. Love comes from the heart. When we seek love outside of ourselves, we live in a constant state of survival. This is why we suffer. We have the power to end the suffering as we connect to our hearts and commune with God.

You are a child of God and, just like your own children have a direct connection to you, you have a direct connection to God. You've just lost that connection in your zeal to make everyone happy. You've been living from your head, trying to control life, instead of trusting God. Now it's time for a change. As you let go of the controls and give yourself permission to receive love by taking the time to slow down and love yourself, you will feel God's presence. When you honor your heart and the way you were created, you put God first and create a divine connection. Life becomes a joyous flow. No longer will you feel the responsibilities of the world sitting on your shoulders. You surrender them to God.

Most of us don't realize that our ultimate purpose on this planet is to be an expression of love. Love comes as you take time to heal the pain of the past, releasing negative false beliefs that tell you that you are wrong for being who you are. With each release, you open up to compassion, forgiveness, acceptance and love. Your life becomes one filled with abundance. But, instead of taking the time to look within, we push ourselves and deny our hearts, believing this is the right thing to do. In our quest to make sure our children and families are loved, we moms shut down to receiving love. We do everything for everyone else at the expense of ourselves. We lose our connections to God.

Being a martyr is the worst thing you can do for your children. If you don't connect to your heart by honoring and loving the way God created you, Mom, your children will grow up and quickly learn to forget themselves, severing their connections. That's why so many people in our world continue to perform, seeking love. They've learned it from all of us mommas.

If you want your children to have lives of abundance, be an example of abundance. If you want them to have lives of happiness, be an example of happiness. If you want your children to have lives of peace, love and fulfillment, be an example of these things.

> *It's not what we do for our families,*
> *but how we live our lives that*
> *impacts them the most.*

We love our kids so much. We want to protect them. We want to make sure they feel love rather than suffering. So we deny ourselves just like our moms did with us. And as we do, we perpetuate the cycle of judgment, blame, separation and pain all over again.

In *Love Without Conditions: Reflections of the Christ Mind*, Paul Ferrini says, "If you do not take responsibility for bringing love to your own wounds, you will not move out of the vicious cycle of attack/ defense, guilt and blame. Your feelings of rage, hurt and betrayal, all of which seem justified, will just fuel the fire of interpersonal conflict and continue to reinforce your unconscious belief that you are unlovable and incapable of loving." And as you live this way, Mom, your kids will grow up and do the same.

If you're ready to stop this cycle and become an example of love for your family then it's time to take responsibility for your happiness. It's time to heal your wounds. It's time to look within and see who you are and what you believe, not who you think you're "supposed to be." Give yourself permission to love and accept yourself unconditionally. Stand in YOUR truth. And as you do, you walk the path of The Enlightened Mom.

When I first started upon my healing journey, my intention was to be unconditional love. It still is. I knew if I truly wanted to stop the cycle of separation and pain, it had to start with me first. I had spent most of my life being a master at mental games, always judging and beating myself up, especially when it came to motherhood. I wreaked havoc on myself. As a result, it spewed over to my family. And as it blasted them, I became filled with guilt and remorse. The cycle, as my kids would say, really sucked. I broke the cycle when I made a decision to heal.

You are ready to break this cycle. You are ready to be unconditional love, but it has to start with you, Mom. Now you're probably thinking that you already love your kids unconditionally. However, and this is a big however, when you want to mold your children or make them "be somebody" out of your own past beliefs or fears for their future, you are sending your kids a message that says, "You aren't okay just being you." This message is probably similar to the one you received as a kid that said you must seek love and acceptance from the world around you. And to do this, you must deny your heart so you will fit in. The message your kids hear is: love comes only with conditions.

Dictionary.com defines unconditional love as "affection with no limits or conditions; complete love." Conditional love, on the other hand, is when you have an idea in your mind of how a person is "supposed to be" to get acceptance and love. For instance, if you feel as if your daughter has to wear her hair a certain way for fear that people will judge her, this is conditional love. Or if you feel as if your son has to be the best athlete to get ahead in life, this is conditional love. Any time you feel someone is "supposed to be" a specific way in life, this includes how you feel you're "supposed to be," you are expressing love with conditions. These conditions are based in old patterns and programs you took on since childhood telling you how you had to be to receive acceptance and love. When you look back on those beliefs and truly dive into them, you'll most likely realize they aren't your truth. Deep down you are probably holding on to a lot of sadness and pain because you weren't honored just for being you. Now, as a mother, you continue the cycle of self-denial, trying to fit the mold of what you believe a good mother should be. It's time to release that programming and open up to receive love unconditionally.

You can't truly love others unconditionally until you first love yourself unconditionally, Mom. That means taking time each day to get to know who you are. This is the loving thing to do for your family. This is putting God first. By getting to know yourself and finding acceptance and love for all those parts of you that you've judged, you find your heart. Jesus explained it when he said, "Why do you look at the speck of sawdust in your brother's eye and pay no attention to the plank in your own eye? How can you say to your brother, 'Let me take the speck out of your eye,' when all the time there is a plank in your own eye?" *(Matthew 7:3-4)*

By taking the time to connect to your heart and removing the plank in your eye, you create a connection to God and live as Christ did. It is in this space where true unconditional love lives. As you find love and acceptance within yourself, you begin to love all those parts of others that you've judged. The love you feel inside overflows to them. Where there had been judgment, pain, and sadness, there is now overflowing abundance. This is the best gift you can give, and the greatest act of service you will ever do for your family members: being an example of self-acceptance and love, not having to be anything or anybody to be loved.

Unconditional Love = Abundance

The beauty of opening up to receive love simply for being who you are is that as you allow yourself to really move into this heart space, you find your gifts to share with the world. This is true abundance. Isn't that what you want for your kids? You want them to have lives of passion, purpose and love. You want their lives to be filled with abundance. The only way they will truly have this, however, is by taking responsibility for their own happiness and living authentically from their hearts by putting God first. It's up to you, Mom, to live your life like this, setting an example for your family. And to do that, you must get to know yourself. That means spending time meditating, journaling, playing, and loving yourself.

Honoring yourself as an act of love goes against the grain of what we've been taught, but it's the truth. If you're reading this book then most likely the old way of being isn't working for you. It's time for a change and that change begins with loving and accepting yourself first.

Loving Yourself is NOT Selfish

Leslie is an old client of mine. She is an amazing woman and has an absolute heart of gold. Her life before children was one of success, power, and abundance. Now she's the mother of twin little girls. Her greatest desire is to make her children and husband feel loved.

I had been working with Leslie for some time when she came in to see me for a coaching session. In spite of the work we had been doing, Leslie still struggled with loving herself due to the belief that said it was up to her to make her family's life perfect. She constantly felt as if she were failing.

Leslie settled back in her chair with tears welling up in her eyes. "I know you're tired of hearing this story," she said. "But I feel as if I'm angry at everyone. I know it's my problem, but I can't seem to get over it. I feel as if I need to run away."

Do you ever feel as if you want to run away, Mom? If you do, that's God trying to tell you that you need a break. You're not honoring the messages in your heart and taking care of your needs. Therefore, you don't feel loved. Leslie continued to deny the messages she received because she believed that to love herself was selfish. She was wrong.

Loving yourself is not selfish. It's about listening to your heart and putting God first. True selfishness is when you walk around angry, taking out your pain on everyone else. You were created to be a unique being. The reason you feel angry, sad or frustrated with life, or are trying to make your kids "be" a certain way, is because you aren't honoring your uniqueness. Therefore, you can't honor their uniqueness.

Put God first and get to know who you are so that you may share your gifts with the world and be an example for everyone. This isn't selfish. This is love. Be a channel of God's love. As long as you continue to deny yourself, you will never know this kind of abundance.

Leslie's pain continued because she wouldn't honor this truth. Through the tools she learned in our work together, she constantly got messages to honor and take care of herself. But she wouldn't listen due to the false belief that said she would be selfish if she acted upon the messages.

As I worked with Leslie that day and saw her pain, I quietly prayed, "God use me. Show me how I might facilitate her healing." I heard a very clear message as the session ended. It said, "When you are judging yourself or not accepting the feelings you are experiencing, ask, 'How can I honor God today by honoring the way I was created?'" That's a pretty potent question. Think about it again. Take it in:

"How can I honor God today by honoring the way I was created?"

I shared this message with Leslie and as I walked her to the door I asked her, "So does that help you a little?"

"Yes," she said. "It helps me feel not quite so selfish."

I hope it will help you see that you aren't being selfish when you love yourself. Dishonoring yourself is true selfishness. When you hide the real you, people are not allowed to enjoy the light you have to shine on the world. When you disconnect from your heart and the love of God, you only create more pain and suffering. It's time to break the cycle of true selfishness and create a divine connection!

What Is God to You?

Before we go any further about creating a connection to God, I want to address an important question: What is God to you? When you imagine God, how do you see that picture? Is God kind, loving and compassionate? Or is God some man sitting up on a throne judging you, determining if you are worthy of being seen or heard? That's what God used to be to me. I was terrified of God. I believed that God was this giant man just waiting for me to mess up. I feared God's judgment and, therefore, was really hard on myself. Compassion, kindness, forgiveness and love were not a big part of my vocabulary when it came to looking at my relationship with God. Thankfully, that has all changed now.

What I know for sure is that we are all energy and are all connected. This is a scientific fact. However, I believe from a spiritual perspective that this energy makes up the whole and we are all a part of it. We make up the body of God. We are all part of the oneness of God. God isn't outside of us. God is a part of each of us. And because of this, I believe God is always with me.

When I call upon God for guidance, I am calling upon all of the loving energy of the universe. I see this energy as The Light. For me, The Light consists of Christ, angels, beautiful spirit guides, the world around me, as well as God's love inside of me, all acting as messengers. I believe that we can call upon that loving energy and ask for help and it is always given. We just have to allow ourselves to receive it. Do you allow yourself to receive? Do you allow yourself to be open to this all-loving presence? What do you believe?

I invite you to spend some time with this question: What is God to you? Check in with yourself and see if what you believe really resonates with you or is it some childhood belief that you took on. I hope you do know, however, that God is love, pure and simple. Just knowing this and living your life trusting that the love is always there will shift your life in monumental ways.

I share my beliefs with you to show you how beliefs can change once we open up to the possibilities and get to know ourselves. I never thought mine would shift, but I'm so glad they did.

The core belief I learned during childhood is that God is punishing and is "over there" somewhere, unavailable when I ask for help. Therefore, I punished myself and didn't allow myself to receive love in most areas of my life because I didn't believe I was worthy of God's love and help. I felt extremely alone, especially with my duties as a mother. But as I have slowed down to get to know what I truly believe, that belief has changed. As a result, I have opened up to an all-loving presence, and now fear and worry have dissipated from my life. I have a peaceful knowingness that the love is always there. We mommas just have to be willing to stop denying ourselves and open up to receive it.

Set an Intention

You've come to this point because you are ready to break the cycle of pain and self-denial that has been handed down from generation to generation. You are ready to open your heart to God and create a connection. Your first step is to set an intention. Setting an intention means to simply visualize what you want for your life and to feel it throughout your body.

Here are three simple steps to create your intention:

1. Close your eyes and visualize how you would like to see your life. Is it filled with laughter, passion, and love? Please don't be just an observer to this picture; be in it. Look down and see your hands. What are you wearing? As you turn your head, what do your surroundings look like? And here's the key point: how do you feel? Has your anger and frustration dissipated? Do you feel a great connection to God and all those you love? Is your life in balance? Is it one of unconditional love? Take a moment and create in your mind a picture of how you want to experience your life.

2.   Imagine bringing this picture into your heart. See it exploding like a starburst, filling up your whole body. As you visualize this picture, say to yourself, "Yes, yes, yes, yes, YES!" just as if you were cheering for your child at some school or sporting event.

3.   Say, "I give myself permission to live this kind of life. God, I open myself up to your guidance and miracles. I THANK YOU for this healing. I thank you for guiding me and showing me the way."

~ ~ ~ ~ ~

Mom, to move deeper into this healing, go to
The Enlightened Mom Meditation CD #1, Track 2,
and set an intention for what you want!

~ ~ ~ ~ ~

*As my gift to you, download this first meditation, **Set an Intention**, for free, or purchase the entire series of 25 powerful meditations, all personally guided by me, at www.TheEnlightenedMom.com/freemeditation*

Mom, I want you to know right now that you can have the image you just created. Know it! By owning this truth, you will start seeing miracles happen. You are a part of God and, in this truth, your natural state is abundance. You are the one who limits this, Mom. To shift your consciousness, all you have to do is to open up and receive it. And that starts with you saying "YES!" to yourself.

You might be questioning your ability to create what you want in your life. Most of us don't believe we are that powerful. We don't tend to believe that we can set an intention for unconditional love and abundance and then create it. But you can. You are that powerful. You are the creator of your life. Most of us have been raised to believe that we are the victims of circumstance. Whether we were told that verbally or by watching our family members complain, we didn't believe we could create our reality. But we are not victims. Every thought you have creates your reality. If you dwell on negative thoughts then this is what you'll bring to your life. For instance, I used to resent my late husband, Steve, for a lot of things. You name it, I resented him for it. The resentment created a wall between us. Then one day I decided I would only focus on the good things about him and acknowledge him for them. All of the sudden the wall came down. No longer was I creating a negative environment for myself, and my family. I created a home of gratitude and love. Our home shifted simply because I changed my thoughts.

Your mind is powerful. It is time to realize that what you think, you create.

Is there too much drama in your life? If there is, it's because you have too much drama in your mind. Try focusing on the positive in your life and the drama will go away. This is the Law of Attraction: what you think, you will bring to your life. Life is a mirror. It's as if the beautiful all-loving presence of God and all of the angels are watching you, waiting to see what you want to create. If you focus on negativity then you will bring negativity to your life. Try focusing on positive things like loving yourself. Miraculously, your world will change.

You are the creator of your life. This is your free will. That's why when you make room for abundance in your life and open up to receive it, you will finally experience the love you've always craved.

Permission to Receive Love

One of the first things I notice as a healer is that most people are not able to create a connection to God because they are not open to receiving God's love. They are shut down. I believe as babies we come into the world ready to receive love, but over time, as a result of watching and learning from our parents, grandparents, siblings, caretakers, and society in general, we begin to live in fear. As a result, instead of trusting God to guide us, we become disconnected. To be connected, we must give ourselves permission to receive love.

My healing journey began years ago with my late husband, Steve. He felt he got a new wife when I made a decision to heal my life. In the beginning of our marriage, I was a control freak. Talk about struggles! There were too many to count. I felt so alone. Steve often found me in his face screaming. I was tough on him and I was really tough on my stepson, A.J. I didn't know how to be a mom. I didn't know how to love A.J., nor Steve, unconditionally. I was tough on them, because I was tough on me. I believed I had to be perfect to receive love. I believed that love came from the outside world. Not from God. God really wasn't in the equation. I believed in God, but didn't feel I could have God's help. I believed I was alone. Then our girls were born. I was terrified of continuing the cycle of pain. I decided to heal my life. That's when I finally gave myself permission to receive God's love, stepping onto the path of The Enlightened Mom.

Opening up to God's love simply comes down to shifting your mindset. You get to choose how you want your life to be. Do you want your life to continue the way it is? Or are you ready to receive God's miracles and abundance?

If you're ready to make a shift, create a quiet space for yourself. Give yourself five minutes to do this. Take a few deep breaths, not from your chest but from down low in your abdomen. Allow your body to relax. Speak these words out loud:

"I give myself PERMISSION to open up to God's guidance and love. I give myself PERMISSION to receive this kind of abundance and love."

When you give yourself permission to receive, you are using the power of your mind to shift from lack into abundance. Just by saying these simple words, you open up your heart and create a connection to

God. However, to truly feel the presence of God in every cell of your body, stay open and take this exercise further.

Grounding in God's Light

Grounding in God's light is a visualization tool to help you release your fears, worries and concerns by letting go of negative energy that you're holding onto. It clears your mind and raises you into a higher vibration so that you can be in tune to receiving God's messages.

"What is a higher vibration?" you ask.

We are all energy and energy vibrates. When you are at a lower vibration, you feel yucky or stuck and often feel confused and uncertain. When you raise your vibration, you immediately feel better because you've created a connection to God.

Grounding in God's light, combined with giving yourself permission to receive God's love, sets up a foundation for all the exercises you'll be doing in this book. I invite you to practice this daily. It will help you create the life you want. And it will be one of the greatest gifts you ever give to yourself, as well as to your family.

Grounding in God's light is simple and fun to do. At first, I'm going to give you a full description of the different steps, how to do them, and how they affect you. Then I'll follow these guidelines with a short recap. Read through this a couple of times and allow yourself to play. We'll start with the first step as I discussed above.

Step 1: Create a Quiet Space

Find a quiet place to sit. Give thanks for the healing that is about to take place. By giving thanks, you rest in the knowingness that you are loved and supported. Say, "I give myself PERMISSION to open up and receive God's love and guidance."

Step 2: Your Energy Body

Imagine sitting in an energy field that looks like an egg. This is your aura. It extends around your body about arm's length. Visualize it above you, below you, on either side of you, in front of you and behind you. You literally look as if you're sitting in an egg.

When you open up to God's guidance, keeping your aura at arm's length is key. Otherwise, your energy is sapped if it is overextended, often making you feel scattered and anxious. Or if the aura is pulled in too tight, you feel as if you're smothering.

Jeff is a top dog with a television network. I noticed one day when he walked in for a session that his aura was literally all over the place. It felt like the old movie, *The Blob*, big, gooey and smothering to me. I can only imagine what it felt like to him.

I asked Jeff to imagine bringing in his aura to arm's length all the way around him and to start practicing this every time he walked into a room for business meetings or in social gatherings. The next time he came to see me, Jeff said he couldn't believe how calm and centered it made him feel. This will work wonders for you, too!

If you're scoffing at the idea of having an aura, please ease your mind. Not only does science tell us that we are all energy, but there is a way to actually see auras with your own eyes. It's called Kirlian photography. When you have a Kirlian photograph taken, not only will you see the energy surrounding you, but you will also see it in vibrant colors. It's really quite fun when you see it for the first time.

Step 3: Create a Grounding Cord

The next step to getting grounded in God's light is to create your grounding cord. Imagine a huge column of light attached to the outer edge of your aura at about hip level. Visualize it shooting down from your hips. It is firm, but flexible. See your grounding cord connecting to the center of the earth. I like to imagine the center of the earth as a big peach pit.

I can't begin to tell you how many times I've seen people walk in for a healing session and look as if they're floating up above their bodies. They are scattered and feel out of control. If you ever feel this way, or if you feel as if your brain left town a long time ago, it's probably because you're not in your body. Check in with your grounding cord. By visualizing it, you will bring yourself back to the present time and fully envelope your body.

Step 4: The Light of God

It's time to bring in the light of God and allow it to emanate throughout your body, your aura and your grounding cord. All of these parts of you have the ability to hold onto both negative and positive energy. As you bring in the light, you wash away worry, fear, and darkness. You create a connection to God and raise your vibration.

Imagine a beautiful iridescent golden light coming down from the universe. This is God's love and wisdom waiting for you to tap into it.

Visualize the crown of your head opening up like a camera lens. As it opens, feel this light flooding into your whole body via the crown. See it flowing all the way down to your fingertips and toes.

Imagine opening up your palms and each fingertip, just like camera lenses again. Allow all of the darkness you've been holding onto to pour out of your hands and into your aura. Do the same for the energy that's drained into your feet. See the balls of your feet opening up and allow the darkness to dump below them into your aura.

You are so full of God's love now that the light is spewing out of the top of your head and overflowing into your aura. Allow all the fear and worry to drain to the bottom of this egg of energy that surrounds you.

Think of yourself now as a beautiful bright light. The only darkness you see is the heavy energy sitting at the bottom of your aura. Imagine opening it up under your feet. Once again, see it like a big camera lens. Allow God's light to push the remaining darkness down your grounding cord. Imagine it being absorbed back into the earth.

Step 5: Gratitude

Gratitude is an essential element in raising your vibration. I find that I create a deeper connection to God when I start my meditations with gratitude and then end with it.

Gratitude moves you out of your head where there is worry and fear, and guides you to your heart. It raises your vibration and shifts you immediately from lack into abundance.

Grounding in God's Light Recap

1. Find a comfy and quiet place to sit. Take a few deep breaths to relax you as you give yourself permission to receive God's love and guidance. Give thanks for the healing that is about to take place.

2. Close your eyes and visualize your aura, as if you're sitting in an egg of energy. See your aura at about arm's length all the way around you.

3. Visualize your grounding cord beginning at your hips on the outer edge of your aura, running down and connecting to the center of the earth. Imagine the center of the earth as a huge peach pit.

4. Open the crown of your head like a camera lens. Allow the light of God to pour into your body, spew out of your hands and feet, and overflow from your head. Have the light push all dark energy into the bottom of your aura. Drain the negative energy down your grounding cord, sending it to the center of the earth. If you feel you're stuck and can't release the darkness, check in with your hands and feet to make sure that they are open. See if the bottom of your aura is open, too.

5. Give thanks once again for the healing.

~ ~ ~ ~ ~

Mom, go to The Enlightened Mom Meditation CD #1,
Track 3, to walk through Grounding in God's Light
step-by-step. And then when you're ready, go to
Track 4, for the meditation.

~ ~ ~ ~ ~

When I first learned to ground in God's light, I found it a little difficult to stay present. I constantly wanted to fall asleep, or my mind would continually race. If this happens for you, give yourself a break. Instead of judging yourself, be kind and allow your mind to relax. Say hello to whatever comes up for you and then take yourself back to the light.

Practice grounding in God's light. Give yourself permission to receive this kind of abundance and create some time to do this for yourself daily. Start with just ten minutes in the morning. It's a great way to begin the day, especially when you feel as if you have to hit the floor running. Set your clock for ten minutes earlier than usual. That's all you have to do to start this daily practice. As you allow yourself to receive love first thing in the morning, you set up your whole day with an intention of love.

If you find yourself beginning to feel anxiety-ridden as the day progresses, ground in God's light again. You don't have to take a full ten minutes. You can do it anywhere in about 30 seconds. Just allow yourself to open up the crown of your head and feel God's golden light pouring in.

Be flexible with grounding in God's light. I've given you this step-by-step guide to help familiarize you with the different aspects of grounding and why it's so important to do them. However, there is no right or wrong way as to which step comes first. I've used this tool so much that most of the time I simply visualize my crown opening up and then flood my body with the light. That's when I check in with my aura and grounding cord to make sure I'm dumping out all of the darkness. Then there are other times when I realize that I'm out of my body and start with my grounding cord first. Allow yourself to play with this.

I've had many women come to me after using this grounding tool for a week and tell me that friends and family have asked them if they are on Prozac because they are all of the sudden so calm! That's how effective grounding can be once you've committed to doing it.

I'll never forget the time I first used this grounding exercise to help me with a chore around my home. We had just moved into a new house and the back porch light had burned out. I pulled out a ladder to get to the light and noticed that it had eight pieces of glass, each pane connected by a piece of metal. On each strip of metal was a little knob. I thought this was how the fixture opened. Well, lo and behold, as I began to unscrew one of the knobs the whole fixture started to come apart in my hands. I knew I was heading for a disaster! I quickly screwed the glass back together and took a deep breath. I did my grounding exercise and said a little prayer. Suddenly I knew that I had to climb higher on the ladder. I did, only to find that the top of the fixture had an opening that unscrewed to replace the bulb. Wow! A simple task was about to become a catastrophe. But by grounding in God's light and opening myself up to receive the guidance, I was able to get the answer I needed to make my life a whole lot easier!

One of my favorite times to get grounded and fully connected to God is while I'm sitting at a stoplight. Often when we are driving, we are thinking about what we have to do next. Our minds are going 90 miles a minute. This is a great time to slow down and breathe.

Not only do I see myself being grounded, but I visualize my car grounded as well. I imagine a beautiful light surrounding my car and visualize a grounding cord for it, dumping out all of the dark energy that it is holding onto. Try this exercise. You'll be amazed at how much safer you feel driving your car.

Another area you can ground is your home. Visualize it just as you would for yourself with a beautiful golden light above it. See a grounding cord connected to all the corners and edges of your home, or if you have land surrounding it, see the corners of the land. Then flush your home and land with the light from above, sending all of the negative energy to the center of the earth. The difference in your home will shock you! I remember when I first started grounding my home. A friend of mine who was sensitive to energy came in one day. As she stood in the foyer, she said, "What's different about this house? What are you doing differently?"

At first I said, "Well, the windows are open today."

"Nope, that's not it," she said.

I had to think about it for a minute and then remembered what I had been doing to my home on a daily basis. I guess I didn't notice the energy shift so much because I was living in it...kind of like gaining weight. It creeps up on us without seeing a big change. Thank God, grounding your home is a good kind of shift!

I told my friend that I had been grounding my house. She's not an energy worker, just someone who feels it. She understood immediately. She said, "That's it! Your house feels calm and peaceful. It feels really good."

This is what grounding your home can do for you. Just like grounding yourself, it allows God's love and light to flow through it, cleansing and releasing the darkness, bringing peace, love and light to your family's life and home.

Ground in God's light daily, Mom. By using this tool in all areas of your life, you will release the negative energy that keeps you stuck in worry and fear, creating an opening for you to receive God's loving messages.

Receiving God's love is your choice, Mom. "Ask and ye shall receive." However, most people ask for help, but have no idea of how to receive it. This goes back to that old programming that says to receive is to be selfish. Well, that's baloney! Love is a cyclical flow of energy. To truly be able to give love, you must first receive it by slowing down, listening to your heart, and opening up to create a connection to God. You are worthy of this kind of love. When you allow yourself to really open up to God's love, it takes away your worries, anxiety and pain. You become a vessel of love. What a relief for you as a mom! The key is to trust that you are a part of this beautiful energy of God and it wants to give you what you need. What a revelation! Most of us never believed we could have this kind of love in our lives. But you can when you give yourself permission to receive it.

≈ ≈ ≈ ≈ ≈

CHAPTER 2

God is Everywhere...
Even in Your Washing Machine

om, it is our fear of being alone that causes us to perform and shut down to receiving God's love. Our greatest desire is to experience love. We want to experience love in every aspect of our existence. We want our children to love us, our parents to love us, and our spouses and friends to love us. We do everything for them to make them happy simply due to the fear of feeling alone and unloved. The irony, however, is that as we give ourselves up in the search for love outside of ourselves, we disconnect from God. It's this disconnection that is the true source of feeling alone and unloved.

This fear of aloneness causes great anxiety. It causes you to be angry, sad, and frustrated. It makes you bitter, hopeless, and resentful. This fear makes you want to control everything. You don't trust yourself and the choices you're making. You constantly question yourself. You feel buried in guilt. "Did I do this right?" You ask yourself. "How can I get it all done? Will my kid hate me when she grows up?"

Then you take your pain and fear out on the ones you love. You find yourself screaming, ranting and raving, "You kids are making me crazy!" You hate yourself. You are filled with sadness and guilt for causing them pain.

Mom, life doesn't have to be this way. You are not alone. You are part of this wonderful, loving presence we call God. God is in everything; therefore, you are part of the whole. You are connected to all of it, Mom. When you make the decision to stop performing for love and open up to make a divine connection, you'll realize that you are not alone and never have been.

Most of us know about God in some way or another, but do we really have a connection to God where we feel a loving presence around us all of the time so we no longer feel alone? Do we hear God's messages and allow God to guide us?

Most of us don't.

We don't know how to connect and receive God's loving messages.

We are so buried in our own pain and fear that we don't trust ourselves to hear or see the beautiful messages that are everywhere. And let me tell you, they are everywhere. These messages are here to guide you, bringing peace and calm to your life. You simply have to be willing to open up and receive them and believe that they are there.

I'll never forget the day that I truly realized that God IS everywhere. I can't remember the exact reason I was struggling—motherhood seems to have sapped my memory—but what I do remember is the fact that I was standing over my washing machine praying. Yep, that's right. I was praying over my washing machine. Don't laugh. My daughter, Mackenzie, will tell you that she walked in our house on another day with a friend and saw me sitting on the floor in my fluffy pink bathrobe by a partially unloaded dishwasher with my eyes closed. When she asked what in the world I was doing, I opened one eye and said, "Meditating." She rolled her eyes at her friend, threw her arms up and laughed, saying, "See what I have to live with!"

I tend to meditate and pray everywhere, especially after that day in my laundry room. As I said, I don't remember exactly what I was upset about but do know that I was really struggling with life. I felt so alone. I remember saying to God, "I need to know you are here. I need help."

As I lifted my eyes I saw "Infinite Water Level" listed on my Maytag washing machine. "Wow!" I thought. "That's just like God: infinite." Then I noticed another line on the machine, "Dependable Care Plus/Heavy Duty, 2 Speed, Super Capacity." Yes, I knew I was being told that God is always dependable and will always be there with me with super capacity to take care of me if I will just surrender.

The message went a step further when I noticed the "Wash/Rinse Temperature" settings. I saw "Hot/Cold, Warm/Warm, etc.," you get it, and knew that I was being shown that it is our choice as to how much we allow God to help us. God's touch in our lives can be really hot if we want it to be or really cold if we shut it out.

When I saw the next setting, "Wash/Spin Speed," I knew God was telling me we have a choice to be on our journeys as fast or as slow as we want to be. Our path can be regular or fast, or very gentle and slow. It's always our choice.

The last setting I saw on my washing machine that day was for the 11 different cycles for different types of clothes. This aspect of the message told me that God is there for everybody. No matter who you are, where you're from, or what race you are, that God's unconditional love is everywhere for everyone.

Wow! I couldn't believe I received such an inspiring message praying over my Maytag washing machine! I knew then that God was listening to me. And I knew that God's messages come in all sorts of packages.

Watching for God's Signs

Mom, your day-to-day life is filled with messages from God, just like my Maytag washing machine was for me that day when I prayed for help. God speaks to us in many ways. The messages are gifts to guide us. They give us the answers we seek so we don't feel so alone and buried in responsibilities. By giving yourself permission to create a connection and opening up to receive God's messages, you release the turmoil in your life and become a more loving mom.

Sometimes we ask for specific help and search for an answer, and then other times we don't even really know that we have a question. But our spirits know. And the messages always show up. We just have to be awake to see the answers. For instance, have you ever heard a verse of a song over and over in your head? This is most likely a message from God. Zoom in on the verse and really listen to what it's telling you. I know there is a message for you.

One of my clients was in a failing marriage for a very long time. I have to give Sandy credit. She tried to hold it together and had taken a look at the marriage from every angle, but the marriage was over. Sandy continually dragged it out, however, because she didn't want to hurt her husband. One minute she would tell him that she was done and then the next she would send him a subtle message, keeping his hopes up that it wasn't over. Then she called one day to tell me that she had awakened that morning with the verse of an old song playing in her head. "It's cruel to be kind," is what she heard over and over again.

"That's a message!" I said. "Don't you get it? You think you're being kind to him by dragging this out, but in reality you are being very cruel. God is trying to tell you to follow your heart and love this man enough to let him go."

God sent Sandy a message because this was what her heart wanted. She wanted to let go of her marriage, but her head said, "No." By opening up to see the message, Sandy finally recognized that it was time to love her husband enough to let him go.

Have you ever had a question on your mind for a day or two and didn't know the answer only to turn on the radio and hear a song that seemed to speak directly to you, giving you an answer? You turned on the radio just at the right moment not by chance, but because somewhere deep within, God was speaking to you, giving you a little nudge to find your answer.

God speaks to us through our conversations, too. You have to listen, really listen to hear those messages. Often when we talk with people we're thinking about something else, not really paying attention. Start listening to what people say to you. You will hear

God's messages. I'm sure you've had this kind of experience with a girlfriend. You're yapping on the phone, sharing your woes, when all of the sudden something that you've been dealing with is resolved. There's no coincidence in this. Again, God is working in your life. These kinds of messages are everywhere, Mom. This is why it's so important for you to slow down and listen.

Another way that I like to get messages from God is to take a book in hand, say a little prayer asking God to show me what I need to know for the day, and then I flip the book open. I'm constantly amazed at the messages I receive. The key is that I know I will get a message and I know that I am worthy of this kind of love, so I open up to receive it.

Several years ago while speaking at a convention, a man walked up to my booth where I was selling my books and CDs. He looked sad so I invited him to take my book, *Message Sent,* in hand and ask God what he needed to see for the day. He followed my directions and opened up the book. This big hulking man immediately broke down into sobbing tears. As I held him, I asked, "What's going on?"

"This morning I thought about committing suicide," he said. "I'm a chiropractor and the building where I work has just been sold. I don't know how I'm going to take care of my patients. I don't know how I'm going to make a living. I feel so hopeless. But now this," as he showed me the page he had turned to. "You are Worthy of Living Powerfully" was the title of the page I read. "My friend asked me to come here today," he added. "I didn't know why I was coming, but now I do. God is telling me that it's going to be okay."

That was absolutely one of the most powerful moments I've ever experienced. God spoke to that man through the pages of a book. He will do the same for you. All you have to do is take a book in hand, ask what you need to know for the day, trust, and open up to the message.

Sometimes I like to turn on the television when I eat lunch. Instead of just turning to any channel, I take a moment to get grounded and then ask, "God, what do you want me to see?"

The first time I did this, I got a channel in my mind and turned to it only to find someone playing golf. "Golfing?" I asked. Then I looked a little closer to see what was really going on and what it was telling me. The message became clear. I was being told to get outside and play, that I wasn't having enough outdoor time. I knew that this was the truth, so I listened.

God has no limits when it comes to sending you messages. Whether it's through a song, a conversation, a book or your television, all you have to do is ask and be willing to receive the messages.

People are Messengers

God not only talks to us through conversations with others, but with our relationships in general. Your relationships go much deeper than the human level. All of the people in your life, your parents, teachers, kids, spouse, friends, co-workers, boss, everyone with whom you've had a relationship, are in agreement to play a part for you to get to know yourself, and vice versa. These are your spiritual agreements. These people are part of your soul group to help you find yourself and re-connect to God.

I share a lot of my life experiences in this book. Some are wonderful and some are not so great. I believe as a spirit that I chose ALL of my experiences, not necessarily on a conscious level, but on a deep spiritual level. I feel the spiritual agreements with my parents, and now my kids, have been tremendous gifts in helping me step into my life's mission. We had a lot of love in our family when I was a kid, but there was also a lot of pain. As a child, I chose to focus on the negative and blamed everyone for the judgment and hurt I felt inside. I believe I came in to have that experience so that I could gain the tools to fulfill my life mission. It was only through having those experiences, and then choosing to heal them, that I can now share with you the tools I learned along the way.

I invite you to try this belief on as you make your way through this book. Instead of feeling as if you are a victim of your life, see yourself as a spirit who came in to have an amazing human experience. See every person with whom you have a relationship as an emanation of God. Pretend that God sent them here to help you learn about yourself and remember who you really are. See past their human flesh and recognize the love.

Shelly, one of my Enlightened Mom students, told me that just by knowing we are all in spiritual agreements to re-connect to our hearts, her view of everyone has changed. Shelly shared with our class that when she looks at people now she asks herself, "What is this person here to teach me about myself?" She sees each person as an avenue to re-connect to her heart and the love of God. Each is a messenger from God. Shelly has shifted from being a victim to walking the path of The Enlightened Mom.

Animals as Messengers

Animals are another means to connect to God's messages. Whether it's a butterfly, a crow, a cat, or a rat, if an animal shows up in your space and gets your attention, God is trying to talk to you. Ted [Book] Andrews' book, *Animal Speak: The Spiritual & Magical Powers of Creatures Great and Small,* is a wonderful tool to understand what animals are trying to tell you. For instance, prior to beginning this book, I knew I was preparing to write it as I had been taking a lot of notes with my clients. However, I wasn't really sure when I would strike that first word on my computer. It was right before Christmas and, as many mothers do, I was up late into the night wrapping presents. I walked downstairs to hear crickets chirping. Now you might say, "So what's the big deal about crickets chirping? They do that everywhere." Well, we lived in Southern California at that time and didn't hear a lot of crickets near the beach, especially since we didn't have a yard and neither did anyone else around us. What was even odder is that the crickets were under my refrigerator and had been there for almost a month. I hadn't paid any attention to them and had more or less forgotten about them. But for some reason on that night in the wee hours of the morning, the crickets got my attention.

"Hmmm," I thought. "Those darn crickets have been there a long time. I wonder what they're trying to tell me."

I went upstairs to get my *Animal Speak* book and looked up cricket. It fell under the heading of grasshopper. "When grasshopper shows up there is about to be a new leap forward," is how it was described.

"That's cool!" I thought and read on. "It is important to get off the haunches and move."

I knew God was speaking to me through those crickets. It was time for me to get my act in gear and move. I guessed the message was referring to this book, but wasn't quite sure.

I had left the scissors downstairs and needed them to finish wrapping presents. I went into the darkened kitchen once again and flipped the light on. Creeping across my kitchen counter was a spider. My gosh! It sounds as if my home was crawling with critters! It was that night, so once again I went back upstairs to see what the spider was trying to tell me.

"Spider can teach how to use the written language with power and creativity so that your words weave a web around those who would read them."

God was really speaking to me through those little critters. Wow! I felt as if I had been given the best Christmas present ever. God was telling me to get off my haunches and write! Ironically, my little critter friends left after that. Even the crickets. After a month of listening to them chirping constantly, I finally listened, so they left.

Please realize that, just like you and me, animals are God's children. They are here to help us heal and to see ourselves. Be a witness to God's glory by listening to the animals' messages.

God Speaks to You in Your Dreams

Do you remember your dreams, Mom? Some people know that they dream, but simply don't remember them. Others' dreams are very real. Some dream in black and white, others in color. My dreams are like movies. God speaks to me a lot through my dreams. Prior to writing my first book, I had a very profound dream. I saw myself standing in a big hall. My mother stood next to me. A man at a podium called my name. He said I was to take a trip with Soul and head to San Francisco. I was so excited to be called for this trip but found myself shutting down when I realized my mom stood next to me.

My dreams often haunt me and confuse me. As I awakened that morning, this one stuck with me. I knew I had to take a deeper look.

As I reflected on my life, one memory stood out to me. I had returned from San Francisco a month earlier where I attended a spiritual convention. I had amazing and wonderful experiences there and felt completely connected to God. But when I came home, I gradually lost that connection due to daily life and feeling buried in responsibilities as a mother.

When I meditated on the dream, I was shown that this was why my mother appeared in it. She represented my life as a mom and the fact that I was not being fully connected to God, seen as Soul in my dream, because I kept myself too busy and buried in responsibilities. As I meditated further, I remembered an exercise I had learned in San Francisco at the convention while taking a class from Cheryl Richardson, author of *Take Time for Your Life*. She said to write down the five most important priorities in your life and then to let everything else go. I came out of my meditation and did the exercise. I was shocked to discover that I really didn't want to continue to work as a spiritual counselor at that time. I had a little office that I leased and knew that it was time to let it go.

I called my landlord that day not knowing if I could get out of my lease quickly. She surprised me when she said, "That's perfect. I had someone call today wanting the space. You can get out immediately if you want."

I was thrilled and knew that God was working with me, sending me signs. I was being guided on my spiritual journey. I just had to listen to my dream. Amazingly, I cleared out my life of anything that wasn't a priority and a month later *Message Sent* began. That book was my awakening and was completely guided by God. Through the process of writing it, I began to find the real me, releasing the negative beliefs I held onto about being loved, especially when it came to being a perfect mother. I connected to my soul, just like in my dream, and found my purpose: becoming an Enlightened Mom, sharing my message of unconditional love with families all over the world.

If you don't remember your dreams, don't fret. Keep a notebook or journal next to your bed and tell God that you are open to receiving messages via your dreams. Then rest assured that eventually you will begin to remember them. When you awaken from a dream, don't wait to take a look at it later. You'll most likely forget. Write down every detail: colors, people, buildings, etc.

Mary Summer Rain's Guide to Dream Symbols by Mary Summer Rain and Alex Greystone is a wonderful tool to have at your bedside. I often laugh because it seems that my dreams now come in messages that are referenced in the guide. It's easy for me to break down a dream and find out exactly what it means with this book. I even use it for God's messages that I receive when I'm awake.

I'll never forget the day I unplugged my vacuum cleaner and saw flames shoot out of the electrical outlet. My computer across the room was on and immediately shut down. I thought the jolt of electricity shut it off only for the moment, but I was wrong. My computer wouldn't come back on. However, when I tried other outlets in the room, they still worked.

I walked down the hall to the den to my kids' computers. Neither one of them would turn on either. However, once again, when I tried other outlets in the room they worked fine. I was REALLY frustrated with the situation and went to the garage to find the circuit breaker box. I had to climb up and over all kinds of junk (you know what I mean if you use your garage as a storage room like we did back then). I played with the switches, jiggling them, turning them on and off. I knew this would do the trick. I was wrong! I went through this process three times. I couldn't believe that in two different rooms only certain outlets weren't working and they were the ones connected to our computers. I took a breath as I went back to my bedroom and stood by my nightstand only to look down and see my dream symbol book.

"Hmmm," I thought. "I wonder if God is trying to send me a message." I sat down and began looking up each symbol in the situation. Here's what I discovered:

- "**Vacuum cleaner** indicates that a 'clean up' is needed. This may refer to a situation, relationship, or even some type of negative within self."

- "**Outlet (electrical)** provides one with an available source of energy or empowerment."

- "**Flame** signifies great intensity, usually connected to the emotions."

- "**Computer** connotes a need for analyzation or better understanding."

As I read each definition I knew that a "clean up" was needed within me. I needed to go within and get a better understanding of the emotions I was feeling in my life. I'd been so busy that I hadn't taken any time to meditate in recent days. I had lost my connection to God. My emotions were so intense that I was losing my inner strength and power. That's why the flame shot out of the outlet. I was burning out. From these definitions of the symbols that had been presented to me, I knew it was time for me to climb into the bathtub and meditate.

During this fiasco of trying to get the outlets and computers to work again, I had called my husband to see if he had any suggestions. He didn't, other than jiggling the switches in the circuit breaker box. I reassured him I had attempted that three times and failed. It was time for me to heed God's message and take a look at myself.

I climbed into the bath and began to meditate. Immediately I received a message that my hubby was about to come home and that he would flip the switches in the circuit breaker box, just as I had done, and that the electrical outlets in the house were going to start working again. I was told that God had been trying to get my attention to slow down and meditate, but I hadn't been listening. It took sending flames out of my electrical outlet and shutting down my computers in different rooms to get me to wake up! Thankfully, I did. And wouldn't you know it? My hubby came home, climbed up over the junk in the garage like I did, flipped the switches, and everything started working again. In the past, I would have told myself that I had somehow screwed up and didn't know what I was doing. But I did know what I was doing and I also knew that God's message was for me, not for my hubby. There was no need for him to struggle with anything.

That's how God works. Messages are everywhere. Even in the struggles you experience daily, there is something for you to see and learn. The key is to stay in awareness and be open to receiving, and then use tools that will help you discern the meaning when you can't get it for yourself. That's why using a dream symbol book can be so helpful.

Messages in the Muck

In our quest to create a home of abundance and love, we often discover that life can be a struggle. We feel as if we're stuck in the muck of life, always questioning which way to go. Steven Lane Taylor, author of *Row, Row, Row Your Boat: A Guide for Living Life in the Divine Flow,* says, "When you are in the flow, life ceases to be a struggle. You don't have to fight for what you want, or defend what you have. When you are in the flow your every need is met so easily, so completely, so consistently, there's only one reasonable explanation for it. There must be a higher power at work on your behalf."

Mom, when you feel as if your daily life is a struggle, you are not in the flow. Your life is mired in the muck because you aren't listening to God's messages. You've lost your connection. Be aware. Awareness is key to recognizing when you are flowing with the river of life or when your boat has capsized. For instance, if you are running from errand to errand and nothing is going right, stop. God is sending you a message. Take this as a sign that you are not supposed to be doing these errands right now. Trust that you are being given a message that there is something else you're not aware of which will help you get more productive with your time. Check in with yourself and see what you need and then act upon it. This is how you'll end your struggle.

There was a period in my life where I believed my husband's way was the "right" way for me to live. It was at a time when I struggled with following my heart. Steve's attitude was always one of "MOVE, MOVE, MOVE! MAKE IT HAPPEN!" I had lived by that belief for most of my life as well. However, as I began my journey of healing and getting to know myself, a battle roared inside of me. My heart said, "Take your time, Terri. Steve's way is not your way." My head, on the other hand, said, "Get moving!"

Thankfully, God sent me a message one day to clear this up once and for all. Steve and I had switched cars for the weekend. He was taking our youngest daughter, Kolbi, on an Indian Princess camping

Book

trip and needed my SUV. Steve drove a Mercedes sedan, one with all of the bells and whistles. I didn't like driving his car back then because he was still attached to his toys. They defined him. Well, wouldn't you know it? I took his car and decided to run it through a car wash. I sat patiently, contemplating my weekend ahead, when all of the sudden I saw four men rolling Steve's car out of the wash. I could not believe what I was seeing! The car was dead. I sat for over an hour-and-a-half waiting for a tow truck to pick me up. I knew God was sending me a message. When I FINALLY arrived home, I opened up to receive it through meditation.

"Terri," I heard while meditating, "cars are symbolic of the physical journey you are taking. Steve's car dying is telling you that as you continue to follow his path and his way of doing things, you are not following your heart. You are dying."

Whoa! I couldn't believe what I was hearing but knew instinctively that it was the truth. God wanted me to know without a doubt that it was time to follow my heart instead of Steve's way of being.

God speaks to us in many ways. Some messages come wrapped in a beautiful gift like a song on the radio. And others, well, the packages aren't quite so pretty like Steve's car breaking down that day. Stay in awareness, Mom, and watch for God's messages. They are guiding you. Know that you are worthy of this kind of love.

Connecting to God through Meditation

The world around you is filled with messages. However, some of the most profound messages come when you open up in meditation. Meditation takes you straight to your heart and the voice of God.

If you're questioning meditation and what its value is, please know that, just for starters, it is something every person on this planet can physically benefit from. Many of our major medical hospitals are now using meditation for their patients. Studies show that meditation decreases stress levels and causes heart rates to slow down. That's a HUGE benefit for you, Mom! I learned this firsthand when Mackenzie, my firstborn, was a baby.

I had not yet learned much about meditation when Mackenzie was born, but, instinctively, every time she cried I held her to my chest and wouldn't say a thing, nor would I get upset by her tears. Then I would slow down my breathing. Immediately, she would match my breathing and completely relax, stopping her tears. My meditative breath raised my vibration to calmness. She matched my breathing and vibration, thus, relieving her stress. What an awakening this was for me! Not only did I learn more about meditation from this experience, but I also got to see how my actions affect my children. Mom, take the time to meditate and you will set the example for your kids to learn how to relax and do the same.

Some people think that meditation is scary and "New Age." It's not "New Age" and has been around for centuries. For instance, meditation is talked about in many books of the Bible including *Genesis 24:63* where Isaac "went out into the field one evening to meditate..." The intention of meditation is not to take you away from your religion or beliefs, but to help you find a greater connection to God.

I've had clients tell me that they have a hard time meditating. It wasn't easy for me either when I got started. I took a weekly meditation class. Each week my homework assignment was to meditate daily. For the first three weeks or so I found myself not meditating at the beginning of the week and being very lax about my commitment. But because I knew I had to show up at class at the end of the week, by mid-week I would kick into gear again. Pretty soon, however, I wanted to meditate. I loved how peaceful I felt. My goal was to meditate for 30-minutes a day. During that time, I would first get grounded in God's light, allowing it to flood throughout my body. I kept my attention on this energy washing away all of my pain, fear, and negativity, and then I would stay in awareness of the pictures I saw in my mind, the feelings I had, or the messages I heard in my ear. If I wasn't sure what something meant, I would ask questions. I felt like a detective! I loved the adventure I was on and still do! I never know what messages will come to me. That's what makes meditation enlightening and fun!

Some of my clients tell me that they do an active meditation like walking and running. This is great if you're doing it by yourself. If you choose this way, I would like to invite you to still take some time each day to sit quietly with God. It will give you great peace and tranquility.

Another way to meditate is to simply focus on your breathing like I mentioned earlier when talking about my daughter Mackenzie. Breathe in the light of God and breathe out all of the darkness that sits within you. Just release.

As you're reading this you are probably wondering, "How in the world am I going to make time for meditation? I've got laundry to do, errands to run, kids to schlep. How am I going to get it all in?" I get it. Please take my word for it that this will be one of the greatest gifts you will ever give yourself and your family. Meditation will give you answers to calm your life. Where you might have spent hours worrying about something, causing you to expend a lot of energy, meditation will help you get your answers quickly.

Getting started meditating is often the hardest thing to do, especially if you have kids at home all hours of the day. When I first began, it was a little trying for me to create boundaries with my kids. Kolbi, my littlest, was three. I remember telling her that it was time for me to meditate and that she had to leave the room. This was mommy's time. Because I knew I was doing something not only for myself but for my family as well, I stood my ground when she wanted to come in. She handled it very well. I believe she handled it well because I felt no guilt about taking this time for myself. I quickly realized that I was a better mom when I took time to meditate. My husband saw how it made me feel and completely supported me by watching our kids.

I remember the day when Kolbi quietly opened my bedroom door to peek in. I opened one eye and smiled at her and waived, whispering "shhhh" to her. She smiled and waved back, saying nothing, and shut the door. Not only was I taking care of my needs, but I was also teaching her to respect my boundaries.

Meditating has been a wonderful example for my kids to create boundaries for themselves, too. Mackenzie was having a rough day some years ago. Junior high was taking its toll. When I asked her if there was anything I could do, she said, "No." Then she told me, "Mom, I just need some quiet time to be alone." I was so grateful that I had set the example of taking time for myself so that my daughter could express herself this way. Mackenzie had learned from me that it is okay to take a time out and love yourself. Yeah!

I invite you to try meditation. As we move further into this book, I will teach you my favorite meditations through some of the exercises you'll do. They are a lot of fun and will take you straight to your heart. For right now, however, I invite you to simply create a quiet space, give yourself permission to receive God's love and guidance, and do the "Grounding in God's Light" meditation we talked about in Chapter One. If you find yourself worrying about something as you do this, imagine handing the reins of your life over to God. Surrender. Feel your body and the energy that is flooding through it. Then take the exercise one step further.

Watch any pictures that come into your mind, any thoughts you hear, or sensations you feel. If you have a question or concern about anything, ask it. Rest in the knowingness that it will be answered. Your answer may come during the actual meditation or it may come during the day through messages from your outer world. Just stay open and allow yourself to receive.

When I'm struggling with something in my life, I go straight to meditation. I create a quiet space and then set an intention. In Chapter One, we talked about setting an intention to be unconditional love. I set intentions for everything in my life. So if something is bothering me, after getting fully grounded and opened to receive, I set an intention for what I would like to heal. Instead of trying to control how a healing might happen, I set the intention that it is already done. I feel it in my body. I see myself celebrating and giving thanks for the healing, even though I have no idea how the answer will come to me. I take a stand for trust and know that the answer will be given because I know that I am worthy of receiving one. Then I breathe, relaxing deeper into the meditation, allowing God to guide me.

Please know that there is no right or wrong way to meditate. There are so many ways to go within and connect to God that I can't name them all here. If you would like to explore different types of meditation, go to your local bookstore, post office or coffee shop and look at the community board. Often you'll see meditation classes being offered in someone's home. This is a wonderful way to learn to meditate and meet others who are doing the same.

No matter what your meditation practice looks like, just by taking a time out for yourself, Mom, you will slow down and relax. And as you surrender to the process, you will open up and receive amazing messages from God.

Angels as Messengers

There are countless ways to connect to God's messages, Mom. One of my favorite ways is to talk to the angels. We all have beautiful angels watching over us. Most people believe in angels. On the other hand, many don't believe they can communicate with them.

When I first began my training at a school for energetic healing, I took a class in which we were taught to bring in our healing masters and connect their energy into our hands. I quickly learned that allowing the healing energy to flow through my hands was one of my gifts. I had no idea! The way we were introduced to our healing masters was by sitting in meditation and then imagining someone walking up to us. I immediately saw what I thought of as a man. My teacher guided the class to ask the "spirit" in front of us his or her name. My healing master's name was Michael.

Over the next few months Michael and I created an amazing relationship. The thing I loved most about him was that he had a crazy sense of humor and made me laugh. You probably think I'm a little off my rocker right now if you don't believe in this kind of relationship. That's okay. I didn't believe in this possibility either. But I was willing to try and loved imagining Michael in front of me. The more I worked with him, the more I believed in him and that he was my guide. If I needed a parking place in a busy crowded area, I asked for help. The more I knew he would help me, the more parking spaces were presented to me. It became a game. I was on an incredible adventure! Michael became one of my best friends and was always there to help me with my life, and to help bring healing to others.

Right after I started working with Michael, the movie *Michael* came out, starring John Travolta. I love movies and I loved this one. I loved it so much that I saw it FOUR times! That is not my norm. If I like a movie, I'll see it once and then watch it again on DVD. But to go to the theatre and pay to see a movie that many times was crazy! I didn't understand why in the world I was doing this, but felt driven to go. So I did. Then my dear friend Linda, who is also a healer and was taking the classes with me said, "Don't you think it's kind of ironic that you keep going to see a movie about the archangel Michael and your healing master is Michael?" I knew immediately that my Michael was the archangel Michael. I couldn't believe it! What I soon learned is that many people work with Michael. He is a loving, funny, dynamic angel and is there to help us heal.

Upon finishing my book, *Message Sent*, I sat down to meditate. I have no idea why I decided to tape my meditation that particular day, but I did. I wanted to talk out loud about what I was learning. During the meditation, Michael came to me. All of the sudden I saw him pick me up under his arms and sit me down with a plop. Then he handed me a contract and said, "Sign this." I visualized opening up the contract and read it out loud on the tape. It said:

I am a spiritual warrior.
I stand for truth and integrity.
I stand for being who I am,
Living from my heart and what I believe.
No other person's judgment shall hurt me,
For God is my authority.
This is who I am.

I was absolutely blown away when I went back and listened to the poem on the tape. That poem sits at the beginning of *Message Sent* and to this day is my life's theme. Michael, my beautiful, loving, funny angel friend had helped me once again, giving me guidance to find my truth.

Over the years Michael and I have continued working together. I hear his messages fairly easily now. In the beginning, however, I questioned myself. I found a great way to communicate with him by using Doreen Virtue's *Healing with the Angels Oracle Cards*. This is a beautiful deck of cards that is so simple to use, but the messages are absolutely profound. I have used them when I struggled with making decisions about my kids, or for just about anything. They bring great comfort. They also help you start trusting yourself.

When I first began my healing journey, I would get answers during my meditations but not trust them. Then I would pray over my angel cards asking for assistance. I found tremendous comfort when the card I pulled validated the message I had received in my meditation. With each time that I pulled a card telling me what I had already discovered for myself, it deepened my confidence in the messages I was receiving on my own through meditation. Now I hardly ever use the cards, but keep them to remind me that the angels are always there, watching over me.

My late husband, Steve, watched me working with Michael and, like me, had often been astonished at the help I received. Again, I'd like to point this out; I received the help because I knew I was worthy of this kind of love. And, I opened myself up to receive it. I gave myself permission. That's all it took. Steve, on the other hand, didn't quite believe he could have this kind of help. Then one day we went to our local coffee shop. When we went to order, we noticed a big silver platter with dice sitting on it. The girl behind the counter said, "Roll the dice. If you get a seven or an eleven, your coffee is free." I grabbed the dice, asked Michael for help and threw an eleven. "Your coffee is free!" the girl cheered. I was thrilled. Once again Michael had helped me. I turned to Steve and said, "I asked Michael for help." Steve took a quick breath and threw the dice.

"Wow! It's a seven. Your coffee is free, too!" The girl couldn't believe we both hit the jackpot. I looked at Steve and asked, "Did you ask for help, too?" He shook his head yes.

"Do you realize what just happened? Do you realize that the angels are here for you, too? You finally gave yourself permission to ask for help and receive it. They're here for you, Steve!" I exclaimed. "They are here for YOU. This is so cool!"

I knew in my heart that Steve had a tremendous shift in consciousness that day at the coffee shop. He finally realized he was worthy of this kind of love, too. That little incident changed his whole mindset. It wasn't too long after that wonderful gift that Steve and I drove up into the hills one night to look at the stars. He was struggling a little and felt very alone. I walked him through a healing meditation and asked him to call his angel before him. He invited one in and imagined it standing in front of him. I guided Steve to ask his angel friend what his name was. I told him whatever name came to mind was the right one and not to question it. Steve hesitated and flinched a little. Again, I asked him for a name. He said, "It's stupid. It's a stupid name."

"There are no stupid names," I said. "It doesn't matter what your angel's name is." My feeling is that angels don't really have names. I believe they are vibrations of energy that we can't even fathom. We give them names to make them more humanlike and so that we may call upon them. "What's your angel's name, Steve?" I asked again.

"Ralph." He seemed so disappointed. "Ralph. It's a stupid name for an angel, but it's Ralph." I guess he was expecting some poetic, profound, noble name, but instead he got Ralph. What he didn't realize was that Ralph was Raphael, the archangel that heals the physical body. When this happened Steve was fighting cancer. He had called on help from the angels and had no idea that he had called on one to help him heal his cancer. Steve didn't realize this until much later after spending many hours sitting on our front porch smoking cigars and talking to Ralph. He envisioned Ralph having a smoke with him. Steve found great comfort in this and got tremendous information from this healing space. And for the record, his cancer healed.

I'd like to invite you to give yourself permission to open up and receive help from the angels. When you do, you will be absolutely amazed at how they will help you. And as you give this gift to yourself, your family will benefit as well.

To invite your angel in, sit quietly and close your eyes. Get grounded in God's light and breathe. Give yourself permission to receive this kind of love. Then say, "I invite my beautiful angel guide to step before me." Now imagine your angel before you. That's all you have to do! The angels have always been there, right beside us. We just didn't know to look. But when we give ourselves permission to look and to receive, they reveal themselves to us.

Ask your angel, "What is your name?" Whatever name comes to mind is it. Don't question it. I've heard names like Sabrina, Glenda, and Tawanna come out of my clients' mouths. Again—IT DOESN'T MATTER! This name is for you to call upon your angel friend.

Now that you've called upon your angel and gotten its name, imagine crawling up into your angel's arms and feel the love. It feels soooooooo good. If you allow yourself to really sink into it, you might feel a tingling run throughout your body or a slight vibration. Over time the intensity of the feeling will build.

One of my favorite things to do is to lie on my bed and tell Michael, "I'm ready to raise my vibration to a higher level of love. I open myself up to receive your love and healing." As I breathe slowly and relax my breathing deeper into my abdomen, I begin to feel an intense energy flooding into my body from the top of my head. Pretty soon my whole body is enveloped in this energy and I literally feel as if I am vibrating. Sometimes the energy gets so intense that I can't move my arms, legs or face. I feel as if I'm glued to the bed.

I hope my description of raising my vibration doesn't scare you. As I have surrendered to this kind of healing from the angels and allowed myself to feel the energy, I have healed. And in that healing I have found so much love. When you allow the angels to help you raise your vibration, you feel as if you literally change the energy of the cells in your body.

Surrendering to the angel's healing is something you may want to work up to. When I first started working with the angels, I didn't believe or even know that this kind of healing was possible. But over time with each healing and with each message I've received, I've learned to trust the love that is there for me. That love helps me through each day. It helps me get through the struggles of being a mom and brings fun and adventure to my life where I often feel there is none.

I received a call one day from my client Sandy. "Terri," she said. "You're not going to believe what happened to me last night. Remember how we were working with my angel yesterday in our session? Well, last night I went to my friend's home clothing party. She always has a raffle at these parties and out of all the parties I've attended, I've never won. So, last night I called on Regina, my angel, right before the raffle was called out and said, 'This would be a fine time to help if you'd like to help me.' The next thing I knew I had won! I couldn't believe it! She really helped me!"

That's how the angels work if you are willing to receive their help and guidance. Another client, Elaine, told me a similar story. She and her husband had tickets to a baseball game in Anaheim, California. That's about 45 minutes from where she lives in Southern California. Elaine told me they were running late heading for the game and knew they were going to be stuck in evening traffic. What would normally be 45 minutes driving during the day would now be a good hour to an hour-and-a-half. They were going to miss the beginning of the game. Instead of fretting, however, Elaine called on her angel to help. As she shared her story with me, she was literally glowing with happiness. "Terri, I couldn't believe it! We got to that game in record time, faster than we normally would during the lighter traffic hours. It was as if the traffic just opened up!"

I have heard miracle story after miracle story about how the angels help people. Give yourself permission to open up and play with them, Mom, receiving their abundant love and healing. There is great comfort in realizing that you are not alone. Resting in that knowingness helps you to face each day. As moms, we feel alone a lot of the time. We feel a great burden resting on our shoulders to make sure that our family members' lives run smoothly. We get tired. We get frustrated. But it doesn't have to be that way. You can call on your angels at any time for love, comfort, and guidance. They are waiting to hear from you.

Spirit Guides

I can't tell you how many times I've guided people to connect to their guardian angels when, instead, a dead relative shows up. It's wonderful to know that our loved ones who have passed on are watching over us. Be open to all possibilities. You may be surprised as to which spirit reveals itself, especially when it's a guide you've never known before.

I was in shock when I first started meditating years ago. I saw the most beautiful Indian's face. I didn't ask to see him. He simply appeared. He was old and weathered. I felt immense love for this Indian. As his face disappeared, I almost cried. There was such a familiarity with him. I didn't want him to leave.

I call my Indian friend Waichuka. I have no idea if that could be a real name or not, but it is the name that came to me when I asked him what I might call him.

After seeing Waichuka in my meditation, I suddenly flashed on my life and realized that it must have been him who had guided me to Los Angeles. I had felt drawn to the city since I was in high school in Arkansas, but had never been. Something said I had to go to L.A. When I finally did, I rented a furnished apartment. It was clean but had furniture I didn't like. I wanted to make the best of the situation, so I went to the local drugstore to find some pictures to hang on the walls. I surprised myself when I chose a beautiful Indian's face. Every time I looked at that picture I felt a sense of peace and love. After seeing Waichuka in my meditation and remembering back to those first days in Los Angeles, I knew Waichuka had been my wonderful, loving guide to help me get there.

It doesn't matter whether you work with angels or spirit guides; it is all the same. These messengers from God are here to show you that you are not alone and never have been. You might see an angel, a dead relative, Christ, or an Indian guide. Open up to the possibilities that these spirits are all a part of God's loving energy and are here to help you through life.

~ ~ ~ ~ ~

Mom, if you're ready to call on your guardian angel or spirit guide, go to The Enlightened Mom Meditation CD #1, Track 5, to connect to God's guides.

~ ~ ~ ~ ~

You are not alone, Mom. God is with you at every moment of every day, sending you messages. As you continue to read this book, you'll see how all the different tools I've just shared with you have helped me receive God's guidance and love.

You, too, can have this kind of support. Give yourself permission to slow down and ask for guidance. Be aware. As you do, you will open up to the love that is always with you. At first you may get some answers and then you may not. It's okay. You've most likely spent a lifetime not listening, so this may take a little training. Be patient. You will begin to experience all kinds of beautiful, divine messages. Just by honoring your heart, you will open up a space in your life to finally see that you're surrounded by love. These messages will guide you and help you bring more peace, love and light into your life, making you a happier mom.

≈ ≈ ≈ ≈ ≈

PART II

Your Heart...
God's Greatest
Messenger Of All!

CHAPTER 3

The Pathway to Your Heart

$\mathcal{S}$ome years ago as a part of a Mother's Day event with the self-help website, ConsciousOne.com, we sent out an e-mail to members asking them if they had trouble with their moms and if they did, to please send me their stories. Upon receiving their messages, I sent them each a letter sharing how I had healed my relationship with my mother. Seventeen hundred people responded over a two-day period! Most of them told me stories about how their mothers wanted them to be something other than who they really were. As a result, the vast majority of the members said they didn't feel loved.

I understood every response we received. What these individuals told me was that they were still in pain and felt like victims of their mother's negative emotions and judgments. My impression was that each person still blamed his or her mom and hadn't taken full responsibility to heal. If they had, they might have realized that it wasn't their mothers they still blamed; they blamed themselves. Let me explain.

When our parents judge us, blame us, control us or try to mold us, it is because they are in pain. They are living from false beliefs that tell them they must act a certain way or be a particular way. They must perform for love. These beliefs run deep and are handed down from generation to generation. Unless this chain is broken and our parents heal themselves, they inflict their pain and false beliefs on us without knowing it. As a result, we take on the message that we are the problem and that there is something wrong with us. Therefore, we feel we are to blame for their pain and, as a result, we feel unaccepted and unloved.

To mask our pain, we blame the ones who judge us. And yet, we take their actions and words to heart and make them our truths. We believe we are not lovable. We can't forgive those who hurt us because we have to forgive ourselves first.

Forgiveness comes when we release the standards of how we think we "should" be. It comes when we give ourselves permission to stand in our truths, to honor our hearts and the way God made us. But since we live in a world that is more worried about what other people think, self-acceptance seems very far away.

The overall message I heard from those 1,700 people who responded to our Conscious One e-mail was that they had not forgiven nor accepted themselves. They were all in pain because they took their moms' pain and made it their own. Each of their mothers was hurting and took her wounds out on her kids. Instead of being loving adults, the moms were coming from a wounded child space. They didn't take responsibility to heal, so their actions sent the message to their kids that they were the problem. The wounded child inside each of the moms was hurting terribly and, thus, the pain was handed down to their kids.

As I grew up, my mom had a lot of knee-jerk reactions to me. And in those heightened moments, she said some pretty harsh things. Then there were those times that I felt I couldn't do anything right. I felt my mom had extreme expectations for me to perform by being the good little girl. That's because she had extreme expectations for herself.

Mom constantly judged herself and created a perfect picture in her mind of how she believed she had to be to receive love.

Mom lived from a subconscious belief that said the avenue to receive love was to perform for everyone. The standards that ruled her mind caused her to lash out at times, especially at my sister and me. It was in those moments that I began to believe that I caused my mom's pain. I felt blamed, and in return, I got mad at her. Thankfully, that has all changed.

I don't blame my mom now. I used to so much that when she tried to hug me, I became stiff with anger and judgment. I could not reciprocate her hugs. I wanted to lash out at her for all of the times I felt she expected me to perform. I can't change the past with my mom, but I have forgiven her because I have forgiven and accepted myself. I healed my pain. Instead of looking for my mom's approval, I have found it within myself. And, as a result, my mom is now one of my best friends.

I know in my heart that Mom's pain would have disappeared if she had been aware of the tools I'm teaching in this book so that she could have taken responsibility for her own happiness and healing. Instead, the little girl inside of her remained wounded.

Recognizing my mother's pain is how I opened up my heart to her. As I began to heal my life and nurture the little child inside of me, I was able to see the wounded little girl inside of her. I believe Mom lashed out because she didn't know how to love her inner child. She didn't have a role model for this kind of love. Most of us didn't.

We live in a world where it is easier to blame everyone else for our unhappiness, our lack of success, and our lack of abundance. That's why there is so much turmoil and anger in our world. Everyone is blaming everyone else. To stop the pain, we must take responsibility for our own happiness. And it starts with you, Mom.

When you take the time to get to know yourself and stand in your truth, you will stop the abuse that has been handed down to you. I'm talking about self-abuse that pours out from you onto everyone else. That's right. For instance, when you have knee-jerk reactions to your kids, in essence, you are abusing them. You have those uncontrollable reactions because you are living from false beliefs that were pushed on you. You felt forced to be a certain way and now you immediately react when a situation reminds you of that pain. You're not living from your truth.

Please know that I'm not trying to make you feel bad about yourself. I'm trying to enlighten you to the fact that the way we have been conditioned in our world is abusive. We're all suffering and lashing out due to a lack of loving ourselves.

We have been programmed to believe that we have to fit into a box to be loved. We have to perform to look like everyone else, dress like everyone else, do the same mundane things as everyone else, and believe as everyone else, or we won't be loved. The problem with this is that when you try to be like other people, you disconnect from God. And when you disconnect from God, there is no love and abundance.

We moms have a tremendous responsibility. The example we set affects everyone we love. When we heal, we break down the walls of separation and blame. We become whole, filled with love and acceptance. As a result, the disconnection we have felt with the world goes away. By taking the responsibility to get to know yourself, Mom, you stop the pain.

When you withhold love from yourself, you withhold it from everyone else.

When you don't take responsibility for your pain and continue to withhold love from yourself due to judgment and self-denial, you will withhold love from everyone else. For instance, if you judge yourself about not being smart enough, the chances are you will judge your child if he or she isn't a great student. This is just one example. You judge your kids, your spouse, your friends, your parents, your co-workers, or the stranger on the street because you judge yourself. You are withholding love from yourself, so you withhold it from everyone else. This creates separation and pain. But when you take the steps to get to know yourself and ask what is hurting, you heal.

I know this responsibility to heal sounds like a pretty tough job, but when you see that it is about loving yourself and the way you were created then the job doesn't seem quite so overwhelming. When you learn to do this for yourself and take full responsibility, your actions will teach your children, your spouse and all those you love as well. That's the beauty of healing yourself: you set the example for your loved ones to go within, facing their fears, allowing them a chance to love and honor themselves. By taking full responsibility for your happiness and abundance and by sending that message to your kids, they will grow up not needing to blame others for their pain, but will feel empowered in every encounter to find love in the situation.

It is time to scrape away all the false beliefs you took on since childhood and discover your truth. Peace, abundance and love are created by going within and embracing who you are and what you believe, giving yourself permission to stand in your truth and be unique.

Who are You?

It's time to get to know the real you. "The REAL ME?" you ask. "Who's that?"

In *Children Are From Heaven: Positive Parenting Skills for Raising Cooperative, Confident, and Compassionate Children*, John Gray, Ph.D. tells us that children tend to lose themselves when they don't know what they want, because they take on the wants and desires of others. And, as a result, they eventually disconnect from the powerful, passionate people they were created to be and lose their sense of direction.

Mom, if you want your kids to have wonderful, abundant lives, they have to learn what is right for them, not what is right for you. Your kids have to get in touch with their hearts, creating a connection to God. This is where they'll find their gifts to share with the world. THIS is why it is so important for you to get to know yourself, Mom. It's not your responsibility to make your kids happy. You can't make anyone happy. Happiness is a choice you make by going within to connect to your heart. All you can really do as a mom is to put God first in your life by honoring and loving the way you were created. You've got to dive deep within your heart and discover your truth. Jesus said, "I will ask the Father and he will give you another Counselor to be with you forever—the Spirit of truth. The world cannot accept him, because it neither sees him nor knows him. But you know him, for he lives with you and will be in you." *(John 14: 16-17)*

The spirit of truth is inside of you. As you give yourself permission to stand in your truth and embrace it, you live as Christ did. You become kindness, compassion, forgiveness and love. You commune with God. It is here that you will finally experience the abundance and joy you've been seeking your whole life.

I'll never forget the day I started my first book, *Message Sent*. I knew I was about to write a book but had no idea what it was going to be about. As I lay on the floor in deep meditation, I saw in my mind's eye a little child standing before me. This child was little Terri. Boy, did I sob! I had never noticed her before. I had never acknowledged her wants, desires and dreams. I didn't know her truth. I had lived my life continually performing, doing what I thought was right for everyone else and what I thought would make people love me. Because I denied myself, I was constantly angry, resentful, sad, and frustrated. You name it; I was filled with sheer pain and negativity. Don't get me wrong. On the outside you would never have known it since I put on my best face for the world to see. But on the inside I was drowning. I was buried in darkness until that day little Terri appeared. That's when I heard in my head, through the midst of all my tears, "Get up and write this, Terri. This is the beginning of your book."

Through the process of writing *Message Sent*, I began to discover myself. I let go of childhood programming that said I had to "act" a certain way to be loved. Instead, I got to know the real me and finally found love and acceptance for myself. The changes were profound! I no longer felt angry, sad, resentful, or frustrated, nor did I feel the need to control people to love me. I finally loved myself! And as a result, my family healed as well. The yelling stopped, my kids started getting along, and my husband, Steve, and I became more connected. Our whole family shifted!

Talking to the child within wasn't something I had ever studied. In spite of the fact that it took me almost a year to write *Message Sent* and the fact that I had tremendous healing, I still didn't get what talking to the inner child really meant, until one day when I went into a local bookstore.

I love God to guide me when I enter a bookstore. Instead of "thinking" what I want to read, I allow God to show me the way. So, on this particular day I had no idea why I was going into my local bookstore. I walked in, stood at the front door and asked, "So what do you want me to see today?" I always ask for an arrow to be shown in my head.

I followed the arrow to the middle of the store and then was shown to take a right. I did. The next thing I knew the arrow was guiding me to go down to the floor. There I was crawling around like a baby, following the imaginary arrow in my head. All of a sudden the arrow pointed at a book on the shelf. It was the only one of its kind. I pulled out the book, which was called *Healing Your Aloneness: Finding Love and Wholeness Through Your Inner Child,* and noticed that it was written by my old therapist, Erika Chopich, and her partner, Margaret Paul. Wow! Of all the books in that huge bookstore, I was guided to the one written by my old therapist. I didn't even know Erika wrote books. At the time I discovered her book, I hadn't seen her in almost 15 years. I sat there stunned, taking it all in.

I asked God, "What do you want me to see?" I got a page number in my mind and turned to it. I was in shock as I read a paragraph that explained that the pathway to higher consciousness is the relationship between the inner child and the inner adult. Oh, my gosh! I couldn't believe what God was showing me. In that message, my work with little Terri, my inner child, was defined in a nutshell. By acknowledging, loving and embracing little Terri, the truth of who I am and how I was created, I took a huge step onto the path of The Enlightened Mom. The irony is that I had never done any of this inner child work with Erika.

Talking to the inner child is the pathway to your heart. It is in your heart where God resides. This is where you connect to the intuitive, trusting, compassionate, creative, loving, kind and wise being that you are. You become enlightened.

"We must become like children to enter the kingdom of heaven." *(Matthew 18:3)* I believe that Bible verse tells us that to truly find the kingdom of heaven here on earth; in other words, to be enlightened, we must release all of our old beliefs taken on through the years and get in touch with the pureness of who we are. We are the children of

God. And, because of that, we are all creative, loving, compassionate, intuitive, kind and wise beings. We've just forgotten this along the way. Now it's time to remember. We remember by connecting to our hearts. Your heart is God's greatest messenger of all. And the little child within is the pathway there.

Connecting to the Child Within

It's time to connect to the child within! It's time to parent yourself the way you've always wanted to be loved!

To connect to the child within, you must first give yourself permission to see this little kid. Permission is key here. Society has told us for ages that to see ourselves, speak up for ourselves, or acknowledge ourselves in any way is selfish. And when we do finally take a step up for ourselves, we tend to feel guilty. It's time to stop the guilt and pain! It is up to you, Mom, to shift the cycle that has been handed down from generation to generation.

Say Hello to Your Inner Child

1. Get grounded in God's light, checking in to make sure your crown is open to receive, pulling your aura in to about arm's length all around you, and bring in the beautiful golden light from above, flushing it throughout your body down to the center of the earth.

2. Say, "Thank you God for guiding me into this healing. I now give myself permission to say hello to the little girl inside of me."

3. Imagine a little kid off in the distance. Notice that the child is walking towards you. As this little kid gets closer, take a look at her face. This is you. You are four or five. See your beautiful eyes, your little mouth, your tiny hands and feet. Notice what you are wearing.

4. Imagine pulling this little kid upon your lap and give her a hug. Tell her that she has permission to talk to you.

5. Get in touch with your inner child's feelings. Ask her, "Are you happy? Are you sad? Are you scared?" Is she mad at you for not acknowledging her for so long? It's okay. Know that whatever your inner child is feeling is awesome! What matters here is that you are finally acknowledging this little girl.

6. Feel everything.

7. Tell your inner child that you love her. Hug her like you always wanted to be loved. By acknowledging this little kid within, you have taken the first step to really loving and knowing yourself.

~ ~ ~ ~ ~

Go to The Enlightened Mom Meditation CD #1, Track 6, to say hello to your inner child.

~ ~ ~ ~ ~

Visualization is a wonderful way to create a relationship with the little girl inside of you. As you begin developing this relationship with your inner child, you may struggle a little. Please be patient with yourself. You've spent a lifetime neglecting her. She needs to feel safe.

Ask yourself, "What will happen if I acknowledge myself?" Allow all of your thoughts, feelings and emotions to arise. Feel everything. Imagine all of your fears draining down your grounding cord.

Some of my clients feel they don't have the gift of being able to see this kind of vision. Anybody can do it! If you're still struggling with this, I challenge you. Take a moment and think of one of your kids as a baby. I want you to remember holding this child and how it felt. Think about how cuddly and wonderful it was to rock your little baby in your arms. I know you can remember this. Well, it's no different when you visualize yourself as a little kid. It doesn't even matter if you've never seen a picture of yourself. The key is that you're creating a connection to your heart. Visualizing yourself as a little kid will make it more real.

Permission to Mother Yourself

When I first began to work with my client Sandy, she wouldn't allow herself to talk to her inner child. For months she ignored this little spirit within. Every time I had her visualize little Sandy on her lap, she said she felt like, "Ugh, not again." She was in complete resistance to loving and mothering the child within. Then one day before our session, after seeing how much pain she had been in week after week, I prayed for God to really heal her and to use me during our session together. Well, God took over.

I was guided to take Sandy through this lifetime. Sandy's mother died when she was six. Her father had to raise Sandy and her sisters all by himself. He had a heavy load. He couldn't replace the love and the nurturing of the girls' mom. Sandy felt extremely alone.

As we walked through Sandy's life, an old memory was revealed. It was one she had suppressed for most of her lifetime. While at her mom's funeral, her grandfather, during an emotional moment, told Sandy and her sisters that they had caused her mother's death. You can only imagine how it made little six-year-old Sandy feel.

I guided Sandy to visualize her grandfather before her, as well as his little inner child standing next to him. I invited Sandy to talk to this little boy and to ask him why he blamed Sandy and her sisters for her mother's death.

Sandy was shocked to see her grandfather's little inner child crying. He told her he was very sad about losing his daughter and was lashing out when he made his accusations at the funeral.

Sandy finally realized that her grandfather didn't nurture his child within and, thus, handed down his pain to her and her sisters. Sandy knew in that moment that for over forty years, she had been living with the subconscious belief that she was somehow to blame for her mother's death and now knew it had all been a lie. As a result, she got to the core of why she wouldn't nurture herself: she believed she wasn't worthy of love.

You don't have to lose your mother to experience the same kind of pain as Sandy. If your mother denied herself and her needs, doing everything for you as a kid, the chances are you, too, are carrying a program that says you are responsible for her pain.

"You are not to blame for your mother's pain." I was in shock the day I heard that whisper in my ear. I couldn't believe what I was hearing. But in that moment, I knew I had a belief that said my mother's pain was my fault. As I mentioned before, she lived her life for my sister and me. She denied herself completely. This denial caused her sadness and pain. And often she would blame us and yell at us, not realizing from where her pain really stemmed. This lashing out was the little child in her reacting and wanting to be loved. It was my mother needing to love the little girl inside of her. But because she didn't, and because she felt her pain was caused outside of herself, I took the blame. Just like Sandy, I believed I caused my mom's pain. So, with my own children, I continued the cycle. I denied myself, judged myself, and continually abused myself, feeling that I was bad, believing that I had to prove myself to my kids so that they would love me and not abandon me emotionally. What I was really doing, however, was abandoning myself, just as my mother did, perpetuating the cycle of self-denial for my children to grow up and do it all over again with their kids.

The cycle of pain is handed down from generation to generation. Our parents, grandparents, and generations beyond didn't have the tools to heal and take responsibility for themselves. They lived in the belief that pain, as well as love, was given by the outside world. They weren't whole. We, as little kids, didn't know any better and took their words and actions as truth. We blamed ourselves. The authority figures in our lives didn't take full responsibility for their actions, so we did. We've carried on the belief that we are bad. Just like my client Sandy did. As adults, we know intellectually that we aren't bad. However, the emotional charges that we took on in childhood still sit in the dark recesses of our minds. That's why we question ourselves. That's why we play mental games, burying ourselves in worry and responsibility. We don't want to cause our family pain. So we deny ourselves, never nurturing ourselves, burying the little child deep within.

No More Guilt!

Do you have a difficult time nurturing yourself? If you do, you're acting out of guilt. And your kids are helping you learn about yourself. I used to be buried in guilt, especially when it came to Mackenzie. She is my firstborn. And like so many moms, we have a tremendous connection to that child when they first enter our wombs. Then as they grow up and move into adolescence, they start pulling away. I hated this feeling with Mackenzie. I tried and tried to make her happy, but most of the time I failed. I felt as if I were losing her. I could have blamed her for my pain, but I didn't. I knew she was showing me something about myself.

Mackenzie has been a gift for me to see myself and to help me release the responsibility pictures in my mind of making people happy. In spite of all of the healing I had done over the years, she said to me one day, "Mom, sometimes I think you're stuck in your childhood. You had a lot of pain and you don't want me to have any. So you keep trying to make things okay. But they are okay. I don't feel what you felt when you were a kid. You're a great mom."

Mackenzie gave me a tremendous gift that day. She was right. I had been stuck in the pain of my past. I was still living from the belief that I had caused my mother's pain. When my mom said things like, "I love you, but I don't like you," or "I wish you were more like your sister," the little girl inside of her was striking out. It wasn't about me. I didn't know that then, so I took her messages personally. I truly believed I caused my mother's pain. I believed that well into adulthood. That negative charge in my brain stayed with me and played a part in every aspect of my life. I denied the little girl inside of me for fear that if I took care of her, I would hurt other people. I was buried in guilt. I didn't believe I was worthy of being loved.

Mom, the little girl inside of you is worthy of being nurtured and loved. It's time to release all of your guilt and shame that says this isn't so. Somewhere deep in your subconscious mind you have a belief that says you are not loveable. You believe that you don't deserve a life filled with abundance. But you do. You deserve a life filled with abundance and love, just like you want for your family. But it has to start with you lovingly mothering yourself first.

Guilt was the topic on a morning television show. The host did a whole 30 minutes on moms and guilt. I couldn't believe this! That is a lot more time than usually allotted for a segment on a morning show. The gist of the story was that moms are killing themselves trying to take care of their kids, giving them everything, sometimes working several jobs just so their children will have all of the "nice" things. The reason behind this insanity was said to be guilt. The story focused on our society and how everyone is competing to have the best and to get ahead first. The story said moms are taking on the responsibility to make sure that their kids aren't left behind. They don't want to do their children wrong. That was the end of the story. It was a good story; however, I think they missed another key point.

Moms work from a space of guilt with their kids because they somehow feel that if they don't get it right for their children, Mom will be blamed for their pain. The fear of being blamed rests in the fear that you will lose your children's love. This innate belief goes back to childhood once again where somewhere in the deep recesses of your mind, you took on a message that said you are bad and are to blame for another's pain and, as a result, are not worthy of nurturing and love. It's time to clean up this programming and move it out of your life once and for all, Mom. Let's get started.

You Are NOT Bad!

Think back to a time when you felt really bad about yourself. You may remember a situation when you felt as if you were being blamed for something and you felt a lot of shame. Or maybe you felt as if you were being unjustly treated, but you still hold onto the pain. Were you possibly spanked or slapped? Spanking or any other kind of corporal punishment is one of the worst forms of punishment and tells the child that he or she is bad and not worthy of love. My parents only spanked me a couple of times in my life. But as I dived deep within the recesses of my mind, I found that I had lost a part of myself in those moments. Many people believe that spanking will keep children in line, when in truth it does just the opposite. It may shut a child up in that moment, but the rage that builds within will have to come out eventually. That rage will surface as self-punishment or lashing out at the world.

In the award-winning book, *Raising Everyday Heroes: Parenting Children to be Self-Reliant,* Dr. Elisa Medhus says there is a difference between discipline and punishment. She says, "Punishment controls. Discipline guides and teaches so that children can learn to control themselves." Dr. Medhus continues by saying, "Punishment often smacks of disapproval. And since disapproval is usually expressed with negative judgments, insults, and threats, the child's self-worth eventually weakens. Once his self-esteem erodes enough, he begins to lose faith in his ability to make sound choices. Eventually he'll put more stock into the choices, opinions, and values of others then he does his own. Needless to say, misbehaviors continue or increase."

Why has your self-worth weakened over the years? Were you blamed for another's pain as a kid? Were you punished and still have a subconscious belief that says you are bad? Is this why you feel you are not worthy of love? Is this why you don't honor yourself and love the child within? As I said, I was only spanked a couple of times, but between those times and feeling I was to blame for my mother's pain, I took on a message that said I was bad and not worthy of love unless I made others happy. As a result, I buried my thoughts, my feelings, and my needs out of fear of losing other people's love.

I finally discovered that I was worthy of love when I released the negative belief that said I was bad and it was my responsibility to make people happy. By releasing this negative belief, I gave myself permission to really love the little girl inside of me.

Release Your Guilt!

1. Find a quiet space and sit with pen and paper. Get grounded, asking for God to help you heal. Give thanks for the healing that you are about to receive.

2. Write in big words: I FEEL GUILTY BECAUSE…. Then write everything down that comes to mind. Why do you feel

you are bad? Write anything about which you feel ashamed. Make a list of all of the guilt you are ready to release from the past. We're clearing out your energy so that you can live powerfully and lovingly in the present. Go as far back in time as you can remember, to your earliest memory of when you were blamed or punished for something, plus, add anything you feel guilty about that is still hidden in your heart, whether someone else knows about it or not.

3. Feel everything.

4. Imagine the little girl within you and take her up on your lap. Tell her you're sorry that she's been holding onto so much pain over the years. Tell her that she isn't bad. All of this is in the past. You didn't have the tools then to love yourself. But now you do! It's time to start fresh.

5. Imagine all of the mental pictures and energy that were released from this exercise being vacuumed into a big beautiful rose. Imagine that rose standing in front of you and visualize all of the darkness being sucked into the head of the rose. When you feel as if everything is gone, imagine closing the head of the rose and then visualize sending it out over the ocean, mountains, or forest and see it blowing up like confetti. This is a wonderful and loving way to release the energy back to the universe.

6. Once you've released all of this dark energy, fill yourself up with golden light, just like you do when you are grounding in God's light.

7. Give thanks to God for the amazing healing that just happened. Start today knowing that you are worthy of abundance and love.

8. Now go to the second part of this meditation and step into compassion.

Sometimes, in spite of the fact that we've done some healing work, we still hold onto negative judgments and can't forgive ourselves. If you find this happening to you, go back to the earliest memory you wrote down. With my client Sandy, I had her go back to the picture where her grandfather told her that she and her sisters were to blame for their mother's death. Take yourself in your mind back to the earliest memory of when you were blamed or punished. Be aware of your body and how it feels and how it shuts down. Stay grounded, making sure your crown is open. Continue with these steps:

Move into Compassion

1. Imagine the person who blamed or punished you. See this person in front of you and then visualize this person's inner child standing next to him or her. Ask the child what was hurting. With Sandy, I had her imagine her grandfather's inner child standing next to him. She asked the little boy why he would say such a mean thing. He said because he was hurting so badly that he needed someone to blame. In that moment, Sandy knew that her grandfather blaming her really had nothing to do with her or her sisters. The blame he was putting on the girls was the little boy inside of him acting out in pain.

2. If you feel you can, imagine taking the little child of the person who blamed you in your arms and say that you are sorry that he or she hurts, but that you will no longer own the blame.

3. Now send the person who blamed you, along with his or her inner child, into a beautiful white light back to God.

4. It's time to stop blaming yourself. Visualize your inner child. Turn to her and say, "You are not to blame for so-and-so's pain. It's time to let this go."

5. Ask your inner child, "What is your truth?" Is she ready to be nurtured? Is she ready to allow love in? Say, "I give myself permission to be nurtured." Or, "I give myself permission to…" Mom, you fill in the blank.

6. Give thanks, filling yourself up with the light of God, and celebrate that you're one step closer to being whole.

~ ~ ~ ~ ~

***Go to The Enlightened Mom Meditation CD #1, Track 7,
to release your guilt and move into compassion.***

~ ~ ~ ~ ~

If you get stuck during this exercise and question yourself as to whether you can see the other person's inner child, please relax. Allow your mind to expand. Check in with the crown of your head and make sure it is open. If you still can't imagine this person's inner child, step away and simply know that this person was in pain. People lash out when they're hurting. By recognizing this truth, your heart will open up to compassion and forgiveness for the person who hurt or blamed you.

For most of us growing up, the adults in our lives weren't enlightened. They weren't whole. When life didn't go the way they wanted, they often lashed out, sometimes by withdrawing from us, or sometimes with an emotional outburst, often heightened with a fist, a slap or a belt. When those eruptions were centered on us, we took on the message that we were to blame for their pain. As adults, if we haven't healed the pain that we took on, we perpetuate the cycle all over again.

It's up to you to release the pain and use the tools in this book to heal. Let's go back to Sandy's story for a moment. If Sandy's grandfather had been enlightened, he would have known that there was no way those little girls caused their mom's death. I'm sure as an adult he knew this wasn't the truth. But in that moment, because he wasn't whole and his inner child reacted, his pain lashed out onto those little girls. He was an adult authority in their lives, so Sandy took his words as truth.

When you lash out at your family, your wounded inner child has taken over. It's as if the adult in you has left the room. This is why it's so important to love and acknowledge the little girl within you. When she feels loved by you, she'll have less reason to lash out at the world.

Most every person on this planet lives by the subconscious belief that they are bad. That's why they judge themselves, and as a result, judge each other. Most don't feel they are worthy of being loved. So they take their pain out on the world around them. When you finally take responsibility for your life and heal the pain of the past that says you are bad, you'll be able to see this for yourself. No longer will you need to take other people's pain personally. You'll recognize it as their journey and that their pain has nothing to do with you. You will have compassion for them, because you've found compassion for yourself. By not taking their actions personally, you will treat them with love, showing them how to treat themselves.

This is what it means to walk the path of The Enlightened Mom. Being an Enlightened Mom means that you learn to re-parent the little child within. You acknowledge her and have compassion for her. You learn to love both her quirks and gifts. It means that you visualize that little child within and love her, no matter what she looks like or acts like or feels like. To be an Enlightened Mom is to love and accept your humanness. And as you do this for yourself, you will love your family unconditionally as well. The key is to stop judging yourself as bad, allowing yourself to acknowledge, love, and nurture the child within. She is your heart, God's greatest messenger of all.

~ ~ ~ ~ ~

CHAPTER 4

Give Your Inner Child a Voice

*Y*our inner child IS God's greatest messenger of all. Creating communication with her is imperative to your healing process. She's been trying to talk to you for a very long time. You probably just weren't listening.

The little child inside of you is that small voice you hear every now and then. I'm sure you can recall a time when you heard something in the back of your mind and acted upon it. The outcome was most likely right on. And then you've probably also experienced those times when you didn't listen. How many times have you said, "Darn, I didn't listen to my gut"? That message you ignored came from the little kid inside of you. You're probably just not accustomed to hearing her so you don't tend to listen.

My little Terri is like an appendage to me. If I'm driving down the street, I imagine her riding in the passenger seat. She is with me at all

..mes. By talking to her daily, I have discovered who she is and what makes her happy.

As you create a relationship with your inner child, you will learn what brings her joy and what saddens her. You'll also be able to ask her questions as to why she's angry with someone and what she's reacting to. That's a great gift, especially when it comes to healing your knee-jerk reactions to your kids!

At times you will see the little girl inside of you as wounded and other times you will see her really alive. You will begin to discern which aspect of her you are talking to as you create a relationship with this little child.

When you find yourself reacting to anything negatively, know that the little girl inside of you is in pain. She's taken on some belief of how she "has to be" to receive love. By going within and talking to her and allowing her to express her feelings, you will unlock the chains of past negative beliefs and discover who you really are. Giving your little child inside a voice is an essential step in healing your life and connecting to God.

For several years every time I went to the grocery store, the bank or anywhere else in public, I felt myself shaking right where my ribs meet. This area is your power center. I couldn't understand why in the world I felt this extremely uncomfortable vibration, much like anxiety, while doing something as mundane as going to the grocery store. I drove myself crazy asking, "Why in the world is this happening to me? I'm a public speaker!" The irony was that I didn't feel like this on stage. This energy drove me nuts. I kept resisting it, telling myself that I shouldn't be feeling this way. Then one day I was guided in meditation. "Terri," I heard in my head. And by the way, the voice I hear is mine. It's not some booming, almighty sound. "Use your tools," I heard. "Embrace the pain. See the gift in this situation."

I knew that this was the truth. I had been resisting my pain. My body was reacting negatively because something inside of me was hurting. I began to give thanks for the pain every time I felt it. Finally, one day while at an office superstore, I felt the anxiety again. I stopped, took a breath, and imagined little Terri standing in front of me with her big brown eyes and her curly blonde hair. I leaned over my shopping cart and asked, "What's hurting inside of you? What are you afraid of?"

"I have to act perfectly when I go out into public or I get into BIG trouble," was her response.

I couldn't believe what I was hearing in my head, but knew it was a fear I had lived with my whole life. My parents had been sticklers for good behavior when I was a kid. They loved me a lot and believed this would get me the most approval. It just didn't help me to love myself. With little Terri's response, I knew that I had been living by a false belief that said I had to act perfectly out in public or else I would get into trouble. I told little Terri, "I am the boss now. You have my permission to do cartwheels down this aisle if it will make you feel better." Of course, my mind didn't need little Terri to do cartwheels. All it needed was permission to let go of this old false belief. And in that moment it did. I have never felt that horrible sensation in my power center again. I had to take back my power. And when I did, I released the emotional charge in my subconscious brain that caused my body to react so negatively. My body was telling me that something was wrong. Little Terri was screaming out for my attention, holding in her pain, creating a temper tantrum inside my body. Thankfully, I finally got the message.

I shared my story about the office superstore with a friend. She asked, "Terri, how do you get such clear answers? I never get them like that."

My friend exercises her body a lot. I told her that just as she nurtures herself in this way, exercising every day, I exercise my relationship with Little Terri. I talk to her every day so that when there is a really difficult situation I can hear what she has to say.

I invite you to make the child within your new best friend. If you can find some kind of reminder like an old picture of yourself to put out in a noticeable location in your home, that would be great! The bathroom and the bedroom are both ideal places. And if you work outside of the home, please put one on your office desk, too. Setting out a picture will help you stay focused on loving and honoring yourself. If you don't have a childhood picture, use something like a stuffed animal, a trinket, or anything that will work as a symbol to remind you of the little girl inside of you. Once you've done this, every time you see the picture or trinket, say hello to the little girl within. Ask her how she's doing. Acknowledge her and love her. Help her to feel safe so that she can communicate freely with you.

Write to Your Inner Child

I love to visualize little Terri and have lots of conversations with her. However, one of my favorite tools to communicate with her is to write to her. I take time each day to get grounded and fully open and then I write in my journal, creating wonderful communication with little Terri. I've found, however, through my own experiences and from watching my clients struggle with this, that it is often very hard to get started with this kind of dialogue. We have been so ingrained with the belief that our writing has to be grammatically correct and written with the proper sentence structure and punctuation that people tend to fight themselves when getting started. I did this, too, and had to constantly remind myself that I wasn't in school. We lose a big part of our creativity because of the rigidity of this programming. I invite you right now to give yourself permission to release these old beliefs and begin to write to the little girl inside of you.

If you really want to test these old limiting beliefs then write with your other hand. In *The Power of Your Other Hand: A Course in Channeling the Inner Wisdom of the Right Brain,* Lucia Capacchione, Ph.D., invites us to write with the "other hand" because it opens us up to the right side of the brain. She writes, "When you realize that the non-dominant hand is governed by the right hemisphere in most people, it is no surprise that the qualities ascribed to the right side of the brain—creative, emotional, intuitive—are precisely the qualities that come out most easily when the non-dominant hand writes."

If you are right-handed, you are wired to work from the left side of the brain. This is the analytical side. When you work mostly from this part of your mind, you will likely struggle connecting to your intuitive, creative self. But by switching the pen to your non-dominant hand, which in this case will be your left hand, you shift to the right side of the brain. You open up to your intuitive self, creating a connection to the wisdom of God's messages. And communicating with the little girl inside of you is a wonderful avenue to get there!

If you are left-handed, you may be thinking that this means you are automatically working from your intuitive right brain. But that's not necessarily the case. Dr. Capacchione says that 66% of people who are left-handed still work from the analytical left brain. If you feel you are one of the 66% of left-handers who are not working from their right brain then writing with the non-dominant hand may be the perfect tool for you.

I am right-handed. After taking a few moments of quiet meditation, I put my pen in my dominant hand, which is my right hand. I write any question that is bothering me with this hand. Then I take the pen and pass it to my left hand, which is my non-dominant hand. The non-dominant hand is the voice of little Terri. I write whatever thoughts come to me. Often the thoughts will be filled with emotion. But as I allow the emotion to flow, whether it's anger, sadness, judgment, or any other kind of pain, I begin to get to the bottom of what I want to know.

Writing with the other hand is invaluable when it comes to letting go of false beliefs. Often when you ask yourself a question, you will get a left brained analytical answer that tells you what you're "supposed" to do. But when you talk to the little girl inside of you, especially when you allow her to speak to you via your non-dominant hand, you get to your truth.

Writing with Your Other Hand

1. Have pen and paper in front of you. Give thanks for the healing you are about to receive and get fully grounded. Open up and give yourself permission to receive God's love, light and guidance with clarity.

2. Write with your dominant hand any thoughts, feelings or questions that might be coming up for you.

3. When you are ready to receive an answer, switch your pen

to the other hand so that your inner child can talk to you. If you get stuck, check in with the crown of your head again and make sure it is open and allowing the messages to flow. Be free with your writing. Don't worry about how it looks, and don't worry about grammar, punctuation, or spelling. Just allow it to flow.

4. Feel free to express everything.

5. When you get stumped with something, ask questions again with your dominant hand and then switch once again to your other hand for the answer. If need be, pretend you are a reporter asking such questions as "Who, what, when, where, why, and how?"

6. Once you are done, give thanks for the healing and act upon any messages that you have received.

I find that some of my clients tend to avoid this exercise. They can't read their writing from the other hand, so they get frustrated. That's okay. I couldn't read my writing either when I first began, but I stayed with it. The key is to be consistent and persistent. Before long you will notice your handwriting getting better and better. Now I can write in cursive with my left hand and it's completely legible. And the interesting aspect of this is that as my writing has gotten more legible, my creativity and intuition have deepened.

Writing with your other hand is a wonderful way for you to communicate with the little girl inside of you. She is the messenger of your heart. As I have worked with this tool, and I use it a lot, I have discovered that I have different handwriting for the various ages of the child inside of me. There are times when I talk to the teenager, being that I have teenagers in my house, and that writing tends to be in cursive. Little Terri's writing looks more like chicken scratch.

Writing with the other hand is also an avenue for you to talk directly to God, your guardian angels, and spirit guides. It is a tool to use whenever you have questions. The key is to create communication that will guide you to the unique, lovable you. Talking to the little girl inside of you is the best way there.

Daily Chats with the Child Within

I love talking to the little Terri. Whether I see her in my mind through visualization or through talking to her with pen and paper, my relationship with her has healed my life. She represents who I really am, not who I thought I had to be. By loving and honoring her, I have found freedom within me!

Create a daily ritual where you talk to the child within. Do this any way you choose. You may communicate with her through writing, listening for her little voice, or visualizing her. Always start with getting grounded.

Make sure you tell the little girl within that she has permission to speak her thoughts and feelings to you, especially if you feel her holding back. And make sure the crown of your head is always open and connected to the beautiful golden light of God. Sometimes when you don't get an answer it's because you've shut down to this connection.

Ask your inner child what she's feeling and what she needs from you to feel loved. If she is in fear, have compassion for her. Remember, she is just a little kid. Visualize giving her a huge hug. Take action with the message you receive.

Commit to this type of communication daily. You want this child to feel safe so that she will speak freely. It is your responsibility to love her and parent her so that she feels safe. Think of it this way: if you went for days not talking to your real kids, they wouldn't like you very much. In fact, they'd probably resent the heck out of you and feel extremely abandoned. Well, that's what happens to the little girl inside of you when you neglect her and don't talk to her.

I invite you to talk to the child within every moment that you can. I imagine little Terri with me all of the time. She is my little friend.

Make your little inner child your new best friend. Get to know her just as you would a new friend. As you love her this way, and give her a chance to speak, you will begin to see just how wonderful and unique God created her to be.

Children Should Be Seen and Not Heard...Baloney!

Creating communication with the world around you is the next step in giving the child inside of you a voice. As you take a stand to love and protect the little girl within by giving her permission to speak, you may find yourself struggling with this. For many of us, we were raised to believe that children should be seen and not heard. We were sent a message that our feelings didn't matter and that our parents knew better than us. But if we truly want to be all that we were created to be, we have to give the little child inside permission to speak freely to others. We have to heal the pain of the past that says we can't have a voice.

Think back for a moment. Do you remember a time when you were reprimanded for speaking? What scares you about speaking up to your family? For some women, they are afraid that if they do this, they will not be loved. If that is the way you feel, where does this fear come from? Did you speak up about something as a child and got sent to your room? Or maybe you were slapped? Or possibly humiliated by a parent, teacher, or friend? I remember being reprimanded in the second grade for talking to a boy. I got sent to the cloakroom. I was absolutely horrified that I was punished this way. You can darn well bet that I never did that again.

Some years ago, my late husband, Steve, and I had dinner with some friends whose children were still quite young. The man was a very attentive father and loved his kids deeply. However, when he told me that he had a rule that his children were not allowed to question him, I felt very sad for all of them. This is another reason we lose our voices. We were told as kids to do things and when we asked why, our parents told us, "Because I said so. Quit asking so many questions." If we questioned them, we were often punished. As a result, we took on the belief that to speak and ask questions led to punishment.

By having an attitude like this particular dad, parents send messages to their kids that it isn't okay to be curious and to ask questions. Therefore, when children grow up, their voices are hidden.

These types of situations make an impact on you. If you don't allow yourself to speak from your heart, you are punishing yourself. God gave you a voice to use. Why do you hide it?

What feelings come up for you when you consider speaking up for yourself? Take a moment and try this exercise.

Give Yourself a Voice—Part I

1. Sit quietly with a pen and paper on your lap. Get completely grounded in God's light. Check in with your aura and grounding cord, making sure you are centered, opening yourself up and giving thanks to God for the clarity you are about to receive.

2. Acknowledge your little child within and imagine her sitting beside you.

3. Ask your inner child why she's afraid to speak her thoughts, feeling and beliefs to others. Ask the question with your dominant hand and remember to allow her to answer you with your less-dominant hand. Or if visualization works better for you, use that tool, or just listen to her.

4. Allow your emotions to surface. Feel everything until you feel as if you've emptied out.

5. Give this little girl permission to speak out to the world. Tell her that it's okay and that you will love her even if others abandon her as she speaks her voice.

6. Fill yourself up with the golden light of God and give thanks for the healing.

The second part of this exercise is to help you release the judgment and blame towards the person who you felt shut down your voice.

Remember, if someone controlled you and the way you were when you were a kid, it is most likely because that person felt controlled and in pain, too.

Give Yourself a Voice—Part II

1. Go back to that time when your inner child took on a message that she couldn't speak. See the situation.

2. Imagine the person who you believe forced you to shut down your voice. See that person's inner child standing next to him or her. Ask the child what was hurting.

3. Tell this other person's inner child that you are sorry for his or her pain, but you have a right to speak your voice and, from now on, you will.

4. Imagine all of the energy from this person that you've held onto for years. Visualize this energy draining down your grounding cord.

5. Give thanks and send this other person, along with his or her inner child, into a beautiful white light. You've just sent them back to God.

6. Now it's time to call back your voice. Ask God to bring this part of your soul, your voice, back to you now. If you want to visualize this, imagine a beautiful light coming from the highest points of the universe. Allow it to re-enter through your head, filling you up from your head to your toes, throughout your aura, and down your grounding cord.

7. You have now taken back the voice that is rightfully yours. Congratulations! Give thanks for the healing and celebrate.

~~~~~~~~~~

Go to The Enlightened Mom Meditation CD #1, Track 8,
and give yourself a voice!

~~~~~~~~~~

After going through the steps of this exercise, you may feel that no one told you to hold your voice in, but for some reason, you do. Chances are, you probably saw another person getting reprimanded as a child for speaking out and then decided from that point on that you would not get in trouble for using your voice. Many of my clients lost their voices that way. Often they had older siblings who were reprimanded, so they made the decision to be the "good child" and hold their voices in. Even though the reprimanding didn't happen directly to you, you may still have a belief that says to be loved you have to stuff your thoughts and feelings deep inside of you.

It doesn't matter where you took on your false belief. You were created with a voice. Now it's time to use it. Stay in awareness of when you stifle your voice. Every time you realize that you're doing this, stop, give thanks to God for helping you see the truth, and then ask the little girl within what is hurting. Continue to remind her that she has permission to speak her truth.

My client Kathy didn't used to give herself a voice. But once we began working together, she started speaking up more. There was still one problem, however. When she talked, it's as if her sentences came to an abrupt halt, often in mid-sentence. I asked her about this one day during one of our coaching sessions. I took her through a guided meditation, talking to the little girl inside of her and asked her what she was afraid of if she was to speak up. She said, "The little girl inside of me is afraid to make a mistake."

Fear of making a mistake or saying the wrong thing is one of the greatest reasons we hold our voices in. Whether it's the fear of being humiliated or embarrassed, or the fear of sounding stupid or wrong, people have all different kinds of reasons for not giving themselves permission to speak their truths. It all comes back to seeking love outside of yourself. If you are constantly monitoring yourself and what you say for fear of what others will think, you are looking for love from the outside world rather than from within. It is only from within that you will connect to God's love, the true source of all love.

Kathy also discovered by going within that one of the reasons she didn't allow herself to speak was because she was afraid she would be seen as arrogant. I had asked her what she felt when others spoke their minds with certainty and she said, "I see them as being arrogant." Some might call that being a "know-it-all."

I heard my daughter Kolbi say something about one of her friends some years ago. I'll call her friend Joanie. Kolbi said, "Mom, it's as if she always has to be right. She thinks she knows everything."

I invited Kolbi to look at how, just possibly, she might have been holding her voice in when it came to her friends. Joanie, on the other hand, didn't. I asked Kolbi if she was afraid of what her friends would think of her if she was different from them and spoke up. I know Kolbi judged Joanie because Kolbi at that time was afraid to speak her voice. It's always easier to judge something than to face the fears that are inside of us. Thankfully, Kolbi now speaks her truth with her friends.

"You're acting way too big for your britches." How many times did you hear that as a kid? This statement is another reason we hold our voices in. As we grow up and start having thoughts and opinions about the world around us, we tend to speak up. But for some reason, as soon as we find our voices, we get reprimanded with this remark. Before you know it, our voices are gone.

I often hear women say they won't speak up because they don't want to rock the boat. Have you ever done that? Have you ever held your voice in for fear that you would create problems by speaking up? What were you afraid of? Do you hold your voice in with your kids? What do you need to say to them? Why don't you speak from your heart? Take a look at these things and get to the truth. Ask the little child inside of you what is hurting. Have compassion for her pain and tell her that no matter what anyone else thinks, even if they reject her, you will always love her.

I held my voice in as a kid because my dad was the voice of our family. I did not want to upset him or cause any conflict with him. I loved him dearly and didn't want to lose his love.

Daddy was the authority in our family. My mom valued Dad's voice more than she valued her own. I learned this behavior by watching them. So when I grew up, I always gave the men in my life the power over my voice. I was afraid to speak my wants and needs for fear they would stop loving me. I did this with my husband, too. What I learned, however, is that I harbored a tremendous amount of resentment towards him due to suppressing my voice. At first I didn't see this as my issue. Instead, I blamed him for our problems.

Resentment and blame are directly correlated to stuffing your voice in. You think you're mad at the people around you. It's not their fault. You have to make yourself happy by giving the little girl inside of you permission to speak up.

The Battle of the Voices Within

My client Jane has been speaking her voice for some time. However, she often comes across abrasive and angry. That's the tug of war going on within her. She knows she has to speak up for herself, but there is a part of her that still feels she doesn't have a right to do this. As a result, when she finally speaks, the battle that is going on inside of her creates negative energy on her words. This energy makes her sound angry and hateful. As Jane gives herself full permission to speak from her heart, this negative energy will go away.

During a coaching session with Jane, she told me that she is constantly helping her boss speak his needs and that he really values this gift she brings. And, yet, she still judges this about herself. However, a light came on for her as I helped her recognize the wonderful opportunity she has to be of service to her boss and co-workers. By giving herself permission to fully speak from her heart, she is setting an example of love for all of them to do the same. Just by telling Jane this, her total consciousness shifted. She walked out of my office with a smile on her face, knowing that she is a gift to those in her workplace.

If you find yourself in a similar situation like Jane where you feel that battle within, know that the little girl inside of you is really scared. She doesn't feel she has a right to speak up. She is afraid that if she does, she will lose the other person's love. Imagine taking her up in your arms, just like you would do with one of your kids, give her a hug and tell her that she is being an example of love by speaking up. The more you make the little girl inside of you feel safe, the more at ease she will be with speaking her voice.

Fear of Abandonment and Rejection

Almost every mom I have worked with over the years has been terribly afraid of speaking up to her family. Most were afraid of causing their families pain. So they gave their power away. For every one of them, their fears were based in negative childhood programming telling them that if they spoke up they would either be abandoned or rejected from another's love.

Are you afraid of being abandoned if you give the little girl inside of you a voice? Are you fearful of being rejected? One of the main reasons we don't speak our truths is that we are afraid to be alone. But the truth is that when you don't give yourself a voice, YOU abandon yourself. You reject yourself! That is why you are angry, sad and frustrated. You have abandoned yourself by not speaking up.

In *Vocal Power: Harnessing the Power Within*, Arthur Samuel Joseph, voice coach to CEOs, doctors, politicians, Olympic athletes, and movie stars says, "While speaking, we open up and reveal ourselves, communicating our innermost selves to the outer world. At the same time, we offer our thoughts, whether simple or profound, personal or general, to the threat of judgment. We thereby risk parental, social, and public censure—or acceptance."

Do you shut down your voice out of a fear of being judged? I did for years. I really, truly believed that I had to stuff my voice in so that I might receive love. I saw both my mom and dad do it with each other for over 30 years. I believed that to hold your thoughts and feelings in was an act of love. They thought the same thing. But it wasn't. By controlling myself this way, I wanted to control others. I expected them to know what I wanted, needed and felt. And when they didn't, boy, you had to get out of my way.

Do you ever feel as if an eruption is about to take over your body? You try to control it and push the emotions down, but for some reason, the words and feelings come exploding out. That's what I did. I suppressed my voice so much that eventually the words came blasting out. It was miserable for me, and for my family. I thought by holding my voice in I was doing them a favor. Instead, I created more pain, not only for myself, but also for my family. I knew that if I didn't change this habit, my kids would grow up and do the same all over again.

Are you denying your voice out of a fear of being abandoned and rejected? Take a moment and think about this. Ask the little girl inside of you what it means to her if she is abandoned or rejected. What does she think will happen to her? Spend some time journaling or writing with your other hand to go deep within and discover what belief you're holding onto. Or use whatever tool works best for you to create communication with the little child within. Remember, you are not alone. God is always with you. Even if the person you need to speak to rejects you, as long as you use the tools in this book to keep yourself connected to God, you will always feel loved.

God gave you a voice. It is time to use it. Start recognizing when you are holding your voice in and ask the little girl inside of you, "What's hurting? What old belief is running your life?" Continue to give her permission to speak up. As you take a stand for your inner child and give her permission to have a voice, you may find yourself really scared. These feelings are the little girl inside of you trying to communicate with you. She's afraid. Let her know you love her and tell her it's okay. Remember, you are learning to re-parent this little kid. She needs to know that it is safe to speak. Have the courage to give the little girl inside of you a voice. Do this for yourself. Do this for your family.

~ ~ ~ ~ ~

CHAPTER 5

You Have to Feel to Heal

hen I first gave myself permission to honor and love little Terri, it scared the "bedoodies" out of me. Yes, that's a word. It's my word and it means that my insides were in major turmoil. I was terrified to be the real me. I felt that if I spoke my needs, my thoughts or feelings, I would be seen as bad. When I did try to express these things, my throat tightened and I felt as if my head was going to explode.

As I became aware of the feelings that were strangling me, I realized they were there to teach me. Just like every other aspect of you, your feelings are God-given. They are in your life to show you yourself. They are messages from God.

By going within and talking to little Terri, I soon discovered that I had held my feelings in most of my life. I believed this was the right thing to do. I watched my dad be strong and I wanted to be just like him. But by holding onto old feelings, I created a wall. It was HUGE and very thick. I created it for protection. Little Terri decided a very long time ago that to hold her emotions in was to be strong. Boy, was she wrong!

As I have traveled this journey to my heart, the greatest gifts I have given myself are to speak and feel. By giving little Terri permission to feel all of her emotions and by making a choice not to judge them, I have opened up to compassion and helped her feel safe.

Does the little girl inside of you feel safe, Mom? Does she have the freedom to feel everything? Or do you suppress her so much that she wants to run away?

John came in for a coaching session with a big smile on his face. This was our first time to meet so he was putting his best face forward. However, as we moved deeper into our session, I soon realized that his smile was a mask. He didn't allow himself to feel. John even told me that when his mom died, he didn't cry. I asked him why and he said he didn't know. We went further into the healing and soon discovered that he had learned this from his dad.

Like John, many of us have taken on the societal programming that says to be strong we must not feel. As women, we tend to have more permission to shed tears than men, but there is still judgment when we feel our emotions. Little girls are often told they are too sensitive.

My client Kathy is a chiropractor. She was made fun of as a child for being too sensitive. Thus, she shut down her emotions. When I first started coaching Kathy, she was going through a painful divorce, but had a hard time allowing herself to cry. When we dove in and asked why, it was due to her past programming. The irony is that Kathy is a healer and to truly utilize her abilities, she's had to re-learn how to feel and give herself permission to be sensitive again. Being sensitive is one of Kathy's greatest gifts and allows her to connect on a deep level to what her patients need.

Then there are the women who cry at the drop of a pin and don't know why. A large part of the time they judge themselves for being too emotional. Many of these women feel guilty for not being happy. They don't understand why they are sad. Instead of diving into the sadness, or whatever emotion is coming up for them, they push it away.

Mom, by FEELING all of the emotions inside of you and accepting that this is what it means to be human, you will turn the darkness in your life to joy.

Give Yourself Permission To Feel

Feeling is to healing as breathing is to life. We must feel to heal. That's why you'll see me write "feel everything" throughout this book. Your feelings are guideposts. If you have positive ones, you'll feel vibrant and alive knowing that you're following your heart. Your negative emotions, on the other hand, tell you that you've disconnected from God.

To unlock the pain and hurt in your life, Mom, you must dive into your negative feelings. Your feelings will take you to the false beliefs you've been holding onto for a lifetime. These are the beliefs that tell you that you are unworthy and unlovable simply for being you. And as you release these beliefs, you create a connection to God and step into abundance.

Your feelings are gifts.
You have to dive deep inside
of them for the gifts to be revealed.

And that's exactly what we're going to do as we move through this book. But first, you have to give yourself full permission to feel everything. Most of us don't have permission to be this authentic. Just like John, we have been trained to mask our feelings and be strong.

Society applauds those who stand strong. That kind of strength, however, is a façade. True strength comes from having the courage to be vulnerable and real, feeling everything.

When we follow society's definition of strength, we bury ourselves. The wall that we create keeps us from getting to know who we really are. We have to break down that wall and feel everything to heal and connect to our hearts.

As moms, we all have bad moments, days for goodness sakes, sometimes weeks and months. Often, we don't understand why. We just feel yucky. Maybe we feel sad. Maybe we feel angry. Maybe we feel hopeless. Then we find ourselves taking out these emotions on our family members, creating a cycle of pain and judgment. We want to stop the pain, but to do that, we have to embrace the feelings that are churning deep inside of us.

When you experience negative feelings, Mom, how do you deal with them? Do you honor the feelings? Do you try to push them away? Or, even more importantly, do you acknowledge that you are feeling anything?

It is vital for your health and emotional well-being to feel everything that is inside of you. So think about this for a moment. Do you acknowledge how you feel? Or do you put your feelings aside to take care of everyone else's? Have you ever smiled when you really felt like crying? Do you judge yourself when you feel angry, sad, or frustrated? Why do you do this? Why don't you allow yourself to feel your emotions? If you're like me, you may judge certain feelings and embrace others. What messages were sent to you as a kid regarding your feelings?

Many of us were raised to put on our best faces. That's the mask I was talking about. We were told to smile even when we felt down inside. We were told that to hold our feelings in was the "right" thing to do. I know you've been to the grocery store and have seen a mother dealing with a crying toddler. Very seldom, if ever, do you see a mom say, "It's okay, honey. I know you're tired. Go ahead and cry if you need to. You'll feel better afterwards." I've only seen situations similar to this a couple of times in all of my adult years. What you usually see is the adult telling the child to be quiet. And the more the child cries out of the need to feel and release whatever is going on inside, the more the mom gets frustrated. The mom is usually concerned about what everyone else will think and doesn't want the child to be a nuisance to the people in the store. However, she's sending a message to her little one that says we must hold our feelings in to be accepted and loved.

We not only send our kids messages to hold their negative feelings in, but also their playful and happy ones. I'll never forget years ago driving in the car with my girls. They were probably two and four. I wasn't paying any attention to what they were doing. I just heard noise, so I told them to settle down and be quiet. Then I realized they weren't fighting; they were having fun together, laughing and giggling. I was so caught up in my own world that I couldn't see the joy they were experiencing.

I took Kolbi shopping for some clothes one day. As I stood in the huge dressing area while she tried on things, two little boys were also there, waiting on their mom. They weren't out of line in any way, but they were jumping up and down looking in the mirror, trying to entertain themselves. I could tell the mom was extremely concerned about what I was going to think about her kids. I laughed at the boys and got playful with them. Immediately, the mom relaxed and grinned at me. She didn't mind that her kids were having fun. It actually made her time go much easier. She was only concerned about what I would think.

Children need to be told it's okay to feel. Whether it's playful feelings, passionate feelings, or any kind of negative feeling, we have to give them permission to be human. We have to do this by starting with ourselves first.

When I was in the seventh grade, our family went snow skiing in New Mexico. We traveled with another family in their big van. I had never been skiing and did very well on the slopes. I did so well that after taking a class for a couple of hours, my instructor told me to "get out of here." So my dad and I headed up to the top of the mountain. I had a great time and was thrilled with how well I was doing. I felt completely alive!

The day we headed back home to Arkansas, we were reliving our experiences on the slopes. I felt very passionate and excited about what I had accomplished. I wanted to share my excitement. However, my exuberance wasn't tolerated.

My dad quickly shut me down. He somehow saw my excitement as bragging. I was simply being a kid expressing the joy of what I had discovered about myself. But Dad felt that I was being inconsiderate and wanted me to be accepted by the other family in the van. I know his intentions were good and he just wanted the best for me, but in that moment I made a choice to believe that my dad was right and to hold my passion in. For years after that I suppressed my passionate feelings. If I found myself feeling giddy and excited about something new, I didn't allow myself to fully feel my emotions. I thought if I did, I was bad.

To be fully human, we must embrace our humanness. We must feel everything and give ourselves permission to express our emotions in a way that is right and unique for us. I'm not suggesting that you express your feelings by lashing out at others. I'm saying to express your feelings in a safe loving way, but in a way that is right for you.

It was a beautiful day and it seemed as if the whole town was out to enjoy the sunset as I took a walk along the beach. As I strolled, watching surfers ride the waves, I heard a loud squeal. I looked further down my path to see a little boy face down, having fallen off of his scooter.

I headed for the little boy just in time to see his dad reach him. "Why did you yell like that?" He asked his son. "You DON'T yell when you fall."

I couldn't believe what I was hearing from this man, and on the other hand, I knew that this was a negative belief handed down through time, probably from generation to generation. The man's words told his son that it wasn't okay to express his hurt and pain. His reprimand said that squealing was not okay. But it is okay. The little boy didn't hurt anyone else. Obviously, this is how he needed to express himself.

As I walked away from this scene, I wondered how this child would deal with similar situations in the future. Would he allow himself to release the pain with a squeal? Would he allow himself to cry? Or would he hold his feelings in, judging himself for having them in the first place? That moment at the beach could change the rest of his life. I have seen over and over how a situation just like this one can dramatically alter how a person deals with pain.

When we judge our human feelings, we create more pain. I've had people write me about how depressed they feel about being depressed. My response is to embrace the depression instead of judging it. Love it and let it tell you what's hurting inside of you. That's the gift of your emotions. By feeling all of your pain and allowing yourself to go within to see what is hurting, you are able to heal past wounds and negative messages.

The worst thing you can do with any emotion is to shut it down. By shutting it down, you get stuck in life. You must embrace the feeling and allow it to flow. You have to release the old negative programming handed down to you from parents, relatives, teachers and friends, telling you that it's not okay to feel.

My dad used to tell me to hold my anger in. This was the worst thing he could say to me. He thought he was doing me a favor and helping me cope with the world. But he wasn't. By stuffing my anger in, I only got angrier to the point of hitting people. My anger was a red flag telling me that something wasn't right in my life. Now with my family and my clients, I encourage them to feel the anger and talk about it.

What feelings are you holding onto, Mom? Are you angry? Do you need to grieve something? Are you frustrated with your life?

Your emotions that keep welling up are the little kid inside of you hurting. That child feels as if you are not hearing her. You're not acknowledging her. To make the pain go away, you must have compassion for this little child's hurts and embrace her pain.

Imagine this: your daughter walks up to you crying hysterically. In her hands, you notice her favorite little guinea pig wrapped up in a blanket. As you pull back the blanket, you realize that her tiny pet is dead.

Now imagine telling your little girl that she isn't allowed to cry and that she has to go sit in a dark room by herself.

I'm sure you're horrified by this vision and can't understand why in the world I would ask you to imagine this. Well, I want you to see what you do to yourself, the little girl inside of you, when you push your feelings to the side and don't acknowledge yourself. In essence, you are telling the child within that she doesn't matter and are stuffing her into a corner. It is this feeling of being ignored that keeps your inner child in pain.

If you don't allow yourself to feel your emotions, you most likely took on some kind of message as a child that said you had to act a certain way. In our need to please those around us so that we might continue to receive their love, we, as children, took people's messages as truth. We believed that we had to act the way they told us or we would lose their love. But those messages were wrong. We have to break the myth of how we "should be" and allow ourselves to be who we are. That's where true joy comes from. It sits beneath the pain and emotions. You have to peel away the pain to get to the joy, abundance and passion you deserve.

Permission to Feel—Part I

1. Create a healing space for yourself. Sit quietly with the phone turned off and have a pencil and paper ready. Get yourself grounded and open yourself to receive God's love and guidance. Tell yourself that you have permission to receive this kind of love.

2. Imagine the little girl inside of you sitting on your lap. Tell her that she has permission to feel.

3. Ask her, "What scares you about feeling your emotions?" Then ask her, "What are you feeling right now?" You can either write this conversation, going back and forth between your dominant and non-dominant hand, you can visualize it, or just hear it. Do what works for you.

4. Visualize hugging this little girl inside of you, making her feel safe. Emotions will most likely surface. Feel them all and just keep loving her!

5. Give thanks for this beautiful healing and fill yourself up with the golden light of God.

As you went through this first exercise, did you have memories surface from your childhood telling you that it wasn't okay to feel? As I wrote earlier, my dad told me to hold my anger in. I had no idea that by holding it in I was only creating more anger. It wasn't until I did this next exercise that I was able to understand and release my dad's message. Plus, I moved from a space of judgment towards him to a place of understanding and compassion for his pain.

Permission to Feel—Part II

1. Think back to your earliest memory of when someone told you to shut down your feelings. Your feelings could have been ones of sadness, pain, fear, happiness, joy or passion. It doesn't matter what the emotion was.

2. Write about this situation, going back and forth between your two hands. Or visualize the situation, or listen for the conversation. Allow your feelings to flow. If you feel the need, scream, yell, or do anything else to express yourself. Please just do it in a safe way.

3. Now close your eyes and imagine the person in front of you who gave you this negative message. See this person's inner child standing next to him or her. Ask the person's inner child why that message was given. What was hurting inside? Recognize that this person's pain was really about him or her, not you. When people send us negative messages, it is simply because they are in pain and are often scared to death of what others will think.

4. Now tell yourself, "I give myself permission to release any and all negative messages that tell me I cannot feel." Drain off all of the energy from this person's negative message, plus any other energy you're holding onto that says you can't feel. Allow the energy to flow down your grounding cord.

5. Give thanks to this person and his or her inner child, and send them off into the white light of God.

6. Ask your inner child what she needs to be able to heal this. For instance, if she was told not to cry, then she most likely needs permission to cry. If she was told not to be too boisterous and

you now find yourself holding your laughter back, then give her permission to laugh, laugh, laugh!

7. Fill yourself up with the golden light of God and give thanks for this amazing healing!

~ ~ ~ ~ ~

Go to The Enlightened Mom Meditation CD #1, Track 9, and give yourself permission to feel everything.

~ ~ ~ ~ ~

I invite you to do this exercise as soon as possible so that you might really open up your heart. Be in awareness at all times, asking yourself if you're suppressing your true feelings in any way. Remember, we have to feel to heal. Feeling is the pathway to God.

If you've spent a lifetime denying your emotions, prepare for the floodgates to open. This exercise will help you open up and release all of the pain you've been holding onto. Whatever you do, please don't judge the process. It is real and what is needed to heal.

I held my feelings in for years, so when I finally allowed myself to open up, it seemed as if the dam had burst open. If this happens for you, make sure you share with your family what you're doing. Let them know that you don't need any of them to fix you or to heal you. Tell them that this isn't about them, but about you releasing negative feelings so that you can make room for happiness in your life. Tell them that you are celebrating this release and to please be patient with you.

There was a time when my late hubby, Steve, felt as if he had had enough with my tears. He said, "Sometimes you are hard to live with, Terri." I knew my tears were hard for him because he had a negative programming that said he was responsible for making me feel better and had to fix everything. I told him, "Honey, this isn't about you. I love you. I don't need anything from you but to allow me this process." When he realized that it didn't have to be his burden, he got okay with my emotions. He saw that I was taking full responsibility for my life and was allowing myself to feel so that I could heal and be happy. Over the years, Steve saw how going through this process made me a much more loving and nurturing person, not only to myself, but to him and our kids as well.

Negative Feelings Sap You

Have you ever considered why you're so tired as a mom? I'm sure you feel tired or run down at times. There aren't many moms who don't feel this way. Of course, the main reason you feel you are exhausted is because you're doing everything for your family. Right? Well, it goes deeper than that.

Tap into your feelings for a moment. Do you feel guilty about how you're dealing with your kids? Are you angry about something? Are you sad? Do you feel there is no time for yourself? If you don't take the time to look at each of these emotions and FEEL them, giving yourself a chance to get in touch with the belief that is causing them in the first place, these emotions will sap your energy.

If you're feeling stuck in a rut and mired in negativity, it's because you aren't allowing yourself to feel. Negative feelings are the little kid inside of you screaming out to be heard and loved. They are messages from God that something isn't working in your life. They are very real and, when ignored, literally drain you of your power.

Dr. David R. Hawkins, renowned psychiatrist, researcher, expert on mental processes, and spiritual teacher, explains in his book, *Power vs. Force: The Hidden Determinants of Human Behavior,* that there are different levels of human consciousness, each at a different calibration. Dr. Hawkins tells us of his scale that measures the "power of the energy of different attitudes, thoughts, feelings, situations, and relationships." In other words, every emotion you feel, every thought you think, and every attitude and belief you have has a certain energy related to it. It has a vibration. Dr. Hawkins explains that all the negative emotions you feel actually sap your life force energy.

If you're tired as a mom, there is a strong chance that you are holding onto some lower level energies like anger, frustration, guilt, blame and shame. You may not even recognize that you have some of these feelings inside of you. I didn't. The only thing I recognized as a part of my life was anger. Not until I decided to heal and get in touch with my feelings did I see all of the negativity I was holding onto and how it was sapping my energy. For instance, I was molested when I was 15. Shame was buried deep within me and I didn't even know it. As I dug into my feelings, I realized that the shame I held onto not only sapped me of my energy, but was partially the reason I kept myself from going out into the world, not only with the work I was doing, but also with life in general. I'm talking about just being social. I found myself always working diligently, trying to be good, but never having fun. I felt I had to prove that I wasn't bad and that I was good enough to be loved. This drive to hide my shame kept me exhausted.

I was also a master at judging myself and early on as a mom felt great guilt for what I might be doing wrong with my kids. This guilt literally kept me frozen in fear. It kept me exhausted, as well. I constantly stayed busy, doing everything for my family simply due to my fear that I might make a mistake with them. In my mind, if I made a mistake, I would lose my family's love. I thought that my "busyness" was what kept me so tired. It was a part of the problem. The real issue, however, was the lower vibration of the guilt I held onto.

I can't tell you how many women have come in to see me for coaching, complaining of constantly feeling rundown or sick. Each of these women struggled with loving herself. Self-denial was always the main culprit brought on by guilt, shame and fear. The more these women denied themselves, the sicker they felt. But as each took responsibility to honor and love herself and to release the guilt, she became energized and more fully alive. These women had the courage to heal.

Courage is the point that Dr. Hawkins says "power first appears" and where we bring life force energy to us. He adds, "At the level of courage, an attainment of true power occurs; therefore, it's also the level of empowerment. This is the zone of exploration, accomplishment, fortitude, and determination."

You are reading this book because you are ready to heal your life and become an Enlightened Mom. To do this, you must be willing to explore your feelings. This is courage. As you question yourself and sit in doubt as to whether you can commit to the path of The Enlightened Mom, think about how all of the negative emotions are draining the life right out of you. It's not your family draining you; the reason you feel so tired is because you are not doing anything for yourself out of old false negative beliefs, and the energy related to those beliefs is wiping you out.

Mom, it's not what you're doing for your family, but what you're not doing for yourself that makes you feel so exhausted!

It wasn't until I mustered up the courage to go within and explore all of my negative emotions that I truly healed. As I released the energy that was sapping me, my attitude towards being a mom changed. I feel more energized and alive than I've ever felt. I now face my family each day with more humor, happiness, and peace than I could have ever imagined. That's because I finally got in touch with my feelings.

Mom, it is only by getting in touch with your feelings and the beliefs that are causing them in the first place that you can truly release them. And when you do, your energy soars because you're finally loving the real you.

I know it's scary to look at yourself and to dive deep into your emotions. It is, however, these negative emotions that are sucking your life force from you. They are telling you that you are saying "No!" to your heart. It's time to say a great big "YES!" to you.

Please recognize that the reason you have been guided to this book is because you finally have the courage to heal. And if you are stuck in negative emotions and are not paying attention to yourself then every task you do is going to be met with resistance. That's the little girl inside of you taking a stand, telling you that she needs YOU to hear her and love her. And the way to move out of this resistance is by allowing the little girl inside of you to feel.

Recognizing Negative Feelings

1. Create a healing space with pen and paper in hand. Get grounded and give thanks to God for the healing you are about to receive.

2. Write the first question below and then fill in the blank and expand on your answer. Do this with each question. If you want, put each one on a separate piece of paper. Notice how I use the words "I feel." By saying "I feel," you take yourself into your heart. Most people say "I think." This is your brain talking. The key to healing is to tap into your heart. By saying "I feel," you move into this space.

    I feel angry because _____

    I feel resentment because _____

    I feel frustrated because _____

    I feel fearful because _____

    I feel sad because _____

    I feel hopeless because _____

    I feel guilty because _____

    I feel shame because _____

Are there any other negative emotions that you'd like to write about that I haven't listed here? Please take some time to explore those before you move on.

What did you discover about yourself after doing this exercise? Are you holding on to some lower level emotions that you didn't know you had? If you recognize some, congratulations! You have just taken a HUGE step into healing. You have moved into AWARENESS. Being aware of what's going on inside of you is key to healing.

Now let's take this exercise one step further.

3. Go to the question that really got you "lit" up. By this I mean the one that you felt your nerves were on fire. Allow your feelings to flow.

4. Now ask the little girl within what this reminds you of in your childhood. For instance, when I had a participant in one of my classes do this exercise, she said she felt frustrated with her life because she always wanted her home and family to be perfect. When she asked herself what this was about, she was taken back to her childhood. At that time in her life she lived in a nice neighborhood. However, she lived with her sister and her mom. They struggled to make life work, whereas everyone else in the neighborhood had what she believed to be a great life filled with abundance. I asked her what feelings were coming up for her with this memory and she said, "Humiliation."

5. After you've tapped into the childhood memory, write about it. Write everything. Hold nothing in. Allow all of your feelings to flow. Let it all go. Feel the pain that you've been holding onto since you were a little kid. As you write your feelings and go through this healing process, please give thanks the whole time.

6. Ask your inner child, "What false belief did you take on in this situation that is causing your negative emotions?" This belief may be connected to what you think you deserve or how you think you're "supposed to be" to receive love, just like the Enlightened Mom in my class. The frustration she felt about her home stemmed from a belief that said she would be humiliated if it wasn't perfect. Spend time unlocking your hidden false beliefs, Mom. You may get an answer immediately or it may come later. Be okay with your process. Sometimes beliefs are buried so deep that we can't see them at first.

7. Ask your inner child, "What is your truth?" Give her permission to stand in this truth, and, as you do, open yourself up to receive God's love, allowing the beautiful golden light to flood throughout your body. Celebrate and give thanks for the gift you have been given.

Notice how in step five I invite you to give thanks the whole time you are expressing your feelings. The reason I invite you to do this is that as you sit in gratitude, you immediately begin to raise your vibration from negative energy to positive energy. I invite you to do this with every exercise in this book. This attitude will help empower you, rather than feeling like a victim. My intention for you in all of the exercises is to help you see that you are the creator of your life and to help you release false beliefs that are hindering you and blocking your joy. When you give thanks for a healing as it is occurring, you shift your attitude from feeling like a victim to being empowered.

For years you've been walking around like a wounded child. It's now time to empower yourself and think of yourself as the mother to your own inner child. It is time to pay attention to the little girl inside of you just as you do to your kids. When you feel any negative emotions, know that this little girl is hurting. Become the loving adult and allow this child to feel. Give her permission to feel everything. Tell her there are new rules; from now on she is allowed to feel all of her emotions. Tell her that it is wonderful to be fully alive and heal. The next time you are sad about something, visualize pulling the little girl upon your lap, hugging her and loving her. Give her full permission to be who she is, a child so alive that she is no longer numb from controlling her feelings.

We've been told that our feelings don't matter or that we're being a burden to others if we're not wearing our "happy face" masks. So we hide out of our need to be loved and, thus, control our feelings. But it is in hiding and controlling our feelings that we separate from love. We become angry, resentful and filled with pain. But to experience love, Mom, you must give yourself permission to feel everything.

～ ～ ～ ～ ～

CHAPTER 6

Say "YES!" to Your Heart

*Y*ou know the old saying, "When momma's happy, everybody's happy"? Well, the way to make momma happy is to make the child inside of you happy. And that starts by talking to her and asking her what she wants and needs from you. If you're still struggling with this idea, remember, putting God first in your life is the avenue to peace, abundance and love. And the way you do that is to honor your heart.

Your feelings of being overwhelmed, burdened, and wanting to run away are direct results of you disconnecting from your heart and denying the child within. When you REACT to life this way, it is the little girl inside of you who is hurting. She feels as if she is alone. She needs someone to love and honor her. That someone is YOU.

It's time to start looking at what makes the little girl inside of you feel happy and alive so that you may bring positive energy to your life. It's time to say "YES!" to your heart and create a connection to God.

I know it's scary to take a stand for yourself. You've been denying yourself for so long that you probably have no idea what you want or desire. Please remember, you set the tone for your family. You can't make them happy, but you can be an example of unconditional love and abundance for yourself, allowing the love to overflow to them. Say to yourself, "YES! I am worthy of God's love and abundance. I am an expression of God's love. This is the greatest gift I can give to my family."

Open Up to Abundance

1. Get grounded in God's light. Give thanks for the healing that is about to take place. Ask God for clarity and help with loving yourself.

2. Visualize the little girl inside of you sitting on your lap. Ask her to tell you five things she would do right now if she could choose anything. Ask her, "What would make you feel happy and alive?" Would she take a class? Would she see a friend? How about exercise? What would make her really happy? Possibly a nap? When was the last time you allowed this little girl enough time to sit down and read a book for fun?

3. It's time to be the loving mom to the little girl inside of you. Pick at least one of these things and put it on your calendar this week. Make a commitment to this little girl to love her. If putting this activity on your schedule creates a time crunch, see what you can let go of this week. If you're struggling with this, go down each item on your "to do" list and ask yourself, "Is this something I really FEEL I want to do, or is this something I think I'm 'supposed' to do? Am I performing again?" If your answer lands in the latter category, recognize that it isn't your truth, and let it go.

4. Once you've determined what you are willing to release from your schedule so that you can honor the little child within, set

an intention. Visualize yourself doing your activity. Be in the picture. What's going on around you? Now take that image and bring it into your heart. Feel the excitement in your body for having loved and honored yourself. Give thanks to God for giving you this gift and say, "Yes, Yes, YES!"

5. Go for it! Take action and create what you want. Sit in the knowingness that you are doing a great service for yourself and your family by honoring and loving the feelings in your heart and by taking action. This is truly creating a divine connection!

~ ~ ~ ~ ~

***Go to The Enlightened Mom Meditation CD #2,
Track 1, and open up to abundance!***

~ ~ ~ ~ ~

This exercise is terrific in creating abundance in your life. You are going to feel absolutely wonderful for taking time for yourself. By releasing old negative feelings of how life "should" be and giving yourself permission to follow the feelings in your heart, you are going to feel so energized, you won't know what to do with yourself!

You may be someone who takes time exercising, but does nothing to get in touch with your heart. To be truly whole and feel abundant, you must honor every side of yourself: the body, mind and the spirit.

For me, it has always been hard to honor the physical side. I did for a while, playing tennis. But it didn't bring me a lot of fulfillment. When I found myself on a spiritual journey, I was hooked and let tennis go. I couldn't believe the adventure I was on and how loving and wonderful I felt. However, I still felt something was missing.

I don't believe I truly felt empowered and abundant until I added exercise back into my life, keeping a balance with my spiritual life. I was already good about honoring my mind, probably too much so. It was my body that suffered. Now I try to honor each side of who I am, knowing that this is what makes me feel happy and alive.

As you check your weekly or daily calendar, see if you are following your heart. Is there balance between the things you feel you need to do for your family and the things you want to do for yourself? Are you saying "YES!" to your heart at least some of the time? I used to think that balance had to be done every day. What I soon realized, however, is that some days would be filled with kid stuff, and others would be for me to take some personal time. Just like pediatricians will tell you about kids eating: don't look at the daily intake. Look at what is consumed for the whole week. This is the same for balancing your life with what you want and need, and still taking care of your family.

I Don't Know What I Want

Every client I have ever worked with has said at one point or another, "I don't know what I want." That's because they have spent a lifetime not paying attention to the feelings in their hearts. So when they ask themselves what they want to bring to their lives, they have no idea. Even when they ask the little child within, they sometimes don't get an answer. If, after doing this last exercise, you feel as if you are lost, too, try this: think back to when you were a little kid and remember the things that brought you great joy. For me, it was reading or being outdoors with friends, playing sports. I was also intrigued by the spirit world. I didn't allow myself to go there much out of fear, but nonetheless, it was something in which I had a deep interest.

"What made me feel happy as a child?" Keep this thought in mind whenever you get stuck and don't know what you want. Another question to ask is, "What would lift my spirits right now?" Shakti Gawain mentions this question in her book, *Creating True Prosperity.* As you walk through each day and find yourself stuck in a rut, both of these questions will help you get in touch with your heart.

You are Worthy of Abundance

Listening to your feelings is the avenue to creating abundance in your life. Your feelings are messages from God. However, after doing the last exercise on abundance and tapping into what would really make you feel alive, did you possibly hear a little voice in the back of your mind saying, "Well, I'll never be able to have that in my life"? Or maybe you heard, "You can't have that. Moms don't do that."

That is the wounded little girl inside of you running some old negative belief that says she isn't worthy of this kind of love and abundance. But she is. She simply bought into an old belief that was either passed on by society or one that she took on from her family.

I grew up with a belief that a woman's job was to stay in the home and be mom for everyone, including the husband! How many times have you heard a mom say that she has three kids she gave birth to, plus her husband, which totals the number to four? I can't tell you how many times I've heard that remark. The numbers are always different, but the message is the same. We moms are mothers to everyone but ourselves.

When I first got married to Steve, I played the mom role very well. He worked extremely hard as a garment manufacturer of women's clothing. He was off and on planes regularly, sometimes gone for two weeks. He worked hard and he played hard. When he was home, he liked to unwind on our boat or by riding motorcycles. I resented the heck out of him. He was having all of the fun.

Over time, after a lot of griping and moaning, Steve started to back off with his playtime. I wanted him home, believing that by being home he would be acting as a father "should" act. So I let him know it. He couldn't stand my wrath anymore. He began to believe my message that said he was the problem and was making me unhappy. So, he stopped playing so much. What happened, however, is that he shut down to me. He resented me and blamed me for no longer being happy.

The anger and walls that grew between us almost ruined us. That's until I decided to heal. I soon learned that I had to love and honor myself with things that I loved. I had to take full responsibility for my happiness. I gave little Terri a voice and started protecting her and loving her by taking care of her needs and wants. I began to have more fun by listening to my heart and tapping into the things that made me feel happy and alive.

I soon realized that Steve had been right all along. He had known how to have fun. The problem was that I didn't. But the more I honored little Terri's feelings and gave her a voice, I became a much more loving and nurturing mother not only to myself, but to my whole family. The walls between Steve and me came tumbling down. Ironically, it took a long time for Steve to get back to having fun. He had gotten really shut down to life out of guilt and feeling responsible for my past pain. But as he saw me heal and take full responsibility for my happiness, I set the example for him to do the same. It wasn't until Steve decided to heal that he finally gave himself permission to have fun again.

True happiness comes from within. And the way to tap into that happiness is by giving the little kid inside of you as much love as you possibly can and by asking her what she needs and wants.

Take Inspired Action

It's one thing to finally get an answer as to what will make you feel energized and alive. What you have to remember, however, is that nothing in your life will change if you don't take action. In fact, sometimes when you do get an answer and then don't act upon it, you feel even more depressed. Look at it this way. You ask your son or daughter what he or she would like to do for the day. Your child is thrilled that you've finally asked this question. "I want to go to the movie," is the response you hear. You say okay, but then the phone rings. Your attention turns to the person on the phone and the next thing you know you've forgotten your plans. Now your child is sulking and mad, not understanding why you asked for a suggestion in the first place.

When you take the time to ask the little kid inside of you what would make her feel alive and she gives you an answer, or even if she doesn't speak up but you get an answer when you ask, "What would lift my spirits right now?" take action. You can darn well bet the little girl within is going to be really mad if you deny the request. That anger will no doubt land on the people around you. But YOU have the power to stop this cycle of pain, Mom, when you take action. This is "inspired action." That's because your inner child's answers are from God. You're listening to your heart. By taking "inspired action," you create a life of abundance.

Permission to Receive What You Want

Sharing your feelings with others and telling them what you need and want is an important aspect of nurturing yourself. I had a belief for years that if I asked for what I wanted, I would be told "no." I didn't feel I could receive that kind of love.

Do you fear being told "no" if you ask for what you want? Do you feel emotional just by thinking about this question? Is this what keeps you from taking action and following the messages in your heart?

If you feel you can't have what you want, it's because you still haven't given yourself permission to receive this kind of love. I know that if I'm afraid someone is going to tell me "no," it's because I haven't given myself permission to receive a "YES!"

Where does your fear of being told "no" come from? Who told you that you couldn't have what you wanted? Were you told that you were being selfish for asking? Or did you not ask for what you wanted because your role models never asked? As little kids, our parents were the authorities of our lives, so our wants and needs were determined by them. But you're not a little kid anymore. The whole point of walking the path of The Enlightened Mom is to re-parent yourself.

Do you have permission to ask and then receive what you want? Ask yourself this question right now: "Do I feel I can have what I want?" You might hear the response, "Sometimes." Or you may even hear a loud "NO!"

What is your belief? Do this next exercise to release the false belief that says you can't receive a resounding "YES!"

Permission to Receive a "YES!"

1. Go into your meditative space, getting fully grounded, opening up to God's love and guidance. Give thanks for the healing you are about to receive.

2. Bring your inner child upon your lap. Ask her to take you back to the earliest time in your memory where you didn't feel as if you could receive a "YES!"

3. See the other person involved and imagine his or her inner child standing there. Ask what was hurting in this child so much that you, in turn, were told "no." What was this child's belief?

4. Give thanks and send this person and his or her inner child off into the beautiful white healing light of God.

5. Ask yourself if you are still holding onto this belief. If you feel that you are, tell the little girl inside of you that it is time to let it go. Visualize a rose and imagine holding it by the stem. See the head of the rose opening up and sucking in all of the dark energy from this old negative situation. Send the rose out over the ocean, mountains, etc., and blow it up like confetti, sending the energy back to the universe with love.

6. Allow God's light to flood throughout your body, aura, and grounding cord, filling you up with love. And as you do, say to your inner child, "I give you permission to receive a YES!"

7. Give thanks for the healing and celebrate, now knowing you're worthy of a "YES!"

~ ~ ~ ~ ~

***Go to The Enlightened Mom Meditation CD #2, Track 2,
to give yourself permission to receive a "YES!"***

~ ~ ~ ~ ~

Mom, if you don't feel anyone told you "no" in the past, but shut yourself down to receiving a "YES!" anyway then ask your little girl within whose approval she is seeking. Do some introspection with this.

The key to creating the life you want is to bring yourself into awareness and always ask yourself if you have permission to receive a "YES!" Remember, God is the one who is guiding you to ask for what you want in the first place. It's up to you to say a big "YES!" to yourself.

It's Time to Speak Your Needs to Your Family

You've taken some time to get in touch with your feelings and know your truth, and you are ready and willing to love and say "YES!" to yourself and the messages that God has given you. However, you find that you're doing so much for your family that there is literally no room for you. Have you realized that your whole life is out of balance? Do you hear, "Let's go, Mom," just a few too many times in a day or a week? In other words, is your chauffeuring job keeping you just a tad bit crazy? How about your maid job? Does that one have you tired and exhausted by the end of the day? I'm sure your counseling job has your mind swirling. And what about your job as your spouse's little sex kitten? That one probably went away a long time ago! It doesn't have to be that way. When you start honoring and loving yourself, all of these things will become much easier.

Our family dynamics are one of the main reasons we don't honor the little girl's feelings deep within. We spend all of our time taking care of our loved ones' needs, believing this is what a "good" mom does, so the little girl inside of us is once again put in the corner. Now it's time to look at your family dynamics.

We know you're overwhelmed with all the different jobs I mentioned before, or at least some of them. Those jobs are just part of the territory of being a mom. However, as you look at your family's calendar, what needs to be released there? Check in with your feelings. When you look at the list, does your body tighten on any specific item? Or do you feel some resentment? Your feelings are talking to you and will help you create a conversation with your family.

Balance in the family is vital to having abundance in your home. This will not only allow you to be the kind of mom you want to be, but it will also allow your family some growth and freedom.

Balancing the Family Scales

1. Go through your family's daily schedule. Are your kids' lives booked to the hilt, making no room for you or them to breathe?

2. Talk with your kids and see what part of their lives they really love and let any other extracurricular things go. You may have to draw the line at some point. When I did this exercise years ago, I discovered that my kids had a tendency to want to do everything because their friends did them. I had them cut their schedules down to one or two things a week, knowing that they would be better off having down time, learning to create their own happiness. Plus, they had to take a good look at what was right for them, not what was right for their friends. This was a great tool for them to connect to their hearts. We soon found out that my kids were much happier having more time for themselves. They had kept their schedules busy because, one, that's how I had originally taught them to be, and, two, because everyone else was doing it. It was as if they were in some kind of competition to get ahead in life. But as we cut down all of the busyness, they found more of themselves and everyone became happier.

3. Ask another adult, your spouse if you're married, to share some of the "kid responsibilities" with you. If you're not married, find a friend to do trade-offs with the kids. When my kids were young, our neighborhood had a babysitting co-op. We had a list of names of people with kids who liked to do trades of babysitting. No money was exchanged and we all got to have time to ourselves. If you are married, ask your husband to take the kids one or two nights a week so that you might have some time for yourself.

This exercise will work for you, too, even if your children are grown. Is it possible that you're keeping your life filled with things to do out of some belief that you have to stay busy to receive love? What does the little girl inside of you truly want? How can you balance your life and home? Who do you need to speak to and say what you want?

When you tap into the feelings in your heart and give yourself permission to speak up for the little girl inside of you and say what you need, your family dynamics will change. At first this might be scary and there may be a little resistance from everyone. That's okay. Don't fret.

I was afraid to hand my kids over to my husband, Steve, when I first began this journey. I didn't want to burden him with more responsibility and I was afraid my kids would feel rejected by me. But I found just the opposite. I discovered that when I stepped away from my kids, my absence allowed each of them an opportunity to create a wonderful, loving relationship with their dad. For the first part of their lives, Steve was there, but it seemed only on the outskirts. He wasn't truly involved. But as I stood in my truth to follow my heart and to get to know myself, incredible relationships blossomed for all of them. I gave myself abundance and my family found it as well. Steve was able to really experience fatherhood on an intimate level and our girls got to experience an amazing male role model. What a gift for everyone involved!

Liz is a very successful businesswoman and mother. However, her marriage came to an end some time ago. Wanting to take a deeper look at her life, Liz decided to see me. As we dove in, I asked, "What about making time for yourself? You have a lot on your plate. Are you giving yourself enough downtime?"

"Oh, yes. Now I have several nights a week that are mine because my kids go to my ex-husband. I can do anything I want those nights. It's wonderful!"

"When you were married, did you not share your feelings with your husband and tell him that you needed some time for yourself?"

"No," she answered. "He was always too busy working. It was my job to take care of the kids. Now he rarely works at night and he has a great relationship with them."

I looked at Liz thoughtfully and asked, "What do you think might have happened if you had shared your true feelings and asked for more help back then? Honesty might have saved your marriage."

Liz couldn't answer my question. She was still in a space of blaming her ex-husband for not taking more of the responsibility in their marriage. But it really wasn't her former husband's fault. What I soon realized is that she never shared her feelings with him. She didn't stand up for the little child within. Instead of taking responsibility for making herself happy and asking her husband for help, she held her voice in and then blamed him for feeling unloved. Gradually, a wedge was built between them and, sadly, Liz's marriage ended.

I've heard women say, "Why should I have to ask my husband for help? He should do it without me asking." Well, I used to think the same thing. Then I realized two things. One is that men tend to run the societal belief that they are the providers and women are the family nurturers. Therefore, men tend to believe their job is to go out and conquer the world and bring home the bacon. Most have not been programmed to believe that they are needed to help with anything else. That's because we women do it all and don't ask for help! So we have to train them by telling them what we need and want.

The second thing I learned is that men love to be needed. If you speak to them in a way that they can hear, they love to be the heroes. For instance, instead of asking, "Bob, CAN you take out the trash now?" try asking this way, "Bob, would you mind taking out the trash when you get a chance. I'd really appreciate the help." The second way is a kinder, more loving way and it gives your spouse a chance to make a choice. The first request sounds like a teacher telling your husband what to do.

When you don't stand up for what you feel in your heart, resentments build. Resentment leads to anger and anger leads to a complete lack of abundance in the family. Anything that causes a wedge between you and someone you love is going to take you far away from the kind of life you want. Listen to your feelings, Mom. What are they trying to tell you? Ask yourself what you need to feel happy and alive. Then take action and be willing to share the information with your family. When you are ready to share this information, please take a moment and give yourself permission to say what you feel and need. Otherwise, taking a stand for your truth may come off very angry and brutal to your family. Speak with love to them.

When I am facing a difficult situation and don't know how in the world I'm going to share my feelings clearly and with love, I get grounded in God's light and say:

"Please, God, give me your eyes,
your ears, your voice and your heart,
so that I might speak with love."

I've been amazed over and over at how saying this sentence works and brings me into a loving, neutral space.

Another tool to use whenever you feel anxiety about sharing your feelings with your family is to run earth energy. Earth energy is the same kind of energy you feel when you are outdoors sitting under a beautiful tree enjoying the grass between your toes and under your feet. Earth energy makes you fully present, releasing fear and anxiety, so that you may act out of love.

Running earth energy is very similar to grounding in God's light, only the energy moves in the opposite direction, coming up from the earth.

Running Earth Energy

1. Give yourself permission to breathe and open up to receive God's love and help. Put your feet flat on the floor, sitting upright with the palms of your hands in your lap facing upwards.

2. Visualize opening the balls of your feet like camera lenses. Now imagine that there is a beautiful green healing light that is about to surge up from the center of the earth.

3. Invite this healing light to flood up the middle of your grounding cord and allow it to enter into your feet.

4. Allow the energy to flow upwards into your whole body until you are so full that the light floods out of your palms, fingertips, and the crown of your head, again having each of them open up like a camera lens.

5. As the earth energy flows out of the top of your head and hands, it pours down into your aura. Visualize opening up the

bottom of your aura and send the green light down the outer edges of your grounding cord back to the center of the earth.

6. Run this energy for no more than three to five minutes or else it will make you feel really tired and dense with energy. Once you've done that, stop and reverse the energy so that you are now grounding in God's golden light from the top of your head.

7. Give thanks for the healing and move forward with inspired action, sharing your feelings with your family.

~ ~ ~ ~ ~

**Go to The Enlightened Mom Meditation
CD #2, Track 3, to run earth energy.**

~ ~ ~ ~ ~

Again, running earth energy is just the opposite of grounding. It's very easy. It's a wonderful tool to prepare yourself when you are afraid to share your feelings. You are afraid due to negative beliefs you're still holding onto, wondering how your family will respond as you speak from your heart. But when you run earth energy, it helps you release those fears so that you stay present and stand firm with the love of God.

Running earth energy is wonderful for calming your nerves in all kinds of situations, even during the day when you feel tired and run down from too much multi-tasking as a mom. You can use it anywhere and it only takes five minutes!

You get to choose which tool works best for you to calm your nerves when it comes to facing your family and saying "YES!" to your heart. Please know, Mom, that you are giving your family a tremendous gift of growth by taking care of yourself this way. As I mentioned earlier, they may resist at first. Change can be very scary. But by having the courage to make the first move and speak from your heart, you will set a whole new loving tone in your home and create greater communication for everyone.

Saying "NO" Means "YES!" to You

I had to return a dress to the mall one day. I had a little time on my hands and decided to mill around. As I passed a bookstore, something told me to go in. I had never been at this store and had no idea of the layout. I asked, "God, what would you like for me to see in here?" I followed the arrow in my mind that I like to visualize and saw myself heading for the back of the store. It looked as if I was going to be reading children's books for a moment. I was okay with this, although my kids are well past that age. I guessed that it had to be okay if God was guiding me there. Then all of the sudden the arrow changed and turned right. "Hmmmm," I thought. "I wonder where this is taking me." I looked up to see the Self-Help sign. "That figures," I laughed to myself. "I always get guided to this section in almost every bookstore, even when I'm not familiar with the layout of the store!" I had a good laugh, marveling at how God is my guide.

I followed the arrow to a book by Dr. Judith Orloff called *Positive Energy: 10 Extraordinary Prescriptions for Transforming Fatigue, Stress, and Fear Into Vibrance, Strength & Love.* I flipped the book open and saw the message of how important it is to say "NO!"

"Thank you, God," I said. "Thank you for this reminder. This is a very important part to saying 'YES!' to our hearts."

I used to say "yes" to everything else and "no" to myself. That's when I still lived from the belief that it was my job to make my family happy. I wanted to look like the perfect parent and be involved in every aspect of my kids' lives. I also did charity work. Any time a request was presented, I was the one who jumped up and volunteered. I really believed that the more I did for everyone, at the expense of myself, I would feel loved in return. But I didn't. I felt exhausted! I walked around frustrated and angry, feeling overwhelmed. Then I learned to say "no."

I'm not sure where my awareness shifted, but somewhere along the way I realized that I didn't want to be angry anymore. I didn't want to set this example for my family. I knew if I didn't love myself by saying "no" then I would continue to dump my pain onto all those I loved. So I stopped. I started saying "YES!" to myself by saying "no" to others. It was really scary at first, but eventually I felt great! I saw that by giving myself permission to stand in my truth, my whole family was receiving a tremendous gift. They were learning to say "no," too.

Learning to say "no" is a way for you to speak up for the little girl inside of you and tell her that she matters. She needs to feel protected and safe, and she needs to feel loved. When you run yourself ragged never speaking up for yourself, this little girl is put off to the side and told to be quiet. Aren't you tired of pushing her away? By not protecting this little girl within, you are once again creating a wall of anger, resentment and blame.

How would you like to say "YES!" to yourself by saying "no" to others? I learned to say "YES!" to myself by creating boundaries in my life. I knew I had to do this to protect the child within. I also knew it was imperative for my happiness and healing, especially if I truly wanted to be a loving wife and mom.

The first boundary I created was with my family. I created a time and place for me to meditate. I shared the story earlier in this book about how I stood in my truth and told my kids that I needed time for me. Even though Kolbi was a tiny little thing, she understood that when the bedroom door was shut, it was Mommy's time. It took her only a short while to understand and respect this need.

The second boundary I created was saying "no" to things that didn't ring true to my heart. I pulled away from being the full-time hands-on mom at school and decided to pick and choose those events that excited me and that would give me an opportunity to interact with the kids. My kids didn't even flinch. They never thought a thing about it. This was an act of trust for me. I had been so involved in school because I felt the need to control my children's destinies and to create a vision of the perfect mom. Instead, I became a better mom by creating this boundary.

Saying "no" to drama was the third boundary I set for myself. I made a decision to surround myself with love and pulled away from people who were negative and draining. I had enough drama to clean up in my mind. I didn't need someone else adding to it!

These three boundaries were the beginning steps I took to love myself. I didn't do them all at once. I did them as my awareness shifted into what was the loving thing to do for myself, and my family. The more I said "YES!" to my heart, the easier it was to release the things that burdened me and add new boundaries.

When you create boundaries in your life, you create respect for yourself. This is another way of loving yourself as a mother. It saddens me to see so many parents who have disrespectful relationships with their kids. It's because the parent does not respect himself or herself. It's not about forcing your control onto your kids and making them respect you. Respect comes when you love, honor and respect yourself.

I ran into one of Kolbi's junior high teachers not too long ago. As I reintroduced myself to him, he said to me, "Kolbi is one of the most respectful kids I've ever had in my class. How did you make her so respectful?"

I was a little stumped by his question. Then I said, "I respected her."

"That's the first time I've ever heard a parent say that," was his response.

Most parents try to control their kids and force them to respect people. This only produces more anger and resentment. But when you respect yourself, that love overflows to your kids. You respect them and how they were created as a direct result of respecting yourself. In turn, your kids not only respect you, but also their teachers and friends. But it all begins with you, Mom, respecting yourself first by setting some boundaries.

What boundaries are you ready to establish right now? What's not working in your life? If you're still feeling overwhelmed and tired then it's time to take some quiet time for yourself.

Do you have a friend who is draining you due to her negativity? Are you ready to shift this relationship? If you are, talk to this friend and tell her how you feel when you're around her negative energy. If you love her, let her know how much she means to you but that you can't continue the relationship the way it is. If she isn't willing to make some changes then it's time to create some boundaries with her.

Sometimes when we think about creating boundaries, we feel this is putting up walls. The kind of boundary I'm talking about is giving yourself permission to surround yourself with love.

What other ways can you say "YES!" to yourself? What else are you ready to release from your life? I invite you to go into awareness as you make your way through your daily journey. Ask yourself, "Is this working for me? Is this a positive, loving thing? Or is it draining me?" It's time to value yourself and create a boundary of love.

Boundaries Say "YES!" to You

1. Sit down with pen and paper and get grounded in God's light.

2. What areas in your life would you like to say "no" to? Are you involved in too many other people's lives? Are you taking too much responsibility in your kids' lives or your spouse's? How about your parents'? Your friends'? What about your work? Why are you running yourself so ragged? Make a list of where you would like to say "no" in your life.

3. Now ask the little girl inside of you how she REALLY feels about the items on your list. Which one stands out the most that she is ready to release? Ask her, "Why are you holding on to this? What are you seeking when you do this? Who are you trying to please?" Write about this, visualize or hear the conversation. Ask her what she fears most if you start saying "no."

4. Feel everything. Get in touch with all of your fears. Does an old memory come up for you where you said "no" and felt you were punished for speaking your truth? If so, do as in previous exercises and see the person who punished you as a little child. Ask this person what was hurting and then send him or her to the white light of God.

5. Imagine giving the little girl inside of you a great big hug and tell her that she has permission to say "no" from now on. Tell her that you will not abandon her, even if the person you say

"no" to does. This is about finding love within yourself in spite of what others think.

6. Fill yourself up with the light of God and celebrate that you are finally saying "YES!" to yourself.

7. Take action with the boundaries you have created.

~ ~ ~ ~ ~

Go to The Enlightened Mom Meditation CD #2, Track 4, and create boundaries that say "YES!" to YOU.

~ ~ ~ ~ ~

When you start saying "no," people may go a little into shock. That's because you have been a "yes" person for way too long. The more neutral you can be to saying "no," the easier it will be for others to accept this. It takes great courage to say "YES!" to your heart and say "no" to all those things that no longer ring true for you.

Courage is not what we usually consider as one of the traits of a loving mother. We see her as nurturing, giving, and kind, but courageous isn't usually how we define a mother. An Enlightened Mom is courageous. She is willing to take a step into abundance for her family, healing her life so that her family might heal as well.

I invite you to call forth courage from within and take a stand for yourself and for your family. If you haven't already done all of the previous exercises, please do. Getting in touch with the feelings in your heart will take you to the life you've always dreamed of. As you honor the feelings that make you happy and energized, you will create a life of peace, light and love. Abundance comes, Mom, when you say, "YES!" to your heart.

~ ~ ~ ~ ~

CHAPTER 7

You Are a Gift!

om, you ARE a gift. I bet you don't think of yourself this way. You most likely judge yourself and find fault with yourself, especially as a mom. This is the reason you struggle with acknowledging and sharing your thoughts and feelings. You don't value the gift of who you are. If you're like the many moms I've worked with over the years, you probably have a deep-seated belief that says you're not valuable and, thus, feel unworthy of love.

I lived most of my life judging the way I was created. I didn't value myself, until I decided to heal and live the life of an Enlightened Mom.

People are amazed when I tell them that in that moment of winning Miss USA 1982, I felt confusion and emptiness. I didn't see myself as a gift at all. I only felt judgment. Many people believe that winning a title like that is the epitome of acceptance. But it wasn't for me. I had spent my whole life seeking others' approval. I wanted them to define me. I believed that I was only worthy of good things as a result of what people thought of me. This attitude made me crazy! In spite of being a winner, I felt as if I were constantly losing a battle within. I never felt valued and loved. And I definitely didn't see myself as a gift. After gaining one source of acknowledgement from the outside world, I had to quickly go after another. It was like an addiction. I believed this was love.

I continued this negative programming with my family. I worked from a belief that said I had to do everything right as a mother or else I wouldn't be loved. Again, I was seeking approval from my family instead of finding it within. The truth is that I had so much judgment inside of me that I didn't like myself. And because I didn't like myself, I couldn't value myself.

Valuing yourself means that you find the love within, rather than seeking it from the outside world. You take the time to get to know yourself, and to honor and acknowledge yourself. You embrace your humanness and the way you were created. You recognize the things you love about yourself and have compassion for the things you don't. You love yourself enough to know when it's time to work and when it's time to play. You follow your heart. This is truly loving and valuing who you are.

I went walking one morning after diligently writing for hours and then suddenly finding myself at a standstill. My heart said, "Get out of this house!" So I did. I took my little Maltese, Squirt, and we headed out. I found myself walking towards the horse stables around the corner from our home. As I made my way down the tree-lined street, I saw three bright red cardinals fluttering in the trees. I was intrigued. Their colors were absolutely breathtaking! I felt as if they were singing directly to me as their whistling drew me in.

I watched the birds playing for quite some time and felt tears well up in my eyes. My tears were not ones of sadness, but of joy. I felt so alive to be outside. I had valued myself, and the little girl inside of me that morning, so I took a time out and allowed myself to breathe. I knew there was a message in this scene.

I went home and looked up cardinal in Ted Andrew's book, *Animal Speak*. It said, "Renewed vitality through recognizing self-importance." And that's exactly how I felt when I took my walk! I became more energized by honoring my heart and valuing myself. Wow! I couldn't believe what I read. I felt as if the universe had planted the birds there just for me to see. I had come to a standstill that morning because I wasn't sure what I wanted to write next in this book. I knew this section was about seeing yourself as a gift and valuing yourself, but wasn't sure what I wanted to say. I had surrendered this process to God and understood that if I wasn't clear on the next step to take then I needed to listen to my heart to get some guidance. That's why I took the walk. I knew that if I forced my writing due to old programming that said you must work, work, work, and perform then this book would be frozen in fear. I had to acknowledge the fact that the message wasn't coming while sitting at my desk. My heart wanted to go for a walk and so I did. Miraculously, the message I needed to write in this chapter appeared!

The last part of the book's description of the cardinal said, "When they appear as a totem, they do so to remind us to become like them. Add color to your life, and remember that everything you do is of importance."

Mom, everything you do in your life is of importance. Your life is of value. Most moms don't think of their lives this way. They value their families more than themselves. That's why they don't add color to their lives. They add it to everyone else's and deny themselves.

As I write this portion of my book, I'm teaching an eight-week Enlightened Mom class. It runs one morning a week. Last week I invited the ladies to go to their families and speak their wants and needs. I asked each of them to make a commitment to take a stand for at least one thing and then to come back this week and tell us how it felt. Very few of the moms did it. They all had excuses. The real reason, however, is that they don't value themselves.

Why Don't You Value Yourself?

My client Andrea had a difficult time valuing herself when I first started coaching her. Andrea shared with me that when she saw her little child within, she judged her. She didn't see anything special about little Andrea. On the other hand, Andrea said that when she visualized her daughter, she felt great joy and valued her immensely. Somewhere along the way Andrea decided she wasn't valuable. After a short time of working with her, I discovered Andrea didn't like herself very much.

I asked Andrea one day while in a session why she didn't like herself and she said, "Because I'm too judgmental of others. I evaluate someone new immediately and see if I want to know them better."

"Do you have to see that as a judgment?" I asked. "What if you saw this kind of evaluation as a means to getting in touch with your heart? It's very important for us to know the kinds of people we want to surround ourselves with. It sounds to me as if you are judging yourself for listening to what you want."

"Wow! I never saw it like that," Andrea said. "I only saw myself as being judgmental."

Until that day, Andrea lived her life judging herself for having an opinion of what she liked and disliked. She didn't have permission to know what she wanted, so she judged herself. And as a result, she saw herself as bad and not of value.

I had a similar situation with a male client. Eric is a divorced father of two and a businessman. He not only gets to play the daddy/provider part, but also the mommy one when he is with his kids. He began coaching with me because he didn't like how he was dealing with his work, nor with his two children. He said he was very hard and judgmental not only on himself, but especially with his son.

I was doing some healing work with Eric when I saw a vision of him holding a sign that said, "I don't like being me." I asked him about this and he replied, "There are a lot of things I don't like about myself."

"Like what?" I asked. "Give me some examples of things that people judged you for when you were a kid."

"I don't know," he responded. "Like I was disruptive and hyper, I guess."

"What is the positive side of those things?" I asked. "Wouldn't it be better to see disruptive and hyper as creative and full of energy?"

"I never thought of it that way," said Eric.

I pushed him further. "Give me another way people judged you."

"I was always called too sensitive."

"Sensitivity, to me, means that you are really connected to your feelings," I said. "Eric, people judged you when you were a kid because they had been judged for similar things. You took on a belief that said if others don't like something about you, you must not like it either."

This is what we do as kids. We learn to de-value ourselves because we have been judged and continue to hold onto those past beliefs well into adulthood, until we decide to heal. As children, we either put those judgments on ourselves from watching the world around us, or we take them on from remarks made to us by our parents, grandparents, teachers and peers.

People judge us because they have been judged and are living from negative beliefs. Let's imagine, for instance, that your grandma was reprimanded as a child for wanting to play by herself with her special birthday doll. She didn't want to share it with her sister. Her parents were really hard on her and yelled at her. She felt angry and disappointed for what she experienced as an emotional assault. Her heart just wanted to have some time by herself. She cried and was told she was being selfish.

Your grandma took on a message in that moment that said she was bad. As a result, she spent the rest of her life believing this. She continued to carry this belief even when you were a child. Then one day she came to visit.

Visualize this: it's your birthday. You are so excited to be turning six. You can't wait to open up the box with the big pink bow. Oh, you hope and hope and hope that it's the baby doll you wanted. You have been asking your mom and dad for this special toy for months.

It's finally time to open up all of your presents. You can't stand it. You go straight for the box you've had your eyes on.

Yes! It IS your dream doll!

Some time has passed and the party is over. You have waited patiently all afternoon to play with your doll. Now it is your time to get to know your new baby. The only problem is that your little two-year-old sister wants to play too. You tell her, "No. This is my special baby." All of a sudden your grandma jumps down your throat. You are in shock and can't understand why she is so mad. She tells you that you are selfish and bad.

Your little baby isn't quite so special anymore. All of the wonderful feelings you were experiencing are gone. You've just been given a message that to follow your heart is wrong and that you are not worthy of this kind of love.

Now, as you come back to present time and look at your life, you realize that in that moment, you took on a belief that said you are not of value. Your grandma's actions said to you loud and clear that YOU ARE BAD, YOU ARE SELFISH, AND YOU DO NOT DESERVE TIME TO PLAY BY YOURSELF BECAUSE YOU HAVE TO HONOR OTHER PEOPLE FIRST. But this wasn't the truth. You were simply being a kid who was following her heart in that moment, until you were told you were wrong. Your Grandma judged you because she had been judged. It wasn't the truth for either one of you, but you both took it on, making it a part of you.

This story is just one example of how we take on messages that we are bad. And, in our world, "bad" is definitely not of value. Our world says you have to be "good" to be valued. It's time to visualize putting that belief into a big beautiful rose and blowing it up, sending it back to the universe with love!

Flip the Switch on Negative Labels

Mom, God did not make a mistake when you were created. Your feelings, thoughts, interests, quirks, you name it, are the way God intended you to be. You are special just being you. You are of value. One way to see how wonderful and lovable you are is to flip the switch on the negative labels you took on since childhood.

I was constantly told I was moody as a kid. I hated this judgment. The more I hated myself, the moodier I became. In essence, I was being told not to feel.

I finally learned that my emotions are a gift. I went to see a healer and she painted a picture of how she saw my energy. The picture was abstract, but filled with color. It was absolutely beautiful. This spiritual counselor said to me, "You are so blessed."

"I am?" I asked. "Why?"

"You feel everything. Every emotion runs through your body."

"Well, I've always been labeled moody for this," I replied.

"Terri, you're not moody. Society has shut down to feeling. People tell you that you are wrong for feeling because they don't allow themselves to feel due to their false beliefs."

This woman's remarks were truly a gift to me and gave me one of the first steps to seeing my real self. She helped me flip the switch that told me I was bad for being who I am. But the gift didn't stop there. I eventually discovered that my sensitivity is one of my greatest gifts. By feeling everything, I am able to be a better teacher and healer.

"Procrastinator" is a label I gave myself for most of my childhood and young adulthood. That's because I had a belief that said, "If you don't get it done when I say it has to be done, you are bad, you are wrong, and you are a procrastinator." That belief slowly melted away as I moved into my heart space. However, there was still a part of me that judged myself, until the day I met with Master Astrologer, Jeff Harman. Jeff's sessions are full of information and wisdom, but the most important thing he did for me that day was to help me flip the switch completely on being labeled a procrastinator.

Jeff explained to me that we all have ebbs and flows with energy and was even able to break down in a chart the days of the week that are highly energetic and productive days, and those that aren't. The chart starts with the day you were born. This day is an extremely positive and energetic day. For instance, I was born on a Sunday. Sundays are always filled with energy and are usually quite active for me, especially as I have allowed myself to follow my heart. Tuesdays, on the other hand, are days that I seldom get much done. When you look at Jeff's chart below and imagine Sunday being the day I was born, you'll see that Tuesdays are a low energy day for me. I laughed when I saw this because I had gotten so completely into my flow that I left Tuesdays free from any heavy mental work. Jeff validated me for what I had already learned from my heart!

Below is the chart showing the energies of each day of the week, beginning with the day you were born. If you've labeled yourself or someone you know a procrastinator, hopefully this chart will help you finally let that belief go.

Your Weekly Energy Flow

Day you were born:	+ +	positive energy
Day two:	+ −	neutral energy
Day Three:	− −	negative energy
Day Four:	+ −	neutral energy
Day Five:	+ +	positive energy
Day Six:	+ +	positive energy
Day Seven:	− −	negative energy

Understanding how our energy ebbs and flows helped me completely heal the old label that said I was a procrastinator. I wasn't. I was judging myself for following my heart instead of my head. I also received another wonderful gift from this information: I stopped judging my kids.

When my girls were young and came home with weekly homework packets, I had a tendency to push them to get their homework done early in the week. I found myself wanting to call them procrastinators like I did to myself. However, after discovering this information, I realized my two girls were just like me. They were both born on Sundays, too. Therefore, early in the week was not the best energy to get a massive amount of homework done. In the past, when I tried to force it, homework time was always a battle. But as I allowed them to follow their flow, Thursday nights became the norm of getting homework packets done. And the best thing about it was that homework was finished without a struggle.

I'm so thankful I learned to flip the switch on that old procrastinator label. I not only learned to listen to myself and follow my flow, but was able to help my children stay in their hearts as well. I can only imagine the struggles I might have helped create for my kids had I forced them to push themselves.

We've all been labeled in some way that keeps us from valuing ourselves. Whether we've judged ourselves or taken on beliefs by other people's remarks, those labels affect us and define us. They shut us down to receiving love.

I often hear parents of two-year-olds complaining that their children have minds of their own and label these little ones as stubborn. Don't you want your children to have minds of their own? This is one of the greatest gifts God gave us. But instead, these parents want to tame the minds of their kids and label them. They want to control them and put them in a box. When I hear parents make these remarks, I always say, "Isn't it wonderful? Just think how independent your kid is going to be when she grows up. That independence will help her stand strong when she is faced with peer pressure, especially when she becomes a teenager." That remark usually stops them in their tracks! My hope is that I have helped them flip their switches on what they believe is good and bad. It is the suggestion that we are bad that keeps us from valuing ourselves.

This is why it is so important for you to flip the switch on your labels. To open up to abundance, you have to see yourself worthy of love. If you don't like yourself and view yourself as bad, you definitely won't value yourself. You'll stay shut down to receiving love and never know true abundance.

Mom, if you don't like yourself, you won't value yourself!

I didn't believe I was worthy of love for a very long time. But as I flipped the switch on my MANY labels, my whole life changed! I went from a lower level vibration of judgment and shame to a high vibration of acceptance and love. I shifted my mindset about how valuable and lovable I am, and created an opening to receive God's unlimited abundance!

Mom, your life will shift, too, as you release the labels you've been holding onto. You will finally see that you are lovable. And as you honor the way you were created, your family dynamics will change, too.

Julie is walking the path of The Enlightened Mom. She is one of my former students who attended my weekly classes. Julie is a dynamic, warm and lovely woman. When she enters the room, you know she is there. However, Julie carried a negative belief in her mind that not only affected her life, but how she saw her daughter, as well.

In one of the classes Julie attended, I had each of the women imagine herself as a little child with a big sign hanging around her neck. I asked them to visualize a false label printed on the sign. Julie's said, "Drama Queen." This was a label she had been given since she was a kid. Then I had the women flip the sign over and ask God to show them a sign with the truth. Julie began to cry when she realized her sign said, "Passionate." In that moment, Julie flipped the switch from a lifetime of judging herself to finally accepting herself.

The next week Julie entered the class with the biggest smile and tears in her eyes. "I've had the BEST week," she said. "I realized that my daughter is just like me. I've labeled her a drama queen all these years and it's caused a lot of conflict for us. However, after flipping the switch last week and seeing that I'm not a drama queen, I'm passionate, I see my daughter differently. She has argued with me this week and told me what she thinks, but instead of trying to shut her down, I am amazed at how much passion she has!" Julie's excitement was contagious! It was as if you could see a light that had been dimmed for years now flooding the room. This can be the same for you.

What are the negative labels you hold onto, Mom? It's time to let them go. It's time to start valuing yourself. It's time to flip the switch on those false beliefs and judgments you still hold onto. It's time to embrace the unique lovable you, the way God made you.

Release Your Negative Labels

1. Create a quiet space and get completely grounded, making sure that you've visualized the crown of your head open, allowing God's light to flow through you, checking in with your grounding cord and aura.

2. Say, "God, I'm ready to release the negative label that implies I am bad." Give thanks, resting in the knowingness that an amazing healing is about to take place.

3. Visualize the little girl inside of you. See her walking up to you and notice that there is a label hanging around her neck. Notice what it says. Does it bring back any negative emotions for you? If it does, allow your feelings to flow. If you can't see your inner child and her label then write back and forth between your dominant and non-dominant hands, or just listen for the message.

4. Once you feel as if you've released the emotions from this, ask your little inner child to flip the sign over and see what the truth is. Celebrate your discovery!

5. It's time to do a soul retrieval. Call back that part of you that you lost when you took on the negative label. For instance, if you are like Julie and have a label of being a drama queen, but are really passionate, visualize the passionate side of you that you separated from as a beautiful energy coming down from the highest points of the universe. Say hello to this iridescent energy, allowing it to flood into your head and all throughout your body, saying, "Yes, yes, yes! This is who I am!"

6. Give thanks for the healing and give your inner child a huge hug.

~ ~ ~ ~ ~

Go to The Enlightened Mom Meditation CD #2, Track 5, to release your negative labels.

~ ~ ~ ~ ~

If you feel you hold onto a lot of negative labels, please repeat this exercise as many times as you need. Stay in awareness. As you continue to walk the path of The Enlightened Mom, more old labels might reveal themselves. Just remember that these labels are not your truth and as you flip the switch, you'll discover more of the unique, wonderful you!

I've had some women in my classes who didn't see a negative label after doing this exercise and, yet, they were still stuck in their lives. Most of them told me that they made a choice to be the "good girl" in their families because they saw a sibling being judged. If this is the case for you, ask the little girl inside of you what she hid within herself so that she wouldn't be labeled. The irony is that when we label ourselves the "good girl," we often feel really bad about ourselves and live in fear. The key is to dig deep within and see what you've hidden about yourself. As you flip the switch, you will finally value your true self.

We spend our lifetimes telling ourselves that we are not of value because we have tried to fit in a box, telling us how to be to receive love. And when we don't fit, because none of us do, we feel as if we are wrong. It is only when you take the time to discover the real you, releasing all of the judgments you've felt in your lifetime, that you will truly see the value in you.

Mom, You ARE of Value

You've taken a giant step to inner abundance and valuing yourself by flipping the switch on old negative labels. Now it's time to flip another switch: the one that says you are not valuable as a mother.

There is an underlying theme in our world that says to be a mom is not very valuable. We know this is NOT the truth. This goes back to the martyr syndrome. We seem to have an innate belief that mom's feelings, wants, and needs really don't matter. The only reason this cycle continues is because we allow it!

> *You don't feel valued as a mother because you don't value yourself.*

Here's some food for thought: if you worked for a corporation, would one person do all of the jobs you do as a mom? Or would there be many employees on staff to do this kind of work? I bet if you were part of that corporation, you would get breaks and vacations. You'd probably have a ton of overtime stacked up as well.

Take a moment and think about what you bring to your family. If you need to, make a list of everything you do like chauffeuring, counseling, cleaning, etc. Now add a few more items. Only this time add things that you already recognize as some of your gifts. For instance, I know I am the spiritual grounding cord for my family. Who I am brings emotional healing to everyone I love if they choose to receive it. I also keep a constant awareness in our home for following your heart. Whenever my kids or hubby have an issue about something, my message often centers on this topic.

There was a point at the beginning of my healing journey when I didn't know what value I brought to my family, so I went within and asked each of their spirits. I got grounded and asked God for clarity. I visualized Mackenzie's spirit in front of me and asked her what gift I brought to her. She said I show her that it's okay to be unique and different. Kolbi's spirit said that my life proves to her that it is okay to be an adventurer and a little crazy. She's this way and my example gives her permission to be the same. When I asked A.J.'s spirit, he said that my life is an example to him that it's okay to make mistakes and to change. And, as I went within to ask Steve's spirit what I added to his life, he said, "Communication."

I didn't recognize my value for a very long time. But after doing this exercise, I realized that these gifts I give to my family are all a part of the way I was created. I don't have to try to "be" something to have value. I am valuable just for being me!

When you take the time to see what makes you special and unique, and what you bring to your family, you will finally know that you, Mom, are of value. No longer will you feel the need to try to be the perfect mother and deny yourself. You'll know that as you love and honor yourself, you bring a wonderful and valuable gift to your whole family!

Acknowledgment Comes from Within

When was the last time you heard one of your kids say, "Wow, Mom! I love you so much"? Even if you've heard a statement like this once, or more than once, you probably haven't heard it enough to believe it. And even if you've heard it every day, if you don't value yourself as a mother then you won't believe it anyway. We, as moms, spend way too much time beating ourselves up. Because we've been trained since childhood to seek acknowledgment and love outside of ourselves, we continue working hard trying to gain approval. But approval that comes from outside of us is usually empty. We have to find it within.

Mom, you are a gift! It is time to acknowledge this.

What is special about you? What do you like about yourself? Are you kind? Are you organized? Are you highly creative? Are you a great listener and help others heal? Do you like the way you look? Do you have a great business mind? Are you sensitive to others' feelings? Do you have a wonderful sense of humor? Are you a good athlete? Are you good at explaining things? Are you playful? Are you a nurturer? Do you have a positive attitude? What is unique about you?

Most of us have spent so much time in our lives focusing on the negative, we have no idea what the positive is. If you are such a person, you may have trouble finding things you like about yourself. Give yourself permission to start looking for the good in you. It's time to bring positive, loving energy to your life and value yourself. This happens when you acknowledge and love the unique, wonderful you!

What I Like About Me

1. Take a moment, get grounded and fully centered, and ask God for clarity, helping you see yourself clearly.

2. Tell yourself, "I give myself permission to release any negative opinions that have been haunting me. I'm now ready to open up to my truth."

3. Write down everything you like about yourself, including some of the judgments you flipped the switch on and now see as gifts. Try to write at least 10 things. Read over your list and truly acknowledge this is the way God created you.

4. Give thanks for the healing.

If you have a difficult time with this exercise, ask the little girl inside of you if she bought into some old negative belief that says to acknowledge yourself this way is bad. I've heard some people say, "Well, I don't want to boast." This isn't about boasting. This is about accepting and valuing the real you, the way God created you.

Now if you really want to go all out with acknowledging yourself, create a "Marvelous Mom" journal. This is a journal to sit in gratitude and appreciation for the way God made you, plus it will help you focus on the positive aspects of your life.

Marvelous Mom Journal

1. Create an acknowledgment journal. If you feel like letting the little girl inside of you play, allow her to decorate it.

2. Put the journal at your bedside.

3. At the end of the day, every day, write down in your journal what you felt really good about during the day. This can be a combination of things. For instance, write about a unique quality that you've just discovered about yourself. Or, acknowledge something you accomplished during the day such as making a wonderful dinner, or, even better, acknowledge yourself for realizing that it wasn't your kids that were making you crazy. You realized that you needed a break and you took one. Write at least five things you feel good about every day. Make this commitment to love and value yourself!

When you take the time to love and acknowledge yourself, you stop needing others to approve of you. You stop performing and live from your heart, creating a wonderful connection to God. This is true unconditional love and abundance. You find this when you love and honor yourself, acknowledging the gift of who you are!

The Gift of You

As you shift your consciousness and begin loving and accepting the way God created you, you not only begin to value yourself, but you also open up to seeing and embracing your gifts. This is why you're walking the path of The Enlightened Mom. You want the best for your family. And the best gift you can give them is to love yourself so much that you tap into your gifts, revealing to your family what true abundance is.

Our greatest purpose on this planet is to be an expression of love and to share that love with the world around us. When you tap into the gifts inside of you, you manifest that love in a way that is special and unique to you. You probably have a glimpse of your gift right now after doing the previous exercises. Sometimes, however, our gifts are such a part of us that we don't even recognize them. It's time to open up and see how special you really are!

Claim Your Gifts

1. Have pen and paper ready. Get into a healing space, fully grounded, asking for God's guidance.

2. Set an intention to have your gifts revealed to you. Even though you may not know what they are, see yourself on the other side of this healing space celebrating the fact that you now have an idea of what makes you unique. Say, "God, thank you, thank you, thank you. I open myself up and give myself permission to see the gifts that you've given me. Yes, yes, yes, yes, YES! Feel the celebration throughout your body, resting in the knowingness that your gifts are about to be revealed.

3. Imagine the little girl inside of you and visualize taking her up on your lap. Ask her, "What are your gifts?" and give her permission to tell you what is special about her. If she has a hard time with this, visualize a beautiful rose in front of you and vacuum out all of the negative energy that says she isn't

worthy of this kind of love and then imagine blowing the rose up like confetti. Allow God's golden light of truth and love to fill you up and then ask her once again.

4.   Write down any messages that come to you. If something isn't clear, ask questions.

5.   Give thanks to God for this wonderful healing.

～ ～ ～ ～ ～

Go to The Enlightened Mom Meditation CD #2, Track 6, to claim your gifts!

～ ～ ～ ～ ～

If you work better by writing with the other hand and want to ask the little girl what her gifts are then, by all means, please do. I give you a step-by-step guide to these mediations to make it easy for you. However, the ultimate goal with all of the guided meditations is for you to follow your heart. Do what feels right to you. If, for instance, you don't feel you can get a good answer from the little girl within because she still doesn't feel quite safe to speak, ask God directly, or ask your guardian angel or spirit guide. You can visualize one of them, write with your other hand, or just listen. If you see a picture in your mind and don't understand it, ask what it means. Sometimes we have to dig deeper to get an answer that is clear to us. I work with each of these tools. I like all of them and allow my heart to tell me which way to go. We all have different ways of communicating with God. This is part of the adventure of walking the path of The Enlightened Mom. You get to choose what is right for you!

Create an Affirmation

Your mind is a potent instrument. It can be constructive or destructive. When you focus on what's bad about you, you tear apart the goodness inside of you. It's time to shift this consciousness and use your brain as a powerful, positive tool.

You've just listed the things you like about yourself, you've flipped the switch on some negative labels and you've opened up to see the wonderful gifts inside of you. Now it's time to create an affirmation. Affirmations are constructive ways to focus your mind. Since you've been criticizing yourself for way too long, you need a tool that will turn the tables. A powerful affirmation will do this for you.

After doing the exercises in this chapter and discovering what's unique and special about you, what stands out to you? What did you learn about yourself that you really want to own?

Once you determine the things you want to define you, put them in a sentence that says, "I am...." For instance, my favorite affirmation that I've used for years is, "I am divine light, I am divine love, I am divine creativity, I am divine wisdom." When I created this affirmation, I didn't quite believe these words, but knew they were my truth. I knew I was divine light and love because we all are. I also knew that I was here to tap into my creativity and higher wisdom. So I decided that maybe even though I didn't quite feel these things yet, I was going to own them as my truth. It worked. I can now see these things and know for sure that this is who I am.

Who are you? Who do you want to profess to be by recognizing your gifts? Play with this. Write down a few affirmations. When you get to the one that resonates with you, you'll know it. Then every time you find yourself heading into negative mind games again and tearing yourself down, go back to this affirmation. You will be amazed how quickly it will take you back to center.

Add your affirmation to your "Marvelous Mom" journal. Plus, write five more things telling the little girl inside of you why she is so special. Be a loving mother to yourself. By accepting and loving yourself this way, you will gain strength and fortitude to stand in your truth, honoring the way God created you.

Avenues to Discover Your Gifts

Making a commitment to honor, accept and value yourself is the greatest path to your gifts. It can be a little confusing at first, however, because you still have voices in your head telling you what you "should" do, rather than being the real you.

When I first began my healing journey I often judged myself for my wants and desires. I thought that I was being selfish for wanting to have some of my own interests outside of my family. I continually tried to put myself in the societal box of fitting in with what a good mother "should be," but the shoe never fit. I only found myself more angry and frustrated.

Two tools helped me immensely to get to know myself: astrology and numerology. These tools helped me flip the switch in my mind and learn to accept myself. When I first had my astrology chart and numerology done, I felt as if for the first time in my life that someone knew me, and it was okay to be me. The messages I received from both of these tools validated the person inside of me who had been hiding.

For some people, just the mention of astrology or numerology brings up dark scary visions. If you're one of these people, it's okay. I've heard this fear expressed by many people, but when I ask them why they are so scared, they have no idea. They don't understand it, so they judge it. Or, they feel it is against their religion.

Everything on this planet is a part of God. So when you find yourself in fear or judging numerology or astrology, you have to ask yourself, "What is the intention behind this work? Is it evil? Or is it an avenue for me to create compassion for others and for myself?" With both of these tools, I found them to be very loving because they helped me find compassion and understanding for myself, as well as for my family.

When I talk about astrology, I'm not talking about your horoscope in the paper. This kind of astrology touches on only a very small aspect of who you are, so people often feel it is wrong. That's more or less what a friend once said to me. We were talking about astrology and she exclaimed, "I don't believe in that stuff!" I asked her if she had ever had an astrological birth chart done and she said, "No." Then I asked her if she had only been reading her daily horoscopes in the newspaper. Her reply was, "Yes."

An astrological chart takes you much deeper into who you are, including your struggles and gifts. Remember the judgment I mentioned earlier on being a procrastinator? That was a huge struggle for me. The way I finally flipped the switch on that label was through astrology.

Think of astrology as a blueprint for the way God created you. My dear friend and intuitive astrologer, Patty Kamson, says, "Your astrological chart is a picture of the universe the moment you born."

The universe is in continuous motion. Planets move about, as well as the earth. Since we are all energy and all have different vibrations, including every aspect of the universe, that energy is constantly changing and affecting each of us.

Isabel Hickey in *Astrology: A Cosmic Science* says that at the moment you were born you took on the vibration of that day and time, as well as the vibration of the particular place where you were born. She says you will hold that pattern with you for the rest of your life. Patty explains this further. She says, "As you know, we have free will, but within that make-up, you gravitate to a natural rhythm and flow that is revealed in your chart."

I'll never forget when I hosted *The Family Connection* on Internet Radio. This was a show to help people see themselves and their families from a spiritual perspective. Patty was a regular guest on the show. One night a man called in and was really lost. He had no idea of what he wanted. Patty pointed out to him after looking at his chart that he had a gift for music. He confirmed that he did have an interest in music, but wasn't really doing anything with it. In this instance, the man was aware of his musical interests, but not honoring his gift.

I hope you've done the prior exercise about tapping into your gifts. However, if you struggled with the exercise then astrology is a great way to get a little more clarity about yourself. Does the idea of having an astrological chart done scare you? Ask yourself why? Is this a belief that was handed down to you? Ask where this belief came from. I invite you to open up your mind.

Numerology is another tool I love. Dan Millman's book, *The Life You Were Born to Live: A Guide to Finding Your Life Purpose,* is one of the most informative books that I have ever read. It shares with the reader how to figure out your life numbers and what those numbers mean. And it's easy! His book tells you the life issues you are most likely going to deal with, and it tells you the gifts of who you are and some possible interests. It shows you what your life is like when you are running negative energy and when you are in the positive.

I run the number 29/11. A person who runs this number is here to learn to "bring positive creative energy into the world." Dan says that this creative energy is often expressed in the classical arts like writing, music, painting, etc., or even healing. When I first stepped onto the path of being a healer, I often questioned myself. But once I discovered Dan's book, it helped me to gain clarity as to where I was going until I found that certainty within myself.

I never considered myself a creative being. I thought creativity meant you were only an artist or a singer. Then I realized that my speaking, my healing, and eventually my writing were all creative expressions. Living my life the way I do, just being who I am, is the greatest way I express myself creatively.

One of the greatest gifts I received from Dan's book was to have compassion for myself. As he continues to describe the energy of the 29/11, he says that we are often some of the most creative people on the planet but spend most of our lives getting there due to insecurities. Well, that definitely defined me. Whenever I judged my creative abilities, which was often, I would think of Dan's statement and know that this was a life issue and the best way to handle it was to be gentle to myself. By loving and accepting myself this way, I opened up to whole new levels of creativity.

Both Dan's book and astrology have helped me love myself unconditionally, as well as my family. I've become a more compassionate and loving mom by using these tools to gain understanding about everyone in our family. And I've become more grounded in my gifts.

Mom, I invite you to explore these avenues to get to know more about yourself, and your family, too. Be open to seeing the possibilities. Whatever way you choose to discover your gifts and whatever way you choose to express them is up to you. The most important thing for you to remember is that you are of value. You are a gift! Everything you do is of importance, Mom. You make a difference in the world just by being the unique, wonderful you!

≈ ≈ ≈ ≈ ≈

PART III

Stand in YOUR Truth

CHAPTER 8

Life is a Gift...
Even the Crappy Stuff!

om, finding your heart and the unique, wonderful you may seem like a tremendous task when you look at your day-to-day life and realize you have no time for yourself. But, in fact, the truth is just the opposite. Motherhood is filled with opportunities to get to know who you are and tap into your truth. For instance, you know those knee-jerk reactions you have with your kids? Well, those are gifts. And what about the times you want to tell your hubby to take a hike for demanding way too much from you? Those are gifts, too. And how about when you find yourself overwhelmed, angry, controlling, fearful, judgmental, sad, or whatever emotions rein over you? Yes, those are gifts, too!

Paul Ferrini says in *Love Without Conditions*, "Your primary freedom lies in learning from the experiences that come your way." Your day-to-day life is filled with opportunities to discover who you are and erase the negative beliefs you've been holding onto for a lifetime. These beliefs sit deep within the dark recesses of your mind. Remember, the Law of Attraction says that like attracts like. Therefore, whatever belief you hold onto in your mind is what you'll attract to your life so that you may see yourself. When you react to your kids with knee-jerk reactions, when you blame your husband for expecting too much from you, and when you react to your boss and don't know why, these are all red flags telling you to wake up! You're living from some negative belief that isn't the real you.

Let's talk about knee-jerk reactions so you can see what I'm talking about. Don't you hate knee-jerk reactions? We all have them. That's when you want to drop-kick your kid out the door. You can be the calmest, most wonderful mom in the world, and then all of the sudden you are ready to kill your kid. You know what I mean. You hate yourself in those moments. Or maybe I should say, you pretty much want to strangle your kid, and then quickly begin to judge yourself. It's an awful feeling. And the more you judge yourself about these kinds of situations, the more you want to run away. I have a solution for you: celebrate those difficult times. See your reactions to your kids as gifts to learn about yourself and grow. For example, imagine that when you grew up, your parents had a lot of judgment on hippies. They assumed that people who wore long hair did drugs and were bad. You grew up with this attitude surrounding you. The belief was more or less beaten into your head. Now, all of the sudden, your kid, who has just started middle school and who has always been very clean cut and dressed just the way you liked him to, has decided he wants to grow out his hair and wear sloppy clothes. As he delivers this message, you feel your body tightening. You scream at him and say, "NO WAY!" You go off the deep-end. You feel out of control.

You have two options here. You can stand firm in your old way of thinking and create a battle of wills, or you can give thanks for the gift that is being revealed. The key is to remember that if you are having a knee-jerk reaction and your feelings are out of control, you are not living in your truth. Truth is love and is never controlling. Your out-of-control reaction is your red flag telling you that you've bought into a belief that wasn't really yours. You have to go within and ask for the gift so your truth can be revealed.

You take a moment of quiet meditation, getting grounded in God's light, giving thanks for the healing that is about to be revealed. You ask the little girl inside of you why she is reacting to your son. She says she is angry with him. He wants long hair and that means he'll be a bum. But as you continue to talk to the little girl inside of you, the truth is revealed: she's angry because she didn't feel the freedom to be who she wanted to be as a kid. As you talk to her further, you discover that when you were a kid, you liked the hippies. You thought they were cool. You liked the freedom they represented. But you were afraid to make friends with them because you knew your parents would disapprove. You buried your feelings and shut down what you wanted to do out of need to have your family's approval. You felt you had no freedom to be who you wanted to be. And now, your son is railing against everything you've ever believed and forcing you to look at yourself. Your son is a gift. He's helping you release old anger and judgment, and he's helping you find your truth.

See your children and every person in your life as opportunities to get to know yourself. See your kids as little earth angels here to show you yourself. Be in awareness at all times of when you are judging them or controlling them. Ask yourself, "Am I being a loving example, or am I trying to control them and be the guide?" God is the guide. When you try to control your kids and constantly get angry with them, God is telling you that you need to heal. And when you heal, your relationship with your kids will heal as well.

It is the negative beliefs you're holding onto that cause those horrible knee-jerk reactions you hate, as well as all of your sadness, anger, and pain. That's because you're not following your heart. Instead, you are listening to your head. Your head is your ego and your heart is God speaking to you. To create the joy, peace and abundance that you desire, you must get your head in alignment with your heart. The way to do this is to release the false beliefs in your mind that tell you who you "should" be, and then give yourself permission to be the real you.

Life is a reflection to show you the beliefs you hold onto. When you feel as if no one is hearing you, the chances are that you're not hearing the little girl inside of you. You probably have a deep-seated belief that says you're not worthy of being heard. If you see the people around you expecting perfection from you, you most likely believe you must be perfect to be loved. The list goes on and on.

Chaos in your life is a reflection to the chaos in your mind.

Whatever you are experiencing in your life, whether it is negative feelings, lack or even illness, is a reflection to what is going on in your mind. When your mind isn't in alignment with your heart, it creates stress and chaos in your life. Negative charges in your mind that you've taken on for a lifetime block you from being abundant in all areas of your life. Imagine these charges as magnets. They draw to them people and situations that reflect the beliefs you are holding onto. If your beliefs manifest as drama, pain and negativity in your life then they aren't your truth. The truth is that you are a loving child of God and are worthy of all the abundance, peace and joy that life has to offer.

To truly get connected to the unique, wonderful you and live a life of abundance and joy, you must take back the authority of your life and hand it over to God. You do that by listening to the messages in your heart.

Taking back the authority of your life begins by re-parenting yourself, recognizing and releasing all of the negative beliefs that suffocate you, giving yourself permission to stand in YOUR truth. We often feel that we don't have this kind of power. We continue to carry the belief from childhood that says other people have the final say in our lives. We make them the authorities and never take back our power. But you have a choice, Mom! You aren't a little kid anymore. You can change how you live in the world when you stop reacting and start creating what you want. The problem is that most of the time we don't realize that our lives are a series of reactions. We are reacting to the negative programming in our minds. We have to wake up and break this cycle for ourselves and for our families. This is why life is a gift. Every situation, every relationship, every moment of every day gives you a chance to look inside yourself and see the truth. By seeing life as a gift, you turn judgment and pain, and any other negative reactive emotions, into opportunities to find the real you.

"In my opinion, you don't deserve a break, ma'am." That's what a police officer told me many years ago while at Kolbi's elementary school. Kolbi had been feeling sick that morning so she asked to stay home. But around mid-morning she felt better and decided to go to school.

There is a circular drive that sits in front of Kolbi's old school. My intention was to drop her at the door and let her sign herself in. At the last minute she asked me to go in with her. I pulled forward into what is considered a loading zone for food trucks that deliver to the cafeteria, turned off my car and went in. Upon my return, I noticed an officer standing at the rear of my car, writing a ticket.

"Why are you writing me a ticket?" I asked.

"You're too close to the handicap zone, ma'am."

"Too close to the handicap zone? It's over there, officer," I said, as I pointed at the handicap zone sitting five feet away from me. I explained to him that the spot I was parked in was meant for loading and then asked him why the zone was marked for the food trucks that deliver to the cafeteria if it was against the law for them to park there.

"It is against the law to park too close to handicap zones," he continued as he handed me the ticket.

"Three-hundred dollars?" I exclaimed. I was absolutely in shock and exasperated. I couldn't believe I was being ticketed for parking where people parked every single day. I would never, and I mean never, park near or in a handicapped zone. It drives me nuts when I see people do that who don't belong there. I looked directly at the officer and asked, "Can't you give me a break?"

That's when he said in a very smug way, "In my opinion, you don't deserve a break, ma'am."

Oh, my gosh! His harshness and cold demeanor blew me away. I could not believe he said that too me. I was furious and told him, "I will take you to court."

"You go right ahead," is all he said.

I got in my car, drove around the corner and proceeded to start bawling. I was so angry. I did not deserve this kind of treatment. His words ate at me. "How could he be so smug about this?" I thought to myself. "It's almost as if he enjoyed seeing me squirm."

My anger escalated. My whole body wrenched with sobs. I was mired in darkness. I believed a grave injustice had been done.

Suddenly, the tools that I use everyday to heal kicked into gear.

"God," I said, "I'm really pissed off right now! But I know there is a gift here. Please show me the truth of this situation."

Immediately I heard the little voice in my head, "Terri, you spoke up to the officer. You told him you were going to take him to court."

"Yes," I thought. "I did." I knew this was a big shift for me. Never in the past would I have spoken out to a policeman. At that time in my life, I was really becoming aware of how I gave up the authority in my life, especially to men. I had an old negative belief that said men were the "authority" and I had been working diligently to heal it in my life. So it was huge for me to speak up to that police officer. To me, he was the epitome of an authority figure. "Yeah!" I cheered within and gave thanks to God for showing me this gift.

God had another message for me, but it took some time to be revealed. For three days, I stayed in awareness and continually heard in my head, "In my opinion, you don't deserve a break, ma'am. In my opinion you don't deserve a break, ma'am. In my opinion, you don't deserve a break ma'am." No, this repetition isn't a screw-up in this book. It was what was going on in my head, over and over and over again. It was as if a broken record played in my mind. But each time I heard it I gave thanks to God for the gift that was being revealed. I had no idea what it was, but knew that God was trying to send me a message. I was just having a hard time receiving it.

Finally, the message was revealed. Just like the Law of Attraction says, I attracted the policeman to me so that he could give me a message. When he said, "In my opinion, you don't deserve a break, ma'am," he was reflecting to me how I treated myself. I had been working extremely hard and not giving myself a break. I did this because there was still a negative belief in my mind that said I had to get others' approval to be loved. People's opinions, at that time, mattered more to me than my own. So I worked really hard.

The policeman's words showed me that I was not giving myself a break and was acting like I didn't deserve one. What a gift! I felt as if God had sent the officer to me, just in those ten minutes or so that I had gone into the school to drop off Kolbi, to show me myself. It was no coincidence. I was ready to wake up and quit being so hard on myself. So I invited this situation into my life without realizing it. My head was ready to shift so that it could match my heart. I just didn't know it. But this is how the Law of Attraction works. When you are ready to receive a message and to make a shift, the universe will provide you the avenue to see yourself. That is why life is a gift!

I was so excited that I finally got the message. The situation had been all-consuming. I'm not exaggerating when I tell you that for three days this man's words ate at me. But with every negative word I wanted to say about him, I balanced it with asking, "What is the gift?" I created an opening for the gift to be revealed. By staying open to receive, I discovered something new about me. I got in touch with a limiting belief and recognized that I did, do and will always deserve a break! I took back the authority in my life and gave myself permission to be human. What a gift! And with this revelation all of my anger towards the officer dissipated. I even fought the ticket and lost, but it didn't matter. All the negative emotions I had felt towards him were gone. The police officer wasn't "the bad guy." He was a messenger of God.

Get in Touch with Your Negative Beliefs

Life is meant to be loving and abundant. It isn't supposed to be filled with chaos. It doesn't have to be hard. Your issues with your kids, your spouse, your parents, your co-workers, your boss, and friends, even the little daily crap you deal with, come from the struggles inside of you. Those struggles exist due to the negative beliefs you're holding onto.

Negative beliefs stem down to one thing: how you were created versus how you think you're supposed to be.

Negative beliefs stack up over a lifetime. You probably don't realize that your mind is filled with them. But it is. And those negative beliefs drive your life. They act as a filter telling you how you "must be" to receive love. For instance, in my story with the police officer, I was shown that I had a negative belief that said I didn't deserve a break. That's not the truth! We all deserve breaks. This belief affected every aspect of my life. I learned it through watching my dad, who was a workaholic in the business world, and my mom, who was a workaholic in the home. I also learned to be a workaholic by seeing what was expected of me in school. I believed that I had to work really hard to win others' approval.

I believe that God sent that police officer to me because I was ready to see the gift and heal. As humans, our greatest desire is to experience love, so we put everyone else's opinions and beliefs first, making them the authorities of our lives, believing this will bring us love. That's what I was doing by working so hard. I had a deep-seated belief that told me the way to receive love was by working myself to death. But I was ready to see the truth. I was living my life from a belief that I didn't know existed in my subconscious brain. God sent the police officer my way to wake me up and tell me to look within.

The greatest love you will ever find is when you stay connected to your heart, putting God first. This is what it means to stand in your truth: you take back the authority of your life and allow God to be the guide. If you live your life always trying to please others, you are putting their opinions and beliefs as number one in your life instead of God. You've made them the authorities of your life. This is where your sense of lack and unhappiness come from. All of your daily situations, especially the ones where you feel overwhelmed, tired and wanting to run away, are all opportunities that God is sending you to get in touch with negative beliefs so that you might release them and put God first. Life is a gift! It is an avenue to connect to your heart, the place where God lives.

When you see the gift in everything and know that the person involved in the situation is a messenger from God, you quickly shift from blame into love. That's what I did with the officer. As soon as I received the gift, my anger and judgment completely left. I sent love and gratitude where there had been judgment and hate. I no longer saw him as a bad guy, but as a messenger of love.

I invite you to see every person who comes into your life and every situation as a gift. Know that nothing happens by chance. You are the creator of your life. If there is chaos in your life, it's because there is still chaos in your mind. You are living from false beliefs.

We all have old negative beliefs. These negative and limiting beliefs keep us disconnected from our hearts. They keep us disconnected from God. They are the reason we get so angry, frustrated and overwhelmed with life. We live by these false beliefs and, thus, deny who we really are.

I like to call the negative and limiting beliefs we hold onto "programming." That's because, as children, our minds are literally like computers just waiting to be downloaded. If the programs aren't friendly and loving, they eventually shut the computer down completely. This is what happens to each of us as we take on negative and limiting beliefs. We eventually shut down to the love that is inside of us.

What programming did you take on throughout your life? You have stepped onto the path of The Enlightened Mom by reading and doing the exercises in this book. Most likely you have already discovered some limiting beliefs you've been holding onto over your lifetime. For instance, you did exercises on giving yourself permission to speak and feel earlier in this book. Did you discover that you limited yourself in some way? What are some of the limiting beliefs you've already discovered about yourself?

Recognize Your Limiting Beliefs

1. Have pen and paper ready and get grounded, opening up to receive God's guidance and love.

2. Make two columns on the paper. In the left column, write "My Limiting Negative Beliefs." In the right, write "Permission to Be Me!"

3. List all the limiting beliefs you recognize about yourself, including the ones you've discovered while doing the exercises in this book. Sit with this for a moment. See where your life isn't working and ask yourself what belief is running you.

4. Go within and ask the little girl inside of you, "What is your truth?" By asking her this question, you are connecting to the real you, the way God made you. Do this with each limiting belief. After you get your answer for each belief, tell the little girl within that she has permission to be who she is.

5. Write under the "Permission to Be Me!" column all of the truths you've discovered about yourself.

6. Keep your list. As you move through each day, become aware of how you limit yourself. Add to the list any new limiting beliefs you become aware of. Make sure you ask what is your truth and give yourself permission to be the REAL you!

You are now on your way to fully taking back the authority of your life. It takes great courage and commitment. It takes a kind of strength that only few muster. It means that you must take full responsibility for your life and become aware of how you react to the situations in your life. Then you have to go deep within to see what negative programs you've taken on, giving yourself permission to release them by being the real you. By standing in your truth, you release the chaos in your mind, becoming a happier and more loving mom.

Become the Observer

You've already made a commitment to yourself and have mustered up the courage to take full responsibility for your happiness and clean out the chaos in your life or else you wouldn't be reading and doing the exercises in this book. You've recognized some limiting beliefs that have affected your life. However, there are still many negative beliefs that are hidden in the dark recesses of your mind that cause you to shut down in life. To clean out these beliefs so that you may create the life you want, you must become an observer to your life. Being an observer means that you stay present to everything in your life. You go into awareness, watching yourself and how you interact and react with people and situations.

I'll never forget the first time that I recognized I was being an observer in my life. Steve and I were arguing. I had had enough, so I went upstairs to take a bath. To my dismay, he followed me and continued to push the conversation. All of the sudden, I felt as if I had left my body and were watching the situation as an outside observer. I became neutral to what was going on and immediately knew what Steve and I were each reacting to. The issue that seemed to be a problem between the two of us was really two separate issues that we were each dealing with inside of ourselves. All I could think was, "Wow!" I don't remember what the problem was, it's been so long ago, but what I do remember is that in that moment I shifted the conversation and told him what I was struggling with in my life and what I saw to be his issue. The blame and anger we had both been feeling immediately vanished.

Stay present in your life. Watch your ego in action. See when you are coming from a loving space and when ego has taken over. As you become an observer to your life, you probably won't find yourself going out of your body. That was a one-time experience for me. Now I just watch. I check in with myself constantly and stay present to the situation. If I am reacting in any way and coming from any emotion other than love then I know it's time to go within and retrieve the gift of the situation.

Move Into Gratitude

You are the creator of your life. You have a choice to either be a victim of life's circumstances or to find the gift in them. The processes I'm about to share with you are to help you take back the authority of your life, so you no longer feel like a victim.

I lived the first part of my life as a victim, believing others' opinions ruled my life. That is until I decided to take back the power in my life. I began to realize that if I am the creator of my life then

I must somehow be bringing life's difficult situations to me to see myself. As I embraced this belief, I moved into a space of gratitude. It saved my life.

For most of my life I did not know what it meant to sit in gratitude. I said "please" and "thank you" as I was taught. But I didn't know that life's daily situations are all gifts and avenues to experience God. It was only when I decided to heal and take full responsibility for my life that I shifted my consciousness from being a victim to seeing every situation as an opportunity to discover my true self.

Your life is a series of opportunities to learn and grow. For instance, has someone ever said a statement to you that you rolled over and over in your head, just like I did when the policeman told me I didn't deserve a break? I'm sure you have. We all have. Well, there was a gift in that.

What about your spouse? Teresa is an Enlightened Mom. One of the greatest gifts she received from my class was that she realized that the demands she thought her husband was putting on her were actually demands she expected of herself. This belief caused a lot of resentment towards her hubby. When she realized she was doing it to herself out of some past belief that said she had to perform a certain way, all of her resentment dissipated.

I'd like to invite you to think about a trying situation you've experienced. The first step is to give thanks for it. You are not a victim to this situation. As a spirit, you created it and brought it to you so that you could have a human experience to learn about yourself and grow. If you're holding onto some old belief or emotion that doesn't feel loving, your heart wants to heal it, even if the human side of you wants to deny it. God is in alignment with your heart and, thus, will bring people and situations to help you see your reflection so that you might get in touch with the truth of who you are. You are being sent a message that it is time to make a shift in your life.

Some people have a hard time with this belief. Try it on for size. This wasn't some idea that I decided to play with. I was shown while writing *Message Sent* that we separate from love as we grow up. Our deepest desire is to get back to wholeness. Seeing life's difficult situations as gifts will help us get there. We become empowered by doing this process.

Go back to the trying time you thought about a moment ago. Read through the steps of The Retrieving the Gift of Love Process below to familiarize yourself with them. Then do the exercise for the situation you have in mind. Remember, the key is to release the blame by realizing that if you are reacting in any way, it is because the little girl inside of you is in pain. She doesn't feel she has permission to be who she is, and, thus, reacts negatively. It is up to you to give her permission to live from her heart.

Retrieving the Gift of Love Process

1. Ground in God's Light and create an intention for the healing. Visualize the problem you thought about a few minutes ago as solved. This is not about planning how to solve it, but simply seeing how you want the situation to end. For instance, if you are having a problem with someone and you want your relationship to get back to a loving space, see the two of you hugging and laughing. Be in the picture and feel how joyous and happy you are, giving thanks that all is well now. Imagine this picture bursting in your heart and spreading throughout your body. Say, "YES! Thank you, God, for taking care of this problem. I thank you and I'm so very grateful for this beautiful healing. Yes!" This is standing in faith knowing that at some point, whether it's right now or later, the answer will be revealed and the problem healed.

2. Visualize your inner child and ask her what feelings are surfacing as she thinks about this trying situation. Feel free to write or just visualize this conversation, or hear it. Allow the little girl within to tell you everything. If for some reason you can't see your inner child then talk to your angel, your spirit guide, or God.

3. Feel your emotions that the situation is creating. To be able to release the pain, you must move into it, not resist it. Feel free to write your feelings, or, if need be, beat your bed. Do whatever you need to express yourself in a safe, loving way.

4. See the reflection of the situation. Whatever is going on in your life right now is usually a reflection of a similar situation in the past where you took on the original false belief that is now running your life. Allow the current situation to take you as far back in your memory as possible to a similar situation where you felt the same kind of pain. Ask your inner child what negative or limiting belief she took on in that original picture? For example, many of the moms I work with don't feel as if their hubbies hear them. Most of them blame their spouses. But when they ask what the reflection is, they often discover a childhood belief that says they aren't worthy of being heard.

5. Ask your inner child "What is your truth? What rings true to your heart?" Allow all of her thoughts to come forward, continuing to ask questions to help you get to the bottom of what you really believe is right for you.

6. Give your inner child permission to be who she is.

7. Release all the energy related to the negative belief. See it draining down your grounding cord and fill yourself up with the light of God, saying a great big "Thank you!"

~~~~~

Go to The Enlightened Mom Meditation CD #2, Track 7, to retrieve the gift of love.

~~~~~

You won't have to go through this complete process all of the time. I often get an answer and the truth just by asking my inner child,

"What is your truth?" If that doesn't work then I might ask, "What's hurting inside?" and immediately get an answer. The Retrieving the Gift of Love Process is simply a step-by-step guide when you are in turmoil and don't know where to begin. The main points are to feel everything and ask what is hurting so that you get to the bottom of what's causing your negative reaction in the first place. It's a false belief you've been carrying probably for a lifetime. Let it go. Then give yourself permission to be you. That's it!

Please try to stay in gratitude as you do the Retrieving the Gift of Love Process. If you could watch me as I walk through a healing, you would probably think I was crazy. As soon as I feel some negative emotion, I start celebrating the healing. I don't wait until the end. I begin immediately. I say things like, "Thank you, God. I'm really, REALLY ticked right now. But I thank you for this situation. Thank you, thank you, thank you! I know I am dealing with this CRAP in my life so that it will help me see myself and heal. Thank you for helping me to create it!"

I stay in a space of gratitude, but at the same time I allow myself to feel the negative emotions welling up in me. I visualize myself on the other side of the healing as joyous and at peace. By bringing gratitude to the situation, I move through the healing faster than if I was in resistance to the process.

When I'm feeling stuck in my life and have no idea what's going on inside of me, I use this process to help me get clarity so that I might move forward. A lot of the time I'll simply set an intention, knowing that the answer will be revealed. Then I go into a state of observance and watch for the messages that God is sending me. Sometimes they come through journaling, sometimes with animals, and sometimes on the radio or TV. Other times the messages come through my interactions with the people around me.

Your Children are Mirrors to Your Soul

Your children are often your greatest teachers and messengers. How you react to them is a reflection to the beliefs you hold onto. Stay aware of your interactions with them.

My client Liz came in one day feeling emotionally wrought with pain. She was facing the demons of her relationship with her father. I hadn't seen her for a while and was surprised to see her so distraught. Instead of talking about her dad, however, she focused on her son. Liz said she was absolutely exhausted because he had been getting her up earlier than usual and was demanding a lot more attention than he normally needed. She was very frustrated with the situation.

I reminded Liz that her little boy was trying to show her something about herself. As she looked at the situation and asked for the reflection, she realized that her son was showing her that her inner child needed some attention. This is why she felt so distraught. The little girl inside of Liz felt abandoned. This realization reminded her of her relationship with her father. As she went deeper into the healing and looked at that relationship, Liz saw how she made a subconscious decision when she was younger that said she didn't deserve loving attention. Immediately, Liz knew this wasn't the truth. As a result, Liz's interaction with her son helped her shift her mindset into loving herself.

My kids are often the greatest messengers for me to see myself. For a large part of my life I didn't feel it was okay to have a different opinion than those around me. I also didn't feel it was okay to bicker and work things out. So what did my girls do? They fought constantly and played their parts very well to show me myself. When they fought, I would try to intervene and, inevitably, would make the problem worse. Then one day a light went on. I realized my kids were trying to show me some hidden belief. Instead of getting in the middle of their issues, I became the observer. I finally went within and asked little Terri what was hurting. She revealed that I had a belief that said I couldn't have a different opinion. She told me my girls were a reflection of the relationship I had with my sister growing up. As soon as I realized this, I knew this belief wasn't my truth. I allowed myself to go into the feelings of the past and release them. Then I gave little Terri permission to have a different opinion. My whole consciousness shifted! And not only did I shift, but my girls quit fighting. That's what happens when you take the focus off of what others are doing and become an observer of your life. As soon as you look within and heal the belief you've been holding onto, no longer do you need the reflection of people acting out for you.

Stay aware of your daily life. This is why I invited you in the beginning of the book to open up and receive God's love and guidance. It is everywhere and is very beneficial when healing your life issues. And just like my kids did with their fighting, as you heal, so does everyone else.

Letting Go of the Pain

Sometimes we are so angry, upset, or hurt by another person that we can't get past that feeling to see the gift in the situation. Another way to do The Retrieving the Gift of Love Process in cases like these is to see the person you are struggling with standing in front of you. Go through the process and if you still feel stuck, start here.

1. Visualize the person you are struggling with in front of you. See that person as a little child. If the person you are struggling with is your own young son or daughter then just visualize them in front of you.

2. Talk to the other person's inner child. Ask, "What is hurting inside of you?"

3. Ask this person, "What is the gift of this situation? What are you showing me about myself?" You can do this by writing with your other hand if this tool works better for you. Use your non-dominant hand to have the other person speak through you. Or if visualization and writing doesn't work, just listen for the communication.

4. Ask the other person's spirit what gift you are giving them. Continue to use the tool that works best for you. Just remember, if you are using writing as that tool, the voice of the other person will be written with your non-dominant hand.

5. Once you've gotten your answer, send this person and his or her inner child to the beautiful white light of God.

6. Drain all of the energy related to this situation down your grounding cord.

7. Ask your little inner child, "What do you need from me to heal?"

8. Fill yourself up with the golden light of God and give thanks.

9. Take inspired action with the message your inner child revealed.

~ ~ ~ ~ ~

***Go to The Enlightened Mom Meditation CD #2,
Track 8, to let go of the pain.***

~ ~ ~ ~ ~

Just prior to writing *Message Sent*, I went to the beach to write a letter to a friend. I was angry with her and saw her as a problem. However, as I began the letter, instead of her name coming out of the pen in my hand, mine did. I was shocked and in awe that a message was being sent to me. One of the main points of that letter was that we all separate from love and, when dealing with someone, healing will be created when we see past the resistance to the pain.

Resistance is when you or someone else is being anything other than love. Know that if there is resistance in a situation, there is pain. The Retrieving the Gift of Love Process will heal the pain and move you into a space of gratitude, compassion, forgiveness and love. It is really simple and, after doing it a few times, will become second nature to you. Retrieving the gift of love will change your life. When you recognize that every person in your life is here to help you grow and vice versa, you will see them as an arm of God. You will move from pain into compassion and love.

I coached my client Kathy throughout her divorce. Prior to the marriage's final demise, Kathy and her soon-to-be ex planned a meeting to discuss the legalities of the divorce. Kathy was very nervous about seeing her husband. She had not seen nor talked to him in over five months. What she had done, however, was look for the gift in her difficult divorce.

Kathy and I had been working together for almost as long as she had been separated. From the beginning, every time she wanted to lash out at her ex, I guided her through the healing exercises in this book and invited her to see the gift in each situation. As the weeks passed, she found more of herself. Through this process, Kathy realized that she denied her voice in her marriage. It was when we looked at why she didn't express her feelings to her husband that she discovered why she had denied them in the first place. She was still holding onto a childhood belief that said it wasn't okay for her to speak up and ask for what she wanted.

Tapping into her feelings is just one gift Kathy discovered during her separation and divorce. There are too many to mention here. The point is that by seeing the gift in all of the pain and trauma of her divorce, Kathy healed. She became more joyful and powerful than she'd ever been and found a connection to God that she never knew could exist. And in all of this, she moved from blaming her ex to seeing him as a gift. Amazingly, in that first meeting in five months, Kathy told me she felt no anger or pain towards him. She came out of that meeting feeling empowered and great!

Life is full of gifts! Sometimes they come in small packages and other times BIG ones like Kathy's divorce. Often what seems to be the most traumatic are the biggest presents of all. Kathy mentioned once that she didn't understand why she couldn't let her ex go completely. I told her, "Because you haven't opened up all of the gifts. Imagine this situation with your ex like a big Christmas tree. There are many presents underneath it. These presents are different aspects of yourself that you've lost throughout the years. Whenever you dwell on this situation, continue to ask what the gift is. Stay in gratitude. When you've finally opened all the presents under that tree, you'll finally release your ex once and for all."

Diving Deeper into the Past

Don't be surprised as you begin to heal the pain of the past and dive deep into meditation if you find yourself back in your mother's womb. It may happen. Try not to doubt this. Even though you don't remember being in the womb, your subconscious mind does. The womb sits in the area of the body where we hold our emotions, so you can only imagine how much information you took on when your mom was pregnant with you. For instance, if she was angry or scared a lot during the pregnancy, you may have taken on a message from the lower level vibrations of those emotions that you were not wanted, even if she didn't feel that way. Allow yourself to go into the messages that are revealed and give yourself permission to release anything that isn't your truth.

I have a fun way of releasing the messages taken on while in my mom's womb. I like to visualize her pregnant with me. I see a huge grounding cord connected to her belly. Then I ask all of the negative energy and messages I took on while in the womb to leave, draining them down the grounding cord. I ask what gifts I shut down to, due to those false beliefs, and ask the gifts to re-enter her womb. Then I imagine filling up mom's belly with golden light and give thanks for the gifts that were revealed.

I do this same process all over again when I feel that I need to release pain that came in from both my mom and dad at that moment of conception. Emotional pain based on false beliefs can be handed down from generation to generation. Draining the energy from the womb is a great way to let it all go.

Not only do we take on limiting beliefs as we grow up, while we're in the womb, and even at conception, some of the beliefs that keep you stuck come from past life experiences. Think of it as spiritual DNA. These are beliefs that you've come to work on in this lifetime.

If all of the sudden you want to throw this book away because of what I've just said then I invite you to look at your belief about past lives and where it comes from. As a spiritual coach and clairvoyant, I've seen past lives on most of my clients, as well as myself. If you're having a problem believing in this, I understand. Most of us have been ingrained with the belief that THIS is IT. I used to feel the same way. However, as a healer, I see the past lives that affect us and control us. For instance, one of my Enlightened Mom students, Caroline, was terrified of flying, so much so that she wouldn't eat for 24 hours prior to traveling due to getting sick. Flying was torture to her.

During a healing gathering, Caroline asked me to help her release this. She told me she had no memories of why she would feel this way. So we did a past life regression. I guided her into meditation and asked God to show her the picture from the past that was haunting her life. As she moved deep into the meditation, Caroline shared that she could see herself as a pilot during World War II and was shot down to her death.

I guided Caroline to visualize taking that picture from the past up to the beautiful white healing light of God. Then I guided her to ask God to show her the gifts she had lost in that lifetime. She brought back the love of flying.

Two weeks after we did the regression Caroline wrote me an e-mail saying that she had just taken a trip across the country to see her dad. It consisted of three planes there and three planes back. Not only did she NOT get sick, Caroline said she handled the flight with grace and ease. She was absolutely thrilled and amazed! By healing the past and the belief that flying meant death, Caroline got a whole new perspective on flying and changed her life.

Anna is another Enlightened Mom and revealed to me during a private coaching session that she had a recurring nightmare where she was running with her children, trying to protect them from something. As I looked at the energy of it, I felt this was her subconscious mind sending her a message that a past life needed to be healed.

I guided Anna to get grounded in God's light. Like Caroline in the prior story, Anna found herself during World War II. Only her regression had a different message. Anna saw herself as a Japanese woman running with her two children trying to escape the bombings of the war. She was terrified and didn't know where to run.

Anna sobbed as she watched this movie in her mind. But with her tears came relief. Once we took that past life and sent it to the healing white light of God, Anna came out of meditation and began to laugh.

"I get it now," she said. "I've always been fascinated with Oriental décor and furnishings. Now I finally understand why I am this way!" Not only did Anna finally have understanding, but her nightmares also went away.

I mentioned at the beginning of this book that I have a spirit guide called Waichuka. When I saw him for the first time, I felt a tremendous amount of love for him. What I discovered at a later time was that I had lived a life with Waichuka. We had been in the same Indian tribe and he was the shaman. I learned from him and, as he passed on, I became the shaman. I discovered this information from a clairvoyant. I had gone to a women's healing retreat and asked this woman about my Indian past lives. I knew instinctively that this was a part of my being. I told her about the Indian face I had seen when I first started meditating and how familiar it seemed to me. However, what I didn't tell her was that immediately after seeing his face and feeling such immense love that I saw an animal's face that was very scary. It looked like a wolf or something and had red, beady eyes. It scared me so much that I didn't want to meditate for a very long time.

As I asked about the Indian face, the clairvoyant began to tell me about the past life with Waichuka. Again, I did not tell her about the scary animal. "You had a nemesis in this tribe, Terri," she said. "And he will come to you in the form of a beast." I could not believe what I was hearing! Her description of my nemesis was right on. I knew she could see the past clearly. I knew right then that past lives were real and quit questioning them. I did, however, ask God and all of the beautiful angels to protect me from the dark scary energy. Thankfully, they did and I've never seen the beast again.

I have had many past lives where I was persecuted for being different and outspoken. Those lives deeply affected me and the journey I've been on in this lifetime. It has taken me years to clean up those past pictures and finally give myself permission to be a voice in the world. I started by looking at the negative messages I had heard in this lifetime, and then all of a sudden I found myself diving into the past. I found myself there due to comments I received from people around me in this lifetime. I heard things like, "I'm afraid you're working with the devil," or "What you're doing is wrong." I know my work is about love and compassion and about breaking down the walls of separation. I'm so grateful for those people and their remarks. They helped me get more grounded in who I am and my work, and helped me release the past lives that were keeping me from moving forward.

So what past lives are hindering your life? The following exercise will help you discover the answer.

And if you are leery of past lives or don't believe, that's okay. By doing the exercises you've already learned in this book and the ones that are yet to follow, your life will change in ways that you've never imagined! Past lives are something I believe in and are right for me. My intention is not to change your beliefs, but to help you open up to new possibilities that will enhance and heal your life.

Past Life Regression

1. Get grounded and open up to receive God's guidance and love, giving thanks for the healing you are about to receive.

2. Allow your body to completely relax and say to God, "I'm ready to heal my issue about… Please take me to the original picture in my past that will help release this."

3. Imagine yourself walking through a garden. As you walk through the garden you will come to the edge and find yourself on a ledge of a cliff. As you look down, you'll notice a staircase. Step onto this and as you move down the ten stairs that you see, count slowly to yourself, 10, 9, 8…, sinking deeper into the meditation.

4. Once at the bottom of the staircase you will see a door. Open it, knowing that as you walk through it, you are stepping back in time. Allow yourself to be on a journey. Watch the pictures in your mind. Ask questions like, "Where am I in this picture? What's going on in my life?" You'll know when you've come to the original picture.

5. Feel any emotions that come up for you.

6. Ask what false belief you took on in that original picture. Once you get your answer, imagine taking this picture up to the white light of God.

7. Now ask what gifts you shut down in that past life. For instance, maybe you saw yourself as a homeless man, living on the streets. As you watched this lifetime, you realized that this man shut down to using his creative gifts as a painter and that's why he was homeless. This man had a belief that to be creative was to be weak. The gifts you separated from in that lifetime were ones of painting and joy. Call back these gifts from the universe. Allow the energy of creativity and joy to flow into your heart and say, "Yes!" You have just re-claimed a part of your soul that you lost in another lifetime.

8. Give thanks to God for the healing and fill yourself up with the golden light of God.

~ ~ ~ ~ ~

Go to The Enlightened Mom Meditation CD #2,
Track 9, to dive deep into the past.

~ ~ ~ ~ ~

By getting connected to your heart and by using these tools over and over again to clean out the programming you've been holding onto, you'll begin to discern immediately if you need to do a past life regression or if you're holding onto a negative limitation from this lifetime. As soon as you realize you're moving into a healing space, ask your inner child, your angel, spirit guide or God which exercise is the one that will take you to the original picture that set this belief in motion. Then allow your subconscious mind to take you there.

There will be times when your spirit wants you to understand a situation from this lifetime first, so you might heal the pain between you and another person, and then you may be immediately guided into a past life regression. Or it may take months or years before you're ready to go there. It doesn't matter. There is no rush. The key is to enjoy the journey and to give yourself permission to be on an adventure.

Each of us is a spirit having a human experience. And in that human experience there is pain. Sometimes that pain comes from this lifetime and other times it comes from past lives. But when we love the pain and move into it, embracing our humanness and giving ourselves permission to be unique, we clean out the chaos and move onto a fabulous adventure. That's why it is so important to see life as a gift. No matter how much pain you are in, when you shift your attitude and see everything as a gift and an opportunity to get in touch with the way God made you, you move into a space of gratitude. It is in gratitude where you truly become empowered and heal.

～ ～ ～ ～ ～

CHAPTER 9

Dare to be YOU!

Recognizing and releasing your negative beliefs means you will be different from everyone else. You will be unique. No one on this planet will be like you. That's scary! To be different is the exact opposite of what society teaches us. It says that to receive love you must deny yourself and be like everyone else. You must conform. As a result, you become dependent on others' approval, making them the authorities of your life. This is why there is so much pain and strife in the world. Very few people own the fact that they are perfect just the way they were created. Most live with the belief that says "I have to do things 'right' or 'be the best,' or else I won't be loved." It is this belief that creates competition and the need to get ahead. Instead of us each celebrating one another for our differences and how we were created, we compete against one another, creating separation. When we finally realize that abundance, peace and love come from owning our uniqueness, only then will we stop the cycle of pain and separation.

I was an over-achiever all throughout school. My parents didn't push me. I did it to myself. I believed this would get me ahead in life. I graduated second in my class in high school and went to college on an academic scholarship. By the time I entered college, I had already tested out of 18 hours. You would think that college would have been a breeze for me. It wasn't. I hated school. I was burned out by my second year.

I came to a turning point during the second semester of that sophomore year. I was home for the weekend and, while talking on the phone with a friend, lamented the thought of heading back to campus the next day. I shared with him how miserable I was in school.

"So don't go," he said.

"What do you mean don't go? Of course I have to go."

"Who says?" he continued. "Who says you have to go to school?"

I couldn't believe what I was hearing. I knew he was right. I was living from a false belief that said I had to stay in college to get ahead. Immediately, I made the decision to take back the authority of my life. I got off the phone and went in to my mom and dad and said, "I need to quit school tomorrow. I can't stand it. I will let go of my apartment and move home, plus I'll go find a job if you'll let me quit." There was no argument. They agreed and, within the week, I had moved out of my apartment and found a job selling shoes in a nice department store. I had no idea where I was going in life. All I knew was that where I had been hadn't worked for me. Just by giving myself permission to be different than so many of my peers who followed through with school, my life changed in monumental ways. Four months after quitting school, I won the title of Miss USA.

I don't believe I would have won Miss USA if I had stayed in school and not followed my heart. I had been in the Miss Arkansas pageant during my freshman year and was a top five finalist. At that time, I was already craving a change and wanted to break out of Arkansas with a desire to get into modeling or acting. I saw the pageant as an avenue to get me there. When I didn't win, I made a decision to never be in a pageant again. However, I changed that decision after I quit school when a former Miss Arkansas came into the department store where I was working to buy some shoes.

Suzy didn't recognize me at first. I had cut my hair off really short and had lost about ten pounds. She was in shock to see the changes I had made and quickly asked me if I was going to be in the pageant again. I said, "No. The only reason I ever entered into it was to get a break into modeling."

"You really should enter this year. A production company out of Florida just bought the Arkansas franchise. They do television commercials. You might get a break with them."

I did. My mom made my dress and I entered at the last minute. I won Miss Arkansas and about a month later won the title of Miss USA.

I went completely against the grain of what a good contestant "should be" during the Miss USA competition. First off, I had very short brown hair. I was not your typical looking beauty queen. But what really shocked everyone was my interview in the top 12. I told Bob Barker that I spent summers hanging out at Dairy Queen, sitting on the back of my friend's truck while he played the banjo and while all the guys drank beer and dipped Skoal. I told Bob and the millions of people around the world watching that it was a *real* good time. The next thing I knew, I was crowned Miss USA 1982.

When you release your limiting beliefs that say you must conform to get ahead, and give yourself permission to stand in your truth, miracles begin to happen. I know I wouldn't have entered the pageant that year if I had stayed in school. And I wouldn't have won if I hadn't spoken my truth. Instead, I dared to be different. I aligned my head with my heart. I took back the authority in my life and gave myself permission to be me. It was scary. As I said, when I made the decision to leave school, I had no idea where my life was going. All I knew was that I couldn't allow my life to continue the way it was. That decision was one of the greatest gifts of my life. As I mentioned earlier in this book, I felt emptiness when I won. That's because I was still looking for love from the outside world. However, my whole experience of leaving college and winning Miss USA was the beginning of my journey of allowing God to be my guide. That's because I listened to my heart instead of a negative belief that said I had to be like all of my friends and finish college to have success in life.

Mom, it is only when you look deep within, releasing your fears about being different, that you discover the unique, distinct and lovable you. So what scares you about being different? I invite you to do the following exercise and dare to be YOU!

Dare to be Different!

1. Have pen and paper ready. Get grounded and fully centered. Give thanks to God for the healing you are about to receive.

2. Imagine the little girl inside of you. Ask her, "What scares you about being different?" Write your conversation with her going back and forth between your dominant and non-dominant hands, use your visualization tools, or just hear her.

3. Feel everything. Allow all of your fears to surface.

4. Ask God to release your fears and imagine them flowing down your grounding cord.

5. Look at your inner child and be the loving mother to her. Tell her that she has permission to be unlike anyone else. It is okay for her to be different.

6. Ask the little girl within, "What are you ready to embrace about yourself that is different?" Whatever parts you've disconnected from that make you different is what you want to say yes to. Imagine each one of these things in front of you in a beautiful pink bubble.

7. Bring that pink bubble of light into your heart and say, "YES!" Celebrate this and allow the light to flood throughout your body, giving thanks to God.

~ ~ ~ ~ ~

Go to The Enlightened Mom Meditation CD #3, Track 1, and dare to be different!

~ ~ ~ ~ ~

My 40th birthday was an interesting one. Some friends decided to take me on a night ride on horseback over the mountains of Southern California. I can't remember how many of us were there, but we had a nice group. Our goal was to ride for about an hour-and-a-half one way to a restaurant and then return back over the mountains after dinner. Each of us was assigned a horse. I was so excited! The moon was bright, fully lighting the star-filled sky. My friends were all there. What more could a girl ask for? A BETTER HORSE!

Let me preface this by saying that I am not a very good horseperson. That in itself says enough. THEN I was saddled upon the only mare in the group. I had no idea until later that this is a recipe for disaster. My horse didn't like all those boy horses nudging her on the rump. The next thing I knew, she was kicking and neighing, running for the hills, trying to get away from the pack. As I bounced my way along the ledges of the very high mountains, I held my breath. "This was not what I was expecting," was all I could think. "Oh, God, please help me!"

I hated that my mare was acting out. I wanted to be with my friends. But every time I tried to pull her back, she would rare up, kicking and neighing again. Finally, we made it to the other side of the mountain. "Thank you, God," was all I could think. I had made it in one piece to the restaurant. My whole body yelled, "I need a margarita!"

I had a wonderful dinner with my friends. We laughed about our rumps and then realized that we had to ride back over the mountain for another hour-and-a-half. "Oh, my gosh," I thought. "God, please help me get back safely."

I climbed atop my sweet little mare. Yeah, right. The next thing I knew I was holding on for dear life. One of the boy horses had gotten just a little too close for her. So what did she do? She decided to show him who was boss. Her front hooves flew up high in the air and then the back ones shot out for a quick kick at his face. One of my friends said, "Wow! Terri, you looked like you were in a rodeo." Yep, that is just how I felt. I couldn't take it anymore and got off of that darn horse. I told our guide, "This isn't working for me. I need a new horse." So he gave me his.

An interesting thing happened. No longer did I have the only mare in the group, so there wasn't any kicking and biting. However, I found myself, once again, on a horse that wanted to head out in front of the pack. I tried to hold this horse back so that I could be with my friends just like I had tried to do with the other horse. I felt so absolutely frustrated and finally gave in. I knew there was something going on here. I knew I had to keep myself open to receive the gift of the message that was being sent.

I went home and meditated on my birthday celebration and asked for the gift to be revealed. I discovered a new insight to my truth.

I had lived most of my life in a box, always trying to be like everyone else, holding myself back to fit into the crowd. When I allowed myself to break conformity and the need to have others' approval, it felt good but was always tainted by judgment on myself. I hadn't given myself permission to be different. But just like my horses that night of my birthday celebration, my spirit wanted me to move out of the pack. When I didn't allow myself to be my own unique creative being, I felt suppressed and angry. My spirit, like both horses, wanted me to take off and be different. If I truly wanted to be the person that God created me to be then I had to allow myself to break away from the pack and be the real me. I was born to be a leader and felt judgment for this as a teenager. I kept holding myself back out of not wanting to be different. But we're all different. We're all creative, unique beings.

God sent me a message that night: it was time to allow my truth to shine. By denying myself and holding myself back, I wasn't fulfilling my life mission. What a message! And what a wonderful birthday gift!

As you dare to be different, you summon the courage to take back the authority of your life in every area. I stepped onto this courageous path of connecting to my heart and didn't know where I was headed. I didn't realize that I had a tremendous fear of being different. All I knew was that I didn't feel accepted for being me. So I made that my goal, to love myself unconditionally. However, as I peeled away the layers and negative beliefs, there was always one message that haunted me: "I love you, but I don't like you. Why can't you be more like your sister?" I mulled those words over in my mind for more than 30 years. Those are the words my mom spoke to me in a moment of anger when I was a kid.

Mom's words have been a key driving force for me to love and accept myself. However, it wasn't until many years after stepping onto this healing journey when I took a walk one day and heard those words again that I finally gained complete understanding. Quite honestly, I was sick of that message and was fed up with the fact that it continued to haunt me. That's when I realized that I had never asked myself what belief it reflected to me.

I visualized little Terri walking along side of me and asked her what the belief was that sat behind those words. That's when I heard her say, "It's not okay to be different."

Of course! It was so easy. With little Terri's answer, I realized I had spent my WHOLE life with the belief that says it isn't okay to be different, to be unique. I also realized that my mom had the same belief. But because I've spent years with courage and commitment, taking responsibility to find the real me, I was finally able to get to that core belief which caused me so much pain and suffering. And, I finally let it go. Woo hoo!

Mom, it is OKAY to be different! As you give yourself permission to honor and love your uniqueness, judgment, fear and the need to control will gradually go away. That's because you'll allow others to be different, too! This is an incredible gift for your family!

*Love and honor the real you and, as you do,
you'll love others' differences, too.*

Breaking Codependency

Daring to be different is scary. On the other hand, what's scarier is to live your life trying to please others while denying the real you. I've lived both ways and, let me tell you, I'm a much more loving, giving, and compassionate person when I allow myself to stand in my truth.

When you deny who you are and suppress yourself to win others' approval you are being a codependent. There are many definitions of codependency. The term is often used to define a person who is in a relationship with an addict. Your first instinct when reading this might be, "Well, that's not me! I'm not a codependent because my spouse is a very loving and kind person and he definitely doesn't use drugs or alcohol." Good for you if that's the case. However, you may still be a codependent.

In *Beyond Codependency: And Getting Better All the Time*, Melody Beattie says you live by a set of rules that control you and direct your behavior when you are a codependent. The following are the rules she lists in her book:

- Don't feel or talk about feelings

- Don't think, figure things out, or make decisions—you probably don't know what you want or what's best for you.

- Don't identify, mention, or solve problems—it's not okay to have them.

- Be good, right, perfect, and strong.

- Don't be who you are because that's not good enough.

- Don't be selfish, put yourself first, say what you want and need, say no, set boundaries, or take care of yourself—always take care of others and never hurt their feelings or make them angry.

- Don't have fun, be silly or enjoy life—it costs money, makes noise and isn't necessary.

- Don't trust yourself, your Higher Power, the process of life or certain people—instead put your faith in untrustworthy people then act surprised when they let you down.

- Don't be open, honest, and direct—hint, manipulate, get others to talk for you, guess what they want and need and expect them to do the same for you.

- Don't get close to people—it isn't safe.

- Don't disrupt the system by growing or changing.

Do you recognize yourself in any of these rules? You've already broken some of them just by doing the previous exercises in this book. When you live by this set of rules, you create anger, resentment, judgment and blame in your life. The little girl inside of you is so suppressed that she can't help but feel bad. Instead of recognizing that the hurt you're feeling is coming from within, you take it out on everyone else. This is why you're doing the work in this book: to stop the pain you're holding onto.

By breaking the rules and moving out of codependency, you become a light for your family. This is putting God first and taking a stand for love.

No More Caretaking!

When you follow the rules of a codependent, you are being a caretaker. You think you're doing "the right thing" for others by not saying what you need or want, or by not healing in any way, when in fact you are suppressing another's growth, as well as your own. But as you stand in your truth, you allow other people opportunities to find themselves, too.

I remember when Mackenzie was in elementary school. She had two very close friends. The three girls did everything together. However, there were times when Mackenzie just wanted to play with one of them, not both at the same time, but wouldn't speak her mind for fear that she would hurt the child who was left out. Instead of feeling good about this relationship, Mackenzie began to resent it. She said, "Mom, I really love Elizabeth, but I just want to have some alone time with Katie." Of course, there was nothing wrong with Mackenzie feeling this way. She feared if she said something to Elizabeth that this long-time friend would get mad. Each one of these girls had been a caretaker to the other.

Mackenzie was terrified of losing Elizabeth as a friend. I convinced Mackenzie to speak her truth to Elizabeth. So she called her and this is what she said, "Elizabeth, I want to spend some time with Katie today. I still love you, but I just want to play with her today. I'll see you tomorrow." Mackenzie was right. Elizabeth did get mad. So, I explained to Mackenzie that she had just given each of these girls a beautiful gift: she told them that it was okay for them to express their feelings to her, as well. And that is exactly what Elizabeth did one day.

Elizabeth decided that she wanted to have a play-date with only Katie, so this time Mackenzie would be left out. At first Mackenzie felt a little hurt and then I reminded her that just like she had wanted to have some alone time with Katie, Elizabeth had the right to feel the same. I reminded her that she still loved Elizabeth and that Elizabeth still loved her in spite of wanting some alone time with her other friend. Mackenzie smiled and acknowledged that she had just shifted her friendships into a more loving space. In that moment, Mackenzie became more independent by breaking codependency.

You won't abandon another by following your heart. If that person feels abandoned, it is because they have abandoned themselves. Mackenzie almost abandoned herself when Elizabeth said she wanted to have alone time with Katie. She was about to take Elizabeth's actions as a personal rejection. But it really didn't have anything to do with that. It was merely Elizabeth following her heart that day. It could have been a bad situation for Mackenzie, but it wasn't. She realized that by being honest with her own feelings, she had helped Elizabeth do the same. Thus, any resentment and pain between all of the girls melted away. The beautiful thing about this was that each one of these girls discovered that it was okay to speak their feelings. They are all still friends to this day.

It can be really hard to break codependency, especially when you have loved someone very deeply. It can be extremely scary to express yourself and to take this stand for fear of losing that person completely.

We tend to keep our relationships dysfunctional because we don't want others to feel hurt or abandoned. And we don't want to feel abandoned. We don't want to feel alone and unloved. You will always have a sense of aloneness, however, until you make a connection to God by living from your heart.

You give your loved ones an amazing gift when you break codependency. By stopping the dysfunction and no longer being a caretaker, you allow yourself and others to grow up. Codependency is when we put others first and deny God. Put God first and you end codependency and become an example of unconditional love.

Letting Go of Old Relationships

When you decide to break codependency, you will see some relationships fall away. That's because they aren't ready to take care of themselves. They still need to have people around with whom they can be codependent. That's okay. Let them go.

I often hear my clients talk about their relationships changing as they break codependency. For instance, Kathy, who I have mentioned several times in this book, couldn't understand why her relationship with her husband had to end. For a short time prior to the marriage's demise, she had started expressing how she wanted to create a more dynamic, loving relationship with him. She was at the beginning stages of speaking up for herself. She was shifting into her heart space by having the courage to express her wants and needs. Her hubby didn't want this kind of healing and communication, however, so their relationship ended.

Looking at relationships from an energetic perspective, when you begin to shift your consciousness to one of enlightenment and love, your vibration will change. It will heighten and you will feel more alive than you've ever known. If the people around you aren't ready to shift, they will fall away. Remember, like attracts like. Your vibrations won't resonate anymore and, unless both of you are willing to shift and heal, the relationship will most likely come to an end.

I had to take that chance when I stepped onto the path of The Enlightened Mom. I took a stand for finding myself and putting God first. I knew that my marriage was about to shift in a big way. I set my intention for a loving, open and communicative relationship with Steve, not knowing if he would step up or not. I was tired of always being angry and didn't want to set this example for my kids. Thankfully, Steve did step up and, as I wrote in *Message Sent*, he said he felt better in his skin than he ever had. By breaking codependency with him, I gave him a gift to find himself. Not everyone wants that gift, however. That's when you make a decision to trust yourself and God, and let them go.

I struggled with letting go for a long time. I had a friend that was very dear to me. I was the caretaker in the relationship. She had a lot of difficult things happen in her life and I was always there to pick her up. It was as if I took over the role of being her mom. However, what I really wanted was for someone to love me that way, so I gave up myself to try and win her love and approval. When we had a tiff, I would go within and then come back and say, "I'm sorry. This is what I have learned from the situation. What an amazing gift you have been." It was great that I took my share of the responsibility. What wasn't great was that I never felt she did. She didn't have to. I was always one step in front of her, taking all the responsibility for healing the relationship so that I wouldn't lose her. I continually played this role until I got sick of it.

My friend and I both had huge issues that we mirrored for each other. We came into each other's lives to learn and heal. I believe that was our spiritual agreement. But what I discovered over time was that I didn't feel safe to speak my heart to her. I found that when I tried to express my feelings, she shut me out. I wanted a dynamic relationship where we could really share our innermost fears and thoughts. We had this in most every way, except when it came to dealing with feelings about each other.

There were many times I watched my friend literally get up and walk away after expressing myself to her. I always tried to believe that eventually she would take responsibility for her actions and would go within and heal, and then we would have loving, open communication again. But she didn't at that time. At least not from what I could see in how she interacted with me. I believed my friend didn't want to take responsibility for her pain and needed to blame me for any strife between us. I tried and tried to love her, but eventually realized that by continuing to be in the relationship, I was denying my needs. The little girl inside of me craved open communication with my friend, but she wasn't getting it. So I was guided to give us both a gift: I stepped away.

I struggled internally for two years before making this break. I had been guided to do this through meditation and prayer, but it went completely against the grain of what society says a good friend should do. I felt buried in guilt. I was told I was selfish by my old friend and she condemned my work. But what I soon realized is that she blamed me because I wasn't caretaking her anymore. She still didn't want to take responsibility for her emotional needs and heal, so she had to blame someone else and that someone else was me. She wanted a codependent relationship and I couldn't give it to her.

My dear friend Barb finally shed some light on this situation. She said, "Terri, it's as if you feel like a failure because you couldn't create a loving relationship with her." When Barb spoke those words my whole body trembled. I did feel like a failure. So I went within to get some answers.

I realized I was buying into a societal belief that said if a relationship ends, you are a failure. But that isn't the truth. By breaking codependency with my old friend, I took a stand for loving myself. I didn't need her to love me anymore. I found that love with God. Instead of looking for love from an outside source, I found it within. I broke codependency, took responsibility for taking care of myself, and found a greater connection to God, setting an example for my friend to do the same. That is not selfish. That is an act of love.

My old friend was a tremendous blessing to me. I will always be thankful for her and the gifts she brought to my life. It was an interesting journey with her, sometimes wonderful and at times very painful. But what I discovered is that I don't have to give up myself to be loved by anyone. If a person doesn't love me for who I am, that is okay. That's because I have found the love within and created a divine connection.

Just prior to moving across the country from Southern California to Florida, I ran into my old friend. We got honest with one another for the first time ever about our relationship. There had been some communication in the past that was filled with hurt and blame. I'm the one who instigated most of it, trying to rid myself of guilt and needing to heal my pain. Each of those encounters taught me more about myself and helped me have a better understanding of how to break codependency. That last conversation with my friend, however, was very different. We both had grown tremendously and were able to share our thoughts, our hurts, and our feelings, but without blame. We told each other how much we loved one another, but were glad we had separated as we had both found a greater connection to God. Our relationship and the shift in it helped us each break codependency and find more of who we are. What a gift!

Standing in your truth is not only a gift for you, but it's also a gift for everyone else. It's up to the other person to receive that gift. It can be quite scary at first. There will be times where you feel confused and uncertain as to the choices you're making, just like I felt with my friend. Your heart knows exactly what it wants to do, but your head keeps you confused because you have other people's information and energy on you.

When you are codependent, you tend to mingle your energy with others' energy. This creates confusion and separates you from your truth. Whenever you feel this confusion, first try the Retrieving the Gift of Love Process to see what you can learn from the relationship that is bothering you. If you still aren't clear, use the following tool to call back your energy and create clarity for yourself.

The Vacuum Cleaner in the Sky

1. Sit in a quiet place and get grounded. Say, "I release… (insert person's name) energy from my space." See all the energy flooding down your grounding cord.

2. Imagine a beautiful pink bubble of light above your head. Call back all of your energy from the universe, especially from the person with whom you're dealing. Imagine this light like a vacuum cleaner, sucking and drawing back all of your energy.

3. Once the pink bubble is full, allow the light to pour into the crown of your head, flooding throughout your body, aura and grounding cord, giving thanks for the healing.

~ ~ ~ ~ ~

Go to The Enlightened Mom Meditation CD #3, Track 2, and call back your energy with the vacuum cleaner in the sky!

~ ~ ~ ~ ~

The "vacuum cleaner in the sky" not only helps you stand in your truth, but is also a wonderful tool to use when you feel other people's energy smothering you. It is also great whenever you feel exhausted from the day. As mommas, we tend to leave a lot of ourselves all over the place as we take care of others. Use this tool and you won't feel so drained.

Getting to the Root of the Problem

Mom, are you ready to stop codependency in your life? Are you ready to get real? Are you ready to have the courage to take a stand for the little kid inside of you and give her a gift?

As you walk the path of The Enlightened Mom, you will break codependency with others. Remember, by giving this gift to yourself, you will also give it to the ones you love. It's not your job to try and control whether they receive it or not. All you can do is be an expression of love. They will receive the gift when they are ready.

You've been very courageous by doing the other exercises in this book. You've taken great steps in finding your truth. Now it's time to move deeper into courage and break codependency in all areas of your life. A great place to begin in stopping this madness is to look at your resentments.

If you are resentful of anything in your life, it is because you are doing something to gain someone else's love. You are telling the little girl inside of you that she is responsible for everyone else's happiness and that she must keep her feelings, wants and needs buried within. You have given up yourself and are being a codependent. You're putting others first instead of God. It's time to stop this madness! I invite you to do this next exercise and be an example of love.

Stop the Madness

1. Make four columns. Title the left one, "Resentments." Title the second one, "Why?" Title the third one, "The Reflection," and the last one, "Action of Love."

2. In the left-hand column under "Resentments," make a list of everyone or everything you resent. Be honest. You're not being a bad mom if you list your kids or your spouse. Just get it on paper.

3. Look at your first resentment and ask, "Why?" Really dig deep within to see why you're resentful. You might find as you do this exercise that some of your resentments are things you don't feel you can release from your life. For instance, you might write that your first resentment is doing the laundry. Then you write the reason why and your reaction is to write down that you hate it. I invite you to go deeper than that. Why do you hate it? Is it because you really despise dirty clothes? Or is it because you feel you have no time for yourself? Are you buying into a perfect picture that says the clothes have to be done a certain way, maybe the way your mother forced you to do them, and in your heart you didn't want to do the laundry that way, but still do? Really dig deep to ask why you resent your items on your list and write down each answer under the "Why" column.

4. Go to the third column to look at the reflection. Remember, every situation that is difficult is a mirror to the struggle going on inside of you. To see the reflection, visualize the child within you, listen to her voice, or take another piece of paper and ask her what this situation is revealing to you, answering with your non-dominant hand. Let's go back to the example above, in the case of you hating to do laundry. As you look at it, you realize that you do, in fact, hate this chore because you are still doing it the way your mother forced you to do it. But when you ask the little girl inside of you what the reflection is, she tells you that YOU, not your mother, are still forcing her to do things your mother's way instead of your way. In essence, you are being a codependent, living your life for your mother's love and approval, giving up your own.

5. Go to the final column called "Action of Love." Ask what would be the loving action to take to release your resentment and break codependency. A good way to get your response is to once again see the little kid inside of you and ask her what she needs. Or continue to use your writing tool or just listen. Let's take the laundry situation again. Imagine you realize that your mother forced you to do laundry on Fridays when you were a teenager. She forced you to do it her way and gave you no say in the situation. You hated this. You wanted to be with your friends on a Friday afternoon, getting a jump on the weekend. But your mom said, "No," and you became angry and resentful. When you look at the reflection of your life, you realize that you are still doing laundry on that same darn day you did as a kid. You hate it and would rather do laundry on a Monday instead of a Friday. You decide that the loving action is to take back your power and give yourself permission to do the laundry when you want. This is the action of love. Write down the answer in the last column.

6. Once you have your complete list, take action. You will heal yourself, and the resentments you feel in your many different relationships will fall away.

I had my client Elaine do this exercise. She is the mother of three girls who at that time were two, six, and nine. Under "Resentments," she wrote, "Husband home so late to not help with bedtime." Elaine felt extremely overwhelmed with her family's evening rituals, as her hubby is a lawyer and continually got home very late. When I asked her to write why she was resentful in the second column, Elaine wrote, "Tugged by three kids. Have to be three places at once."

I guided Elaine to go within and look at the little child inside of her. She asked little Elaine, "What is the reflection?"

Little Elaine told her, "I'm responsible for all of my kids' happiness. Someone will suffer." Immediately, Elaine recognized this as a false belief and knew this was codependency. Deep down Elaine feared that one of her kids might suffer and not feel loved, and, thus, would blame her and not love her in return. But after doing this work, and from her own life experiences, she knew this was not the truth. Elaine knew she couldn't make people happy and, in fact, by trying to do so, she finally realized that she was hindering her kids from finding their own happiness and independence.

Elaine and I talked about the "Action of Love" to take. Elaine decided that her older daughter would probably welcome the time to herself to read in bed, rather than mom always having to do it, and that this child could also go to bed a little later than the other two girls. The two-year-old needed mom's full attention, but the six-year-old was already good about falling asleep alone.

Elaine also discovered in this process that it wasn't just about putting the kids to bed that made her feel overwhelmed and resentful of her husband's late arrival, but that it was also her family's bath time ritual. I asked her if the oldest daughter bathed herself and she said yes. However, when I asked her the same about her six-year-old girl, she said no, that she felt it wasn't safe for her child. I asked her if this daughter could swim and she said yes. Then I asked her to get grounded and go into a meditative state, asking for God to give her clarity. I had her imagine her six-year-old daughter in front of her and then had her ask this child's spirit if she was ready to take the responsibility of bathing herself. Elaine saw her little daughter dancing around, saying yes. Instead of being in fear of what was right for her daughter, she went within and asked God to reveal the truth. And in doing so, she released some of the responsibility and gave her daughter independence.

Elaine discovered the loving action to take with each of her realizations. By doing this exercise, she finally recognized that her resentment wasn't really with her husband. It was with herself, due to the belief that it was her responsibility to make everyone happy, as well as make them safe, as in the case of her six-year-old bathing herself.

Elaine walked away from our session that day knowing fully what actions she was to take to break codependency in her family. She knew that by standing in her truth and giving herself a break, she was about to give her girls a wonderful gift: their independence. Not only were her girls about to receive a tremendous gift, but just by doing this exercise, the walls of resentment towards her husband fell away.

When you do this exercise, you may feel that resentment isn't your main issue. Maybe it is sadness or hurt that describes how you feel. That's okay. Be creative with this. Insert whatever word works best for you.

Resentment or any negative emotions you're holding onto are gifts to guide you to the root causes of your codependent relationships. It may take a little digging but it is always worth your effort to go within. For instance, if you find that you resent your father-in-law because he's always telling you what to do and you struggle with feeling you have to please him, this may be the little girl inside of you responding to how your dad used to treat you. Your dad was hard on you and, as a result, you constantly sought his approval. You thought you had to be the good girl to win his love. You were a codependent to him and now you are one to your father-in-law. This transposing of feelings can perpetuate codependent relationships in all areas of your life.

When I first came into the relationship with Steve, I struggled emotionally every time his son A.J. walked into the door. I saw A.J. as the bad guy. When A.J. came to our home, the adult Terri left town emotionally and little Terri took over. That's because I was codependent with Steve to love and acknowledge me. When A.J. arrived, a lot of Steve's attention focused on him. I felt left out, not because Steve or A.J. did it to me. I felt left out because I did it to myself. It wasn't very pretty how I reacted to our situation. The blessing is that I learned from it.

I learned that my resentment really had nothing to do with the present situation. I looked deep into the past and discovered that I was transposing my feelings of my relationship between my mom, sister and me where I constantly felt like an outsider in the relationship, and put those feelings onto A.J. I took on a belief as a child that told me I was always going to be second choice. This drove me to codependency. I lived with this belief until I got sick of it.

I went to the beach one day, sad and frustrated with life and a little jealous of a friend. She constantly had miracles in her life and I felt I didn't. This brought up those "second choice" feelings again. I sat at the beach and asked, "God, why does it seem that my friend is the chosen one?"

"She's chosen to be chosen, Terri."

"What?" I asked, a little stumped.

"She has chosen to be chosen. Each of you has a choice. All you have to do is give yourself permission to receive, and then the miracles will happen."

I had a running life theme that said I would always be second choice. I saw it in my relationship with A.J. and Steve, with my mom and sister, and with too many other relationships to name here. This belief caused me great resentment and fear that I would never be good enough to be loved. That's why I kept my relationships codependent. But after doing a lot of introspection and peeling back the layers of this belief, I was finally ready for an amazing conversation with God that day at the beach.

No one made me second choice. I didn't allow miracles into my life because I didn't choose to be chosen. So I made a choice that day at the beach: from then on little Terri was going to be number one to me. And with that choice, I broke codependency. I knew in my heart that this was putting God first. And as a result, the miracles, many that I've shared with you in this book, manifested in my life. This happened simply by looking at my resentments and doing the introspection I needed to get in touch with my truth.

Looking at your resentments and allowing them to take you as far back as you can to the false beliefs you're holding onto will change your life. You may find that after doing the previous exercise that you also need to go back to The Retrieving the Gift of Love Process and incorporate it into your healing. That's okay. Use all of the tools you've been given in this book to help you heal. There is no right or wrong way to use them. Watch the world around you. Listen for God's messages in everything you do. Have a conversation with God, your angel or spirit guide, or if talking with your inner child works best, do that. It doesn't matter. The key point is that you find your answers so that you release yourself and the wall of pain you've created.

Once you really make a commitment to break codependency and start taking action, you will feel so much freedom. Your whole attitude about life will change. The walls that you have felt between your spouse, kids, parents, boss, co-workers or friends will diminish and eventually go away. And when they go away, there is love. That is why it is the loving thing to do to break codependency and stand in your truth.

Honesty is ALWAYS the Best Policy

It was a gorgeous September day in Florida. I sat outside having lunch with my mom, my Aunt Reneé, and her daughter Robin. We were on a little getaway to celebrate my Mamaw's birthday. We laughed as Aunt Neé shared how crazy Mamaw had been while in the hospital the previous Christmas. Mamaw had gone to visit Aunt Neé, only to end up very sick. The drugs they gave her in the hospital caused her to temporarily lose her mind. Aunt Neé had felt frantic and feared that Mamaw was going to die. She didn't know what to do, so she called her daughter Robin.

Robin is a nurse and lives several hours away from Aunt Neé. During Mamaw's hospital stay, Robin made some calls to the hospital to find out what was going on and, after talking to Mamaw's nurses, felt assured that she would be okay. Robin knew the effects of the medication Mamaw had been given and was also aware that Mamaw had been taken off of them due to having weird hallucinations. The effects of the drug were just taking a little time to wear off.

Some of the hallucinations were quite funny, but as Aunt Neé shared this story with us, I could feel the tension building. Pretty soon it was obvious that almost a year later, she held some resentment towards Robin. As Aunt Neé's tears began to flow, she shared how scared and alone she had felt while taking care of Mamaw in the hospital. Robin said, "Momma, I asked you over and over if you wanted me to come. I knew Mamaw was going to be okay. But when I asked you if you needed me to be there, you didn't say to come."

Aunt Neé responded with, "I didn't want to create a problem for you. I only wanted you to come if you wanted to." That's when both Robin and I interjected and told Aunt Neé that if she had been honest and said what she needed that none of this pain and resentment she had been holding onto for almost a year would still be there.

You have to be honest with yourself and those you love to break codependency. When you get honest, you release old beliefs that tell you that you're not worthy of being loved just for being you. If you're not honest, resentment, blame, anger, judgment, separation and hate build. You don't want those kinds of walls in your life. And I know you don't want them for your kids. The sad thing about it is that everyone is doing it, not just Aunt Neé. She told me that she really believed she was doing the "right thing" so as not to create a burden for Robin. I know Aunt Neé thought this was the loving thing to do. But it wasn't. Aunt Neé, like you, me, and the person on the street, has been ingrained with the belief that says to give yourself up and not speak what you need or want is love. It's not. It's codependency.

It is time to get honest with yourself, Mom. It is time to get honest with your family. When you don't say what you want, think, feel, need, you name it, you live a lie and create codependency, setting an example for your family to do the same. It is time to stop the cycle of emotional pain and sickness that smothers our world. It starts with each of us as individuals to create healing. And that means you, Mom, getting honest with yourself first. That may mean you need to tell someone your feelings and needs, or it may mean that you need to take care of yourself. You make that determination when you go within and look at yourself. Honesty is ALWAYS the best policy and is an important aspect to healing.

Handing Over Responsibilities

Years ago I got honest with myself when I realized how much I hated the anger, resentment and overall negativity I felt in my life. That's when I made a decision to take full responsibility for my happiness and heal. A lot of the pain began sliding away. It was great! That's because I was finally loving and honoring myself. However, there was still one problem: not only did I take responsibility for my own life and my issues that needed healing, but I took ALL of the responsibility. And I mean ALL. I took it from everyone. I thought this was being a good mom. It wasn't. I was still being a codependent. I acted like this out of guilt. I had a core belief that said I was bad and caused others' pain. So I unconsciously made a decision to do everything right.

Imagine a pendulum swinging back and forth, back and forth. It goes from one extreme to the other. Think of one end as being the victim, where you feel everyone is to blame for your pain. Then watch the pendulum swing the other way. On the opposite end is the need to take responsibility for everything. You own so much responsibility that you create a whole new source of pain. By taking responsibility for everyone else, you don't allow others to grow and heal. You become their codependent and allow them to play the part of the victim. As a result, the cycle of blame and pain remains.

My life swung from one end of the pendulum to the next. What I discovered, however, is that by taking responsibility for everything, I still hurt. I still had an agenda. I just wanted to be loved. I wanted everyone to love me, especially my kids.

I took Mackenzie to the orthodontist one day when she was in junior high. Her jaw had been popping for months due to her braces. I was concerned about the onset of TMJ, which can create a lot of problems not only in the mouth, but also in the neck and arms. Of course, because I love my daughter and wanted to help her avoid any unnecessary physical pain, I insisted we talk to the doctor.

I asked question after question to the orthodontist, but never felt I was getting a clear answer. I wasn't sure if I was just being brain-dead for the day as we mommas often do, or if the man just wasn't making sense. I walked out of the office realizing that he didn't have an answer for me. I felt quite frustrated with the situation.

I expressed my concern to Mackenzie when all of the sudden she blasted me. "Why did you have to keep asking him questions, Mom? Didn't you get that he didn't have an answer for you?"

I explained to Mackenzie my concern about any future physical problems with her jaw and told her that I was trying to nip it in the bud before it got too bad. In spite of this explanation, she blasted me again.

I was furious! Then Mackenzie said, "Mom, now you're angry. Why don't you use the tools that you teach?" Those remarks really set me off. I had had enough! I jumped out of the car and slammed the door, combined with a few expletives.

I was extremely torn up by this whole situation. I hated the fact that I had reacted so negatively to Mackenzie. On the other hand, I couldn't understand why in the world she was giving me such a hard time for looking out for her health. My gut knew she was giving me a gift. I just had no idea what it was.

For the next 24 hours, I went into a healing space. I wrote in my journal, I meditated, and I prayed for God to help me heal this situation. I'm really good at owning my responsibility during difficult times, so I went over the whole situation to see what my part was in the drama. But this time the only thing I could see that I needed to look at was how angry I got with Mackenzie when she asked why I didn't use the tools that I teach. As I digested this information, I discussed it with a friend. She asked me, "Does Mackenzie not like to ask questions?"

"Thank you, God," was all I could think. At that time, Mackenzie struggled with asking questions and had for years. When she was four and Kolbi was two, we often went to McDonald's to have lunch. Free tiny kid-sized ice cream cones came with their Happy Meals once they were finished eating. Since no money had to be exchanged, I coaxed the girls to go up to the counter and ask to get their free ice cream. Mackenzie would never do it.

As my kids grew up, I allowed them to gain their independence when they were ready. When Kenzie shied away from asking for something she wanted, like ordering a pizza over the phone when she was younger, I would first ask her to do it and then when she refused, I would step in. I allowed her to grow at her own pace. However, when her insecurity caused her to lash out at me with this ordeal at the orthodontist, I gained a whole new perspective and finally received the gift her spirit was giving me.

I finally realized that I was not the "bad guy." In so many ways, that's how I treated myself when it came to owning all of the responsibility in difficult situations. I would take all the blame and often beat myself up. The reason I got so mad at Kenzie's remarks was because deep down I was still performing for my kids. I was coming from a space of codependency, wanting them to love and accept me. I took Mackenzie's harsh remarks and slid back into the old belief that said I was to blame for her pain. She had been extremely uncomfortable with me asking the doctor all of my questions. That's why she got so mad at me. But after hours of introspection, I knew I had simply been true to myself in this situation and acted as a loving parent. I also knew I had a choice to make. I could either take all the blame as I had in the past, or I could do the loving thing. I did the latter and handed Mackenzie's issue back to her.

First, I apologized for my raging antics. Then I said, "I've taken a hard look at what happened yesterday. The reason I got so angry with you was because I felt as if you were abusing me. I felt you were telling me that I am wrong for being who I am. When I asked the doctor all of my questions yesterday, you got uncomfortable with it. I explained to you why I did this and you still lashed out at me. I don't deserve that kind of abuse."

"Kenz," I continued, "I'm not judging you, but you've never liked asking questions. It's okay. We all have issues to heal. You came into this life to find your power. It is my job as your parent to help you become empowered. So, I'm handing this back to you. You want to do amazing things in this life, you want to have cool cars and great clothes, but if you're not willing to claim your power and ask questions, you'll never have the money to get the things you love." Now I was talking a language she could understand!

I told Mackenzie, "I have an old friend that I used to take a lot of classes with. She struggled with me asking questions. She complained that it made her feel uncomfortable. Then one day she admitted that the reason she judged me was due to the fact that she didn't like asking questions. My old friend said she felt like a burden to others when doing this. However, she said that she realized how much she now appreciated my example of having the guts to ask and that she learned so much from my questions."

"Kenz, I'm handing this back to you, this responsibility to heal your issue," I continued. "Yesterday, you made me the bad guy because I asked so many questions. I was doing what felt right in my heart. This is not my issue. It is your issue and only you can heal it. It's up to you to do with it what you want. You can start facing it now, or you can wait ten years. Or you can choose never to look at it. It is your choice. Just know that I'm here for you. I have tons of tools to help you if you should want or need them. I love you."

I felt so darn free. I couldn't believe it! I wasn't claiming responsibility for her pain. I broke codependency with her in that moment. I gave her issue back to her and gave her a tremendous gift: the next day, something came up and I breathed a sigh of gratitude to God when Mackenzie asked, "Mom, do you want me to make the call and ask the question?"

I took a stand for myself with Mackenzie. Her actions were a reflection of an old belief inside of me that said I deserved my children's wrath if I stood in my truth. I knew by my emotional reaction to her that something wasn't right. So I went within and used the tools in this book to find the gift.

Mackenzie was such a blessing to me through that whole difficult situation. It was as if her spirit was playing the perfect part for me to recognize a belief that was affecting my life in so many ways. I believe that was our spiritual agreement. But by taking a stand and handing her issue over to her, I ended that old agreement.

When I look back on that time, it would have been easy for Mackenzie and me to continue our codependent relationship and to stay in blame with one another. I could have pointed a finger at Mackenzie and scolded her for being a bad girl, repeating the cycle all over again. Or, I could look deep within and see what was going on for both of us. I chose the latter and when I got clear, I was able to talk to Mackenzie with love.

It is imperative for us as moms to take responsibility for the pain and hurt we carry within us. We have to take responsibility for our own healing, but not take it for everyone else's. That's the hard part of being a mom. We tend to believe that taking over everything is a way of showing love. It's not. It's codependency. If you want your family members to really be empowered as they try to blame you for their problems, hand their issues back to them with candor and love. Release your guilt and the need to do everything for them. If you've been practicing taking responsibility in your own life and saying "I'm sorry" for inflicting your pain on others, they will know it is okay to be vulnerable and to heal. This brings the pendulum back to balance. No longer will you have to go from one extreme to the other. No longer will you have to be in an abusive situation. When you break codependency, daring to be you as you stand in your truth, you will, in essence, be handing your family a gift on a silver platter.

～ ～ ～ ～ ～

CHAPTER 10

You Don't have to "BE GOOD" to be Loved!

"World's Best Mom." I saw a vision of a trophy that said this while working with my client Elaine. We were doing some healing work when all of the sudden this vision appeared in my mind. Elaine is a wonderful mother to her three girls. She is very conscious of how she interacts with them and has implemented many of the tools in this book to create better understanding in her family. However, at the time I saw the vision, she still lived by a perfect picture of how she wanted to be as a mother and wife, and constantly felt as if she couldn't meet the standards she had set for herself. It's as if she wanted to win the "World's Best Mom" award.

Do you feel you need to be the world's best mom? Maybe you don't think of yourself as needing to be the perfect mother. I don't think Elaine thought of herself this way. However, in that healing session, we were shown that she was definitely running this mental programming. Are you doing the same?

What are you afraid will happen if you're not "the best" mother?

I feel most moms, whether they think about it or not, have this need to be "the best." It's ingrained in our society to do everything perfectly. For instance, I received an e-mail from a friend one day. It was a questionnaire that asked you to fill in the blanks about yourself. Upon completing, you were then guided to pass it on to your friends. I laughed when I saw one of the questions. It asked, "What do you want to be remembered for?" My friend's response was, "For being the best mom."

Of course you want to be the best mom that you can be. That's only natural. However, it doesn't mean that you have to be perfect. We often associate doing our best as perfection. The only perfection we will ever be is when we honor who we are, letting God take care of the rest.

I know it's hard to believe that it's okay to love yourself this way. This goes completely against the grain of what we've been taught. A good mother is supposed to love everyone else at the expense of herself. Baloney!! This is the myth of the perfect mom.

If you are trying to win the "World's Best Mom" trophy by doing everything perfectly at the expense of yourself, you will never win. I promise you this. You will lose your connection to God. The only way you're ever going to come even close to "winning" is by loving yourself and doing what your heart wants, not what your head tells you to do. When you listen to your head, you have an agenda to receive love outside of yourself. When you listen to your heart, you find it within.

What Drives You to be "The Best" Mom?

We drive ourselves to be "the best" moms to save our children from the past pain we felt. We want them to experience the love and abundance we've lacked in our own lives, and, thus, we deny ourselves.

What pain in your past are you trying to protect your children from? What drives you to be a perfect mom? Think about this for a minute. My old client Leslie made a list of things that made her nuts about her mom. These were the things that she felt caused her the most pain. Leslie's mom always worried about other people's opinions. This put a lot of pressure on Leslie to perform as a kid. As a result, Leslie wanted her mom to stop buying into others' opinions. She also wanted her mother to hear her and she wanted her mother to stop pushing her.

Leslie and I went over her list. Every item on it and the pain associated with each complaint was driving her to be the perfect mother. For instance, Leslie put extreme pressure on herself to listen to every one of her twin girls' words because she never felt heard. It's hard enough to always hear one child all of the time, but twins? It's just not possible, especially two-year-olds. Leslie constantly complained of exhaustion. It was no wonder with the standards she had set for herself. What she really needed was some earplugs!

Leslie's perfect pictures of what a "good mom" should be completely sapped her energy. She left no room for herself. Every time she came in to see me, she cried. The little girl inside of her was tired. She was tired of performing for everyone. Ironically, one of the things Leslie disliked most about her mother, always performing for others, was exactly what she was doing to herself!

Leslie's story mirrors my own. The pain from my past stayed with me and drove me to be the best mom that I could be. But the perfect pictures I set for myself made me crazy. I continually felt like a failure.

It was only when I decided to accept my humanness that my life began to change. I made a decision: no longer would I set an example for my kids to be perfect. No longer would I be driven to do everything "right" as a mother, as a wife, or just as a person in general. Yeah! I got it. I finally realized that I had been doing exactly what I disliked about my parents. I was trying to "be good" to gain people's love. I had watched both of my parents acting this way when I grew up. Both were concerned about other people's opinions way too much. I know they both thought this was love. I did, too, until I woke up. I knew if I were to continue this cycle, my kids would follow my lead and need to do everything "right," too. I knew it had to stop with me.

In one of my Enlightened Mom workshops, I had all the moms write a description of a wonderful mother. One of the ladies said, "She would always be calm." Yes, this is an ideal picture, but to create this kind of standard is setting yourself up for failure.

When I first started my healing journey, I set the intention to be unconditional love. At first I thought this meant to be peaceful and calm all of the time. I set a standard for myself and constantly failed. Then I realized I was still judging myself for not being perfect. I wasn't accepting my humanness. To truly love unconditionally, we have to accept and embrace everything about ourselves. That includes the days we lose it with our families.

An Enlightened Mom is a mother who accepts and embraces her humanness, even when she isn't perfect.

The gift in this attitude is that the more you embrace your humanness, the more peaceful and calm you become. Yes, the ideal is to get to that loving space of peace and calm. The key to getting there, however, is to embrace and love the times that you are not.

What perfect pictures have you set for yourself? What pain from your past drives you to be "the best" mom? Let's take a moment and look at this.

Perfect Pictures Drive You NUTS!

1. Sit down with pen and paper, getting fully grounded and centered, giving yourself permission to be open to receive God's love and guidance.

2. Ask your little child within what you disliked the most about your mother when you were a kid. If you didn't have a mom, think of the person who acted as a role model to you. Who

was the main caregiver? Make a list of all of your dislikes about this person.

3. Ask your inner child, "How are these negative feelings affecting your life now? How are you over-compensating with your family, trying to protect them from the hurt that you felt? What is driving you to be a perfect mother?" Write with your non- dominant hand and receive your answers, or if it feels better to you, continue visualizing or just listen for the answers.

4. Ask your little girl within how the need to be perfect makes her feel. Is she angry? Is she sad? How does her body feel?

5. Allow any emotions to come up for you. Feel everything. The more you allow yourself to surrender and move into the pain of the past, the faster it will go away.

6. Give the little girl inside of you permission to be human. Tell her that she no longer needs to be perfect.

7. Celebrate the healing and give thanks that you are finally finding acceptance for yourself.

～～～～～

Please go to The Enlightened Mom Meditation CD #3, Track 3, to release the perfect pictures that drive you nuts!

～～～～～

After doing this exercise with Leslie, I invited her to go within and ask her mother's inner child why she was so very hard on Leslie. She visualized her mother's inner child and asked her what was hurting.

Leslie saw that when her mother was little she didn't feel acknowledged because she was the middle child of three. She never felt she received much attention. As a result, Leslie's mom felt she had to prove herself to her family that she was worthy of being noticed by creating her own "perfect" family.

When you look at your parents this way and understand their pain, forgiveness comes. I know it did for me with my mom. I saw her as a little kid who just wanted to be loved. Out of her fear of causing others' pain and then possibly being rejected and blamed, she gave herself up. When I was a kid, my mother lived her life ruled by others' opinions and expected me to do the same. She thought this was love.

You've already made a list of the things that drove you nuts about your mom or, if you didn't have a mom, the person who was your caregiver. Now it's time to see what caused this person to act this way. It's time to heal the pain and open your heart to love.

Open Your Heart to Love

1. Get grounded and fully centered, opening up to receive God's guidance. Visualize the relationship with your mom or main caregiver as healed, setting an intention to create this, feeling the loving vibration throughout your body.

2. Go back to your list of dislikes about your mother or main caregiver and focus on the item that caused you the most pain. Visualize this person and her inner child. Tell her how you felt when she acted this way.

3. Ask your mother/main caregiver's inner child what was hurting inside. Use whatever form of communication is best for you… talking, writing or listening.

4. Feel all of the emotions that come up for you. If you feel like crying for this little child then, by all means, please do. You are finally opening up your heart to understanding this child's pain.

5. Once you feel as if everything has been said, give thanks to your mom or main caregiver, and send her to the beautiful white healing light of God.

6. Tell yourself, "It's time to release all the negative energy and programming I've been holding onto from this situation. God, I surrender this to you and open up for the healing." Surrender and allow all of the energy and darkness you've been holding onto to drain down your grounding cord.

7. Celebrate and give thanks for the healing you are experiencing as you fill up with the beautiful light of God.

~ ~ ~ ~ ~

Go to The Enlightened Mom Meditation CD #3,
Track 4, to open your heart to love!

~ ~ ~ ~ ~

This exercise will not only bring healing in your own life and help you release the pain of what drives you to be a perfect mom, but it will also shift the whole dynamic between you and your mother or main caregiver. When you can visualize the ones who you feel hurt you and see their pain, you realize that it wasn't about you. As a result, forgiveness, compassion and acceptance set in. That's why this tool of seeing the other person's inner child is so valuable. It creates healing for all of your relationships, especially the one with yourself. You finally release your need to be "the world's best mom" and realize that you were okay all along.

It's Time to Break the "Good Girl" Rules!

Mom, you ARE okay just the way you were created. You always have been. There is no such thing as perfection except the perfection of following your heart. That can be a problem, however, because our heads usually win, especially when it comes to being a mother.

How many times a day do you say things like "I should do this" or "I need to do that"? These phrases are surefire signs telling you that you have created a perfect picture of how you think you must act in the world.

Perfect pictures are thoughts in your mind that set a standard you believe you must meet to receive love.

Some people are perfectionists and it's obvious to everyone they meet. Maybe their home is immaculate or their desktop at work is always clean. They look stylish in their clothes and, for goodness sake, their cars are always clean! That kind of perfectionism is not a harmful thing unless it becomes obsessive and the person defines herself by constantly meeting those standards. Perfect pictures, on the other hand, can be a little more misleading.

When I write "perfect pictures," you may think, "Well, that has nothing to do with me." You might be surprised. If you have a belief in your mind of how a kid "should" act, that is most likely a perfect picture. If you feel you are "supposed" to get a certain amount of things done in a day, this is also a perfect picture. And if you believe you aren't allowed to make mistakes with your kids then you are living by the ultimate perfect picture.

"Should" is a word that comes from your head, not from your heart. It is a red flag telling you that you are worried about what others will think of you. Several other reminders are "have to," "need to," and "must do." If you find yourself saying these phrases a lot, you are probably living your life from a subconscious belief that says, "Only good girls receive love." You are living your life as a "good girl should," trying to be the "World's Best Mom." But since you've given yourself permission to be human instead of Supermom, it's time to get rid of these negative thoughts.

In *Thresholds of the Mind: Your Personal Roadmap to Success, Happiness, and Contentment*, Bill Harris explains that we take on certain attitudes during childhood as to what a good child is. He says, "Part of the problem is that most good-child messages come in the form of prohibitions—what parents want their child not to become or *not* do." He adds, "A good child is someone who has learned to follow the rules, but in many situations the rule follower, the good child, doesn't have many options." As a result, he says, "Being a good child can make you an unhappy adult."

Do you feel there are times when you don't have an option with how to handle your life? Or maybe you feel you can't make a decision out of fear of doing something wrong? What about all of your jobs as a mom? Do you feel as if you're constantly racing trying to get everything done? If you feel any of these things, you are probably stuck in being a "good girl." You've limited yourself to some old beliefs in the guise of rules that say this is the way it has to be. It's time to take your blinders off.

Many years ago right after Mackenzie turned a year old, and a month prior to getting pregnant with Kolbi, my hubby insisted I get a nanny. "No way!" is what I heard myself say. "No one is going to help me raise my children." In my mind, a good mom would never allow someone else to step in and help raise her kids.

Steve was a garment manufacturer at that time and was constantly on the road. He knew I needed some time for myself since we didn't have any family near us to take up the slack. But I had my blinders on. I struggled with this idea. There was a battle between my heart and my head. My heart truly wanted some help, but my head didn't. Thankfully, my mind eventually shifted. I finally took my blinders off. I hired an amazing nanny. That was the beginning step of releasing my "perfect mother" pictures. I released the standards and rules in my mind of what a good mom should be and started following my heart. Thank God! By shifting this old negative mindset, I was afforded the time to step onto my path of healing and teaching. Not only did I become a better mother, but my children were also surrounded with one more person to love, and who loved them in return. Our nanny, Erly, became a surrogate granny to my kids. What a blessing!

Bill Harris says that if you took on a message that said you had to be a "good child" to receive love, you most likely act as a "good adult." You've set a standard for yourself so others will see you a specific way. But what this really means is that you're still seeking love outside of yourself. You're being a codependent. That's right. The rules that a codependent lives by, which we talked about in the last chapter, are some of the same ones good girls tend to live by.

I've had many clients who, as children, can remember the moment they chose to be good out of seeing a sibling being bad. They took on a message that being good is the "right" way to be. They made their parents the authorities in their lives, which is what most children do. What I'm inviting you to do is to take back the authority in your life and listen to YOUR truth. Act from your heart, not from what your parents or society told you to do. All you have to remember is that when you act from your heart, you come from a space of love.

After taking a look at some of the "good girl rules" I had created for myself, I realized my fear of hiring a nanny was based in the fear that, if I did, my children and other people would see me as uncaring and selfish. That was the "good adult" following all of the rules she took on as a child. Those were the limiting beliefs that kept me stuck in my life. Thankfully, I broke the rules of what a good mother should be and gave a wonderful gift to my whole family. And by the way, Erly still lives with us. She hasn't worked as a nanny for me in years. She works outside of the home now and is simply a part of our family. What a gift!

I was pretty darn miserable trying to be good. My misery caused me to lash out at the people around me. My life was filled with rules. Everything was black or white to me. There was no in-between. In my mind, that was how a "good girl" should be. I believed I had to be good to receive love. I also expected others to follow the same rules. "That's what people should do," was my attitude. Well, that attitude not only filled my life with anger and judgment, it made me a controlling wench. That's when I decided to quit trying to be so perfect, always seeking love outside of myself. Instead I went within and looked at the rules that no longer worked for me. Those are the negative beliefs I've been talking about all throughout this book. As daily situations in my life reflected those rules one at a time, I gave little Terri permission to make her own set of rules. And in that, I found acceptance and love for myself, and for my family, as well.

If you were raised to be a "good girl" then you most likely are still living from the negative belief that says you must be good to receive love. The problem is that as we grow up, the "good child" is still with us. Bill Harris adds in *Thresholds of the Mind*, "efforts to create a good child often produce an adult who copes poorly with life—or an adult hypocrite."

I coped poorly with life, until I decided to break the rules in my mind. I even tried to wring traces of all the "bad" ways from my stepson A.J. I was hard on him because I was hard on myself. I wanted to make him good. I believed that by making him this way, he would then receive love. I was instilling the exact negative beliefs in A.J. that had been instilled in me. It wasn't until I gave myself permission to break all of the rules in my mind that I could finally allow A.J. to be free.

As you read this portion of the book, you may be thinking, "Well, none of this applies to me. I never tried being a good girl. I was very bad." Just by saying those words, you are living by a set of rules and judging yourself.

A friend told me that she was most definitely not a good girl and, in fact, was a very BAD kid. She said she didn't follow any "good girl" rules as a teenager and caused her parents a lot of pain. By defining herself as bad, however, her words revealed that she lives by a set of rules of how a person "should be" to receive love. In my friend's mind, she didn't live up to the standards set by society and her parents, so she was bad. I invited her to see the little girl inside of her with more compassion and understanding. Just talking about this brought tears to her eyes. My friend has a "perfect picture" in her mind of how she believes she should have been as a kid and now the guilt still buries her. This judgment affects her whole life and how she feels about herself, as well as how she treats her kids.

When you live by the rules of a "good girl," you often feel as if you can't meet those standards, and end up feeling guilty and bad, thus, continuing the cycle of self-denial. The darkness inside of you drives you to be the perfect mom so that you might prove to everyone that you are worthy of being loved. It is time to finally let go of the darkness and all of the rules that run your life.

Take Inventory of Your Perfect Pictures

Are you hard on yourself, always beating yourself up? Are you constantly running, never feeling as if you'll catch up? Is your life filled with anxiety and pain?

Think about the example you are setting for your family as you try to be the perfect mother. Do you want your kids to believe they always have to be good children, needing to be perfect to receive love? Do you want them to live from their heads instead of their hearts? I don't think so. You want your children to grow up living lives of peace, abundance and love. The only true way to achieve this is by living from your heart, creating a connection to God. And that means to release all of your perfect pictures of being good, giving yourself permission to be who you really are.

What kind of perfect pictures do you run in your mind? Are you a taskmaster, going from one job to the next? Whose approval are you seeking when you act this way? Why are you trying to be a "good girl" again?

When I first began working with my client Eric, he continually asked me to help him get his priorities straight. Between being a divorced dad of two and running a division of a large television network, he felt like a taskmaster, working constantly, never having any time for himself. During one of our sessions, I asked God for guidance with how to help Eric. This is the answer that came back to me, "Terri, being a taskmaster means that you are seeking approval outside of yourself. Tell Eric his number one priority is to follow his heart in every moment."

That was so simple! Of course, if you want the most productive energy at your fingertips, follow your heart in that moment. I'm sure you know how it is when you are in resistance to doing something. You feel drained and it takes twice the effort to get the task done. But when you follow your heart and act upon what it's telling you, you tap into a flow that makes life exciting and fun.

If you're a taskmaster, meaning you continually move from one job that "has to be done" to the next, the "good girl" is running your life again. Ask the little girl inside of you whose approval she is trying to win.

Are you a workaholic? Where does this programming come from? Most of us believe that the only way to have fun is when your work is done. I can tell you firsthand that when you follow your heart and release the rules that drive you to be a workaholic, your life will be so much happier.

Writing this book has been an adventure in following my heart. In the past, I was a type "A" personality. I pushed, pushed, pushed, always feeling the need to prove myself. But as I've grown in my connection to God, I'm a lot nicer to the little girl inside of me. If I find myself needing to push through this book out of some remnant of an old negative belief, I stop and ask, "What is my truth?" I know that if I'm not standing in my truth when it comes to writing, I've just regressed back into my childhood of watching my dad work himself to death. Just by asking little Terri "What is your truth right now?" I move back into a loving flow. I know this is where love is. It is in my heart, not outside of me. By allowing myself this gift and releasing my perfect picture of seeking love by being a workaholic, I am more productive in a less amount of time. That leaves more time for myself, my family, and my friends. It allows me to have a life and be a wonderful example for my husband and kids.

Have you ever experienced morning anxiety when you think of your to-do list? It's telling you that you're once again trying to win the "World's Best Mom" award by trying to be good. When you feel this way, ask the little girl inside of you, "What's hurting? What's making you so nervous? Whose approval are you seeking?" You might be surprised at the answer.

My client Liz entered my office one day flustered and anxiety-ridden. She said, "Every time I take my son to school, I feel as if I'm racing." Have you ever felt that way? I used to. Then I went within knowing that this, too, was a "perfect picture."

I discovered that my horrible anxiety was a reflection of my school days, trying to win my teachers' approval. I felt tremendous acceptance from my teachers when I was a kid. I was an A+ student and was always the teacher's pet. My focus in school was to be the good little girl so I would win my teachers' acceptance. That also meant never being late for class.

Just like Liz, each day I took my kids to school, I felt myself racing, trying to beat the bell. When I found myself anxiety ridden, it wasn't about my kids, but about myself. My old need to be perfect had filtered over to my kids. As soon as I realized this and told little Terri that she didn't have to please her teachers anymore, the anxiety went away. Little Terri no longer had to be the good little girl to be accepted and loved.

Perfect pictures reveal themselves in so many ways. My client Teresa shared with me that she has a fear when it comes to keeping up her home. She said she feels it has to always be clean and in order. I asked her what she was afraid of if she were to let it go every now and then. Teresa said, "I am afraid of being rejected."

Are you afraid of being rejected if you don't do things perfectly? Whose love are you afraid of losing? And what rule is creating your fear?

One of my most difficult perfect pictures to overcome was the need to be right. Steve and I used to argue a lot, often about who was right and who was wrong. When I went within and talked to little Terri about this, I soon discovered that my need to be right was in direct correlation to how bad I felt about myself. I couldn't admit that I was wrong, because I felt so "wrong" on the inside. I constantly felt I had to defend myself. It was as if I could take away my "badness" by insisting that I was right. In my mind, being right meant that I was good.

As I healed and let go of all of the "good girl rules" and began to accept myself, the need to be right diminished. Boy, did that help Steve's and my communication. It saved our relationship! The need to be right built a wall between us. Ironically, I believed that if Steve saw me as being perfect and never wrong then he would always love me and never reject me. But it was when I could finally admit to being wrong and release my need to be perfect that our marriage healed.

For most moms, our greatest fear is to make a mistake with our kids. This is the "good little girl" inside each of us acting up again. We just want to be loved and we want our children to feel loved. So we drive ourselves nuts, never wanting to do anything wrong.

The need to do everything right by my kids literally drowned me in guilt. I was terrified that I might cause them immense pain, just as I had believed my mom did with me. But as I traveled this healing journey and learned that we are all in this together with spiritual agreements, each of us learning from one another having a human experience, I no longer saw myself as a victim but as a spirit who co-created every one of my life's difficult situations, including mistakes. Mistakes are just more opportunities to learn about yourself and re-connect to your heart.

As I mentioned previously, I was tough on my stepson A.J. when he was little. You could say I made some pretty big mistakes. I used to punish myself about this. I felt immense guilt. But as he got older and as I moved into awareness of how I was interacting with him, instead of beating myself up, I took responsibility for myself and told him that I was sorry for my actions. Talk about admitting that you are wrong! That was HUGE for me. I learned to say "I'm sorry" for taking my pain out on him, and I learned to shift my consciousness to love and compassion by going within to see what caused me to make what I considered a mistake in the first place.

I wrote a letter to A.J. many years after my negative actions towards him. I heard him refer to himself as a "bad child" one night at dinner while he visited over the Christmas holiday. He had just graduated from college and was on his way to a very successful career. Steve and I were so happy for him. It seemed he had his life pretty together for a 22-year-old. However, I knew when I heard him describe himself as a "bad child," that it was time to set the record straight. I thought my changes over the years had done that, but what I realized in that moment was that A.J. was still holding onto a false belief that stemmed from the time when I was controlling and driven to make him a "good child."

My letter was filled with love. I told A.J. I was sorry for the messages I had given him as a child. I told him that I had lived by beliefs back then of how a person "should be" to receive love and now knew those beliefs were not true. I told him what was special about him and what made him unique. His response made me cry.

A.J. wrote back to me that he never knew he needed to hear those words from me. But he did. He said he felt so emotional that he had to go up into the mountains to digest what I had written to him.

I could feel gratitude overflowing from A.J.'s response. I knew this gift from my heart, if he was willing to receive it, would allow A.J. to see himself with a whole new pair of eyes. By the way, just for the record, I never told A.J. he was bad. I simply enforced beliefs upon him that suggested that who he was, was not good enough, and that he needed to be perfect to be loved. And that was a lie.

Parents don't realize that when they paint a picture of how life "should be," that they are setting their children up to feel inadequate and possibly like failures. For instance, I know many parents who will never cry in front of their children. They may cry by themselves, but never in front of their kids. They've created a facade that says life has to always be good. What they're really doing, however, is showing their children that it isn't okay to be human.

It's time to let go of your perfect pictures, Mom. You don't have to be a good little girl to be loved. There is nothing you "need" to do. Just be you. You are perfect just the way God made you. Be an example of love for your family. It's time to burn the rules!

Burn the Good Girl Rules

1. Think about the perfect pictures that run your life and the rules behind them. For instance, are you afraid of making a mistake with your kids? What belief are you holding onto that makes you feel this way? Write each perfect picture on a separate small piece of paper.

2. Give thanks for this awareness and ask the little girl inside of you if she is ready to release these old negative "good girl" rules. If she is, go to your kitchen and get the biggest soup pot you own.

3. Find some matches and get far away from a smoke alarm.

4. Say out loud, "I release all of my perfect pictures NOW and I give myself permission to be human."

5. Now burn every one of the items on your "perfect picture" list. That's right. BURN THEM! What's even more fun than just burning all of them at once is to burn one item at a time. As you burn each one, say, "I release the need to..." (Fill in the blank with the item on your list). Then say, "I give myself permission to ..." For example, if you run a perfect picture that says you have to cook dinner six nights a week and you hate it, especially because you're wanting to take a new art class then say, "I release the need to cook dinner for my family six nights a week. I give myself permission to cook a family meal only four nights a week. I give myself permission to wing the other nights of the week and go take my art class."

6. Celebrate! Woo hoo! Say, "Yes, yes, yes! I thank you God for helping me release all of these negative old rules that keep me disconnected from you. I give myself permission to be the way you created me. I take a stand for honoring you today! Yes, yes, YES! Thank you, God, for this healing!" Feel this celebration in your body as if you just won a ten million dollar lottery.

7. Take action with the new guidelines you've set for yourself.

This exercise is one of the most cathartic gifts you will ever give yourself. As you become aware of more rules and pictures in your mind, feel free to do it all over again. (FYI: when creating your list of the perfect pictures you are ready to release, make sure you don't put each item on a piece of sticky pad paper. I did. Boy, was I in shock after lighting the first piece of paper and it stuck to my hand. I couldn't get it off! I almost burned myself. It's quite funny looking back at it now. There I was in my kitchen with my old soup pot and a pad of bright green sticky paper. I had written each item on my list on a separate piece of paper and put them on my kitchen counter. I picked up the first one, ready to rid myself of this limiting belief, when all of the sudden my finger was hot. "Ow, ow, ow, ow, ow!" I yelled as I pulled the paper off. It kind of broke the seriousness of the healing ceremony. On the other hand, I'm sure the fly on the wall, if there was one, had a great laugh.)

Burning your perfect pictures is a terrific way to anchor this transition in your life. If your kids have passed the kindergarten age, you know that the thought of the day in learning is to allow the child to play, much like my kids did while learning how to spell. They were taught to write their words in shaving cream. It creates an anchor for the child to remember. That's what you're doing when you burn all of the rules. You're not just writing them down. You're releasing the old energy to the universe. Be a kid! Allow yourself to have fun and play with this.

Stop the Punishment

An Enlightened Mom is not perfect. In fact, she is just the opposite. She embraces her humanness. She is real. She releases ALL of the "good girl rules" in her mind and loves herself unconditionally. The problem, however, is that we are so ingrained in our world with punishment for not being good, that we do it to ourselves whether we realize it or not. But now that you've burned the rules, Mom, it's time to end this pain and suffering. This may take a little time and effort. You've most likely been hard on yourself for years. To end the pain, go into awareness of how you punish yourself.

Punishment shows up for me in many ways. For instance, if I don't take a break when I'm tired, that's a form of punishment. When I do this, I know that I'm still sending myself the message that I have to get it all done or else I won't be loved.

Another way I punish myself is when I eat poorly. If I look deep within and ask myself why, I am often amazed with the answer. Sometimes it's because I'm stuffing my creativity down and not expressing it fully. Or another reason is that I am so tired from not taking a break that I need a sugar rush to keep going. Both of these are forms of punishment.

Mental games are one of the greatest forms of punishment. I used to analyze everything in my life. I constantly questioned myself. I would look at a situation from every angle, trying to figure out what was best. I soon discovered that this was a form of punishment. Analyzing about what you "should do" versus "what you want" is a surefire way to see that you are not honoring your heart once again. You are punishing yourself. You're living from the belief that says you must be good to be loved. It's time to stop punishing yourself and live from your heart, re-connecting to God.

Most of us beat ourselves up in one way or another. I knew I had to stop the punishment, so I asked God to guide me. I was shown during meditation that whenever I start this battle in my head, I am to quickly point at the battle and say, "That's punishment. I don't do that anymore. I don't deserve this kind of treatment." This statement literally stops the mental game. You may have to do it a thousand times, but look at it this way: you've spent a lifetime denying your heart, playing head games. This is what your brain knows. It's time to retrain it by saying, "NO MORE PUNISHMENT!"

No More Punishment!

1. Take pen and paper and write at the top of the page, "NO MORE PUNISHMENT!"

2. Make two columns under the heading. On the left-hand side write, "How I Punish Myself." In the right-hand column, write, "What Would Love Do?"

3. Think about all of the ways you punish yourself and write your list. Do you punish yourself by doing everything for your kids? Are you still holding your voice in and not saying what you need? Are you being honest with yourself? Are you walking around feeling sad? Are you angry? Do you feel overwhelmed? Any negative emotion is a sign that you are probably punishing yourself. I invite you to go into awareness, real awareness, every moment of the day, and connect with

how you punish yourself. Are you a perfectionist? Do you need your kids to act a certain way? These are avenues for you to get in touch with yourself and release punishment.

4. Take a look at your list in the punishment column. Think about what the loving replacement action would be for each item and write it down. For example, you've discovered that you lose control with your kids and get angry when they leave a mess everywhere. The loving thing to do would be to give yourself permission to stand your ground, not with anger but with self-respect. Your kids will respect you when you respect yourself. So instead of ranting and raving, you do it differently. You sit them down and very firmly say what you need. You create your boundaries. This is what love would do. Not saying what you need is punishing the little girl inside of you.

5. Take action with your "What Would Love Do?" list.

Check in with yourself on a daily basis and see how you continue this punishment programming. The more loving actions you take to stop the punishment, the more you're going to recognize other areas of your life where you allow abuse. Are you allowing your kids to run over you? If you are, you're still punishing yourself. You don't deserve that kind of treatment. You allow this because in some way you still believe you will cause your kids pain by standing up for yourself. This goes back to being the good little girl once again. You're still trying to win the "World's Best Mom" award. You don't want to be regarded as hurtful, selfish, or uncaring by your kids. So you punish yourself, never realizing that you are setting an example for them to do the same when they grow up.

As your awareness broadens, add any new items to your punishment list with a new loving replacement action. Be conscious of your mental battleground and see how you're treating yourself. Check in with your emotional well-being by talking to the little girl inside of you. See what she needs. Ask her what is hurting. And lastly, check in with your body.

If your body is hurting in some way then there's a chance you're not loving and honoring how you were created and are, thus, punishing yourself.

If you're not loving and honoring the way you were created, you are punishing yourself!

Louise Hay has a wonderful book called *You Can Heal Your Life*. In it is a reference guide for many different types of ailments and what they represent. For instance, there is a tremendous amount of breast cancer among women in our society. When you look up "cancer" in Louise's book, you see that it energetically represents hurt, resentment, grief and hatred. Then when you look up the word "breasts" in the guide, you discover that issues with the breasts have to do with "refusal to nourish the self; putting everyone else first." As you put the two definitions together, you realize that breast cancer is related to hurt, pain and resentments due to self-denial. This, again, is a form of self-punishment.

Hopefully, you don't have breast cancer or any other disease. But if you do have something going on in your body, please take a look and see what your body is trying to tell you.

Have you ever had PMS? *You Can Heal Your Life* explains that this is your body telling you that you're "allowing confusion to reign," or that you're "giving power to outside influences," or, here's an interesting one, "you are rejecting your feminine processes." If you have PMS, ask how you're punishing yourself. Are you punishing yourself by not owning your power and are letting everyone else have the authority in your life, creating confusion for you? Or have you bought into societal programming that says you have to push, push, push to get everything done, which by the way is very male-oriented, instead of allowing your feminine creative energy to flow? If you're denying your female side then you are punishing yourself.

I had horrible PMS for years. I mean horrible. We're talking about throwing up and diarrhea for several days, often causing me to be in bed for at least a day. I resisted my femininity. I hated being a girl when I was younger. I wanted to be a guy. I didn't like the emotions that came along with my menstrual cycle. Every month I resisted this process. Until the day I woke up to the gift that was being presented to me.

I made a huge discovery: the emotions that surfaced with each monthly cycle were feelings that I buried on a regular basis. I often denied myself and held my feelings in. But when my monthly cycle came along, for some reason I couldn't hold them in any longer. I discovered this was a gift. I started looking at the issues that surfaced during this time and made my monthly cycle an opportunity to get to know myself. Pretty soon my PMS was gone. I gave myself permission to feel all of the emotions that surfaced, no longer punishing myself by ignoring them, and, as a result, my PMS healed.

These are just a few ways the body tells you that something isn't right. Whether you're an emotional wreck or your physical body is talking to you or your mind is playing games, when something isn't working in your life, there is a good chance that you are punishing yourself. Remember, when you punish and judge yourself, you send a message to the little kid inside of you that she isn't lovable and that she is bad. You've created perfect pictures of how you think she must be. This is love with conditions. It's time to have compassion for the little girl inside of you. As you release the rules in your mind and accept who you are, you become an example of unconditional love. You become so full of love that it will overflow to everyone.

Stop the cycle of punishment. Your parents punished themselves and, as a result, you felt punished. No one deserves this kind of abuse. We all deserve love. Every one of us.

You don't need to be perfect, Mom. Throw away the rules in your mind that say you must deny your heart to be a good little girl. Honor and love the child within. Your life is going to change in so many wonderful ways. You will be happier, more joyous, more at ease, and you'll be a better mom and spouse. That's because instead of allowing society to rule your life, you will be putting God first. It's time to retrain the brain. Start labeling the ways you punish yourself and find a loving action to take. You and your family deserve this kind of love!

~ ~ ~ ~ ~

PART IV

Living In Abundance

CHAPTER 11

MOMS just WANT to have FUN!

ow do you express your life creatively? We often think of creativity as something artistic like dancing, painting, writing, or singing. But to live creatively doesn't mean that you have to be an artist in that sense. It means to be the artist of your life. Paint the canvas of your life with color. Add dimension to it by allowing yourself to play and be a child of God. Be unique. Be the person that only you can be. Align yourself with the greatest creator of all. Alan Ashley-Pitt says it best in his poem "On Creativity":

> *The man who follows the crowd will*
> *usually get no further than the crowd.*
> *The man who walks alone is likely to find himself*
> *in places no one has ever been before.*

*Creativity in living is not without its attendant
difficulties, for peculiarity breeds contempt.
And the unfortunate thing about being ahead of
your time is that when people finally realize you
were right, they'll say it was obvious all along.*

*You have two choices in life: you can dissolve
into the mainstream, or you can be distinct.
To be distinct, you must be different.
To be different, you must strive to be
what no one else but you can be.*

You've done a lot of work in this book to scrape away old beliefs and be what no one else but you can be. As you become more grounded in this truth, how would you like to express your life? How would you like God to use you? Take a moment and think about what makes you feel passionate. Do you have any idea of what that is or have you buried yourself for so long that your passion hasn't had time to surface? It's okay. It will. You have to give yourself time to get to know yourself. And one of the greatest ways to connect to the passion in your heart is by giving yourself permission to play.

Playtime is a Must for Peace, Joy and Happiness

Life is meant to be fun. Our society says, however, that life is about work, work, work. And then when you've finally worked hard enough and done it "good enough," only then can you have fun. Just what "good enough" is has to be determined by the standards you've set in your mind. As we discussed in the last chapter, for most moms, those standards are very high. Therefore, we seldom meet them and, thus, punish ourselves again by denying ourselves playtime. And that's when we get mad. We resent everyone around us. Mom doesn't get to have fun, but everyone else does.

Do you deny yourself playtime because you're worrying about your family too much? Are you still racing, trying to get everything done and working hard to do everything "right"? The little girl inside of you deserves some playtime. The irony is that when you finally do give her permission to play and explore, your worries will go away. By surrendering the controls of your life and allowing yourself to play, you will get the answers you've been looking for.

I often ask moms what they really want. The answer I hear the most is, "I just want to play and have fun." Does this ring true for you? Remember, when you feel something in your heart, it is God talking to you. It's time to listen. You don't have to follow the "good girl" rules anymore. You now know they are not the truth. They keep you from living your life creatively, filling it up with abundance and love.

For my 43rd birthday, many friends asked me how I wanted to celebrate. My normal celebration would have been a birthday lunch. However, when that idea was suggested, I didn't find myself excited in the least. I turned to little Terri and asked her, "What would really get you excited? How would you like to spend some playtime?"

I saw visions in my mind of when I was a kid outdoors playing ball with friends. I knew immediately that I wanted to go to the beach and have a picnic for my birthday, playing volleyball in the warm California sunshine.

I invited about 20 friends to my beach birthday bash. Five showed up. In the past, I might have taken offense to this. That's when I spent my life looking for people to love me. But because of this path I've taken, I was able to be neutral and see the truth of the situation: all of the women who didn't show up were overwhelmed with things they had to "get done" for their families. I heard that excuse over and over. The invitation to my party came a little late and these women felt as if they couldn't shake up their schedules to be spontaneous. I heard, "Oh, I wish I could come. That sounds like so much fun, but…"

My beach party was during the day and each of these women's kids was in school. Nothing was keeping them from having some playtime except the responsibilities in their minds. Most of the women who didn't show up wouldn't allow themselves to play just for the fun of it. Their lives wrapped around their families so much that they had lost the ability to play without them. I understood exactly how they felt when they got my invitation.

For years I buried myself in responsibilities, too. I craved playfulness, but didn't allow myself this freedom. I only gave myself permission to play if a family member was involved and wanted me to join them doing whatever it was that made them happy. Deep down, I resented this. I didn't realize that I was the one who limited myself. When my 43rd birthday arrived, I knew it was time for me to take care of myself and my needs. I couldn't continue to deny playtime for me. Just me. It was time to allow little Terri a chance to play outside again, doing the things that made her most happy.

While at the beach for my birthday, I overheard a man on the next volleyball court say, "Women just suck the fun out of everything. The more fun you want to have, the more they'll suck the energy out of you."

"Hmmmmm," I thought. "It sounds as if he has a wife at home who isn't very happy that he is out having fun. She probably doesn't allow herself enough playtime."

I knew the man's words held a lot of truth. This is what we tend to do as moms. It's part of that martyr syndrome again. It's that message that says, "To be a great mom, you have to deny yourself. You can't have fun."

After seeing my women friends neglect themselves by not coming to my birthday party and hearing what the man on the next volleyball court said, I felt God had given me a beautiful gift. My birthday occurred while taking notes for this book. God was telling me to make sure this was a part of the message that needed to be revealed to moms. This is exactly what I'm talking about when I say that playtime opens you up to receiving messages. I gave myself permission to follow my heart and play and, as a result, received a wonderful message to help me write this book. I moved into the flow of my heart and received a message from God. What a wonderful birthday gift!

Two days after my birthday bash, my family and I flew to Kauai. Little Terri, that curly little blonde inside of me, was really coming out to play. As I danced in the aisles waiting on our flight, my appalled 13-year-old Mackenzie said, "Mom, you need to learn how to relax and be mellow." She was finding my antics a little uncomfortable. She said, "At home you can be a grump sometimes. And when you do relax, you need to learn how to be different."

I knew from hearing Mackenzie calling me a grump that once again a gift was being revealed. Actually, two gifts. One was that I had to continue to bring playfulness into my life. At that time, I did a lot of things for me. What I soon discovered, however, is that one of my greatest joys is when I give myself permission to be outside and feel free.

The second gift from Mackenzie's words was a reminder of what we mommas do to ourselves. We tend to hold ourselves back from being playful for fear it will embarrass our kids. I gave up this belief a long time ago but have seen over and over how moms shut themselves down to make sure they will win their kids' approval. It's time to end this cycle of pain. The more you can act silly and have fun, the more your kids will grow up and have permission to do the same. We think we do our kids favors by suppressing our truly playful selves, but in reality, our actions tell them that life has to be serious. Yes, during their teenage years they might want to disown you. Oh, well. They're going to do that anyway. So you might as well make yourself happy and be playful!

Kids can be very judgmental. This is because they judge themselves. Remember, if you find yourself shutting down or feeling pain due to your kids' attitudes towards you, this is an opportunity for you to look within again. And that's what I did that day. I knew from that point forward I was no longer going to be a grump because of some silly myth that said I had to be a perfect mom to be loved.

Even though Mackenzie told me in her own way "to behave" as we made our way to Hawaii, she's told me for years that I'm different from other mothers—in a good way. That's because I've healed my life and don't get caught up in a lot of life's daily drama anymore. However, the joy that comes from being childlike with friends is a part of me that was missing for a very long time until my 43rd birthday. Don't get me wrong. I did lots of things with my friends. I took weekend getaways with them, and sometimes got together in the evenings for dinner. Those times were few and far between, however. And most of the time, we were doing "adult" things: dinners, movies, etc. But going to the beach for my birthday to play ball with friends allowed little Terri to truly come out and play. It wasn't about being an adult, but being like a kid again. The joy that comes from being childlike with friends was a part of me that had been missing. I didn't want my kids to grow up and deny themselves as I had done, becoming martyrs and taking care of everyone else's needs at the expense of their own. So, as their mother, I took a stand that day for more playfulness and became an example of love.

Stop Denying Yourself and Have Fun!

Are you ready to be the artist of your life by bringing more color and playfulness into it? It's time to stop resenting everyone else because you're not giving yourself permission to play. You are the one doing this to yourself. What keeps you from allowing the little girl inside of you playtime? Are you still buying into the "good girl" rules that say you must be serious to be loved?

I took Kolbi to buy some dance shoes one day. There is nothing like walking into a dance store, seeing all of the sparkly costumes, tutus and dance paraphernalia. The little girl inside of you jumps for joy, at least it does if you like that sort of stuff. As Kolbi was fitted for some shoes, I watched a little girl stand at the checkout with her mother. You could tell by this child's demeanor that she was really excited about her new dance goodies. Instead of being allowed to dance and wiggle as she wanted, the little girl's mother made her stand still and be quiet. That's the message so many of us took on as little kids: to be good, you must be quiet and still. You must be serious.

Why do we applaud children for acting like adults? What is the deal? The deal is we took on that message as kids. It's the same message that tells us we can't be creative and fun as moms. We must be responsible.

I called to wish my grandma a happy birthday when she turned 93. Some of our family had thrown her a big party back in Arkansas. I laughed when she talked about how the kids wanted to play and made a mess all over the room. I love Divine timing. This message was coming in loud and clear right at the time I was preparing to write this chapter. Grandma went on to talk about what a "good boy" my cousin's son is because he stops to clean his hands and he minds so well. All I could think was, "Why does this child need to be a little adult? What's wrong with getting his hands dirty?"

Then that same afternoon I picked up Mackenzie from dance. She was working as an assistant to the teacher for a classroom filled with rambunctious two and three-year-olds. As she climbed into the car to go home, she pointed out some of the kids. I noticed a little girl walking up ahead, dressed in her dance garb. She looked so darn cute I could have eaten her up. Kenzie said, "Oh, she's the best. She's so mature and does everything really well."

There was that message again. No matter how hard I've tried to tell my kids to be kids, the societal message still prevails: the more mature you act as a child, the more you'll be loved. Yikes! Where do you think these kids are getting this message? From us. We moms have to break this cycle and be kids at heart so that our children will continue to have fun when they grow up.

Permission to Play

1. Get pen and paper ready. Sit in a quiet meditative space, getting fully grounded, giving yourself permission to receive God's healing and love.

2. Ask the little girl within you, "What scares you about being silly and playful? Are you afraid that you'll be rejected? Are you afraid that you'll be made fun of and be judged?" Sometimes we have programming from our childhoods that tell us that children need to sit down and be quiet. Maybe your parents were a little reserved. Maybe they were workaholics and didn't play enough. Or maybe as a kid you were quite goofy, but peer pressure got to you and caused you to shut down your playful silliness? Were you reprimanded for this? Are you afraid that your life will go out of control if you are playful? What happens if you allow yourself to let go? Now pass the pen to the other hand and write, write, write all of your feelings and answers. As always, if writing doesn't work

for you, either visualize the little girl inside of you to do this exercise or just listen for her answers.

3. Allow yourself to feel any emotions that come up for you. If you haven't allowed the little girl inside of you to be very playful over the years, she might be a little angry. If you need to take a pillow and beat the bed, do so. Whatever you do, try not to hold back your feelings. You'll just make your little inner child more resentful and fearful. Give her permission to really vent. But remember, give thanks for the healing while you're venting.

4. Tell the little girl inside of you that you are now the boss. Say, "I give you PERMISSION to be playful!"

5. Call back your playful side. Retrieve that part of your soul that you lost as a child. Visualize a beautiful light coming from the furthest reaches of the universe. This is the part of you that was playful. Say hello to this light and allow it to fill you up from your head to your toes. Say, "Yes, yes, yes! I thank you God for this healing. I now own my creative, playful side. I am a child of God."

6. Now give that cute little girl inside of you a great big hug and go play with her!

~ ~ ~ ~ ~

Go to The Enlightened Mom Meditation CD #3, Track 5, and give yourself permission to play!

~ ~ ~ ~ ~

You may feel a lot of sadness or a struggle within while doing this exercise. It's okay. Give yourself permission to feel everything. Bringing playfulness into our lives goes against the grain of what we have been taught as mothers.

Donna is one of my Enlightened Moms. She shared an experience she had at an art festival. Her five-year-old son couldn't wait to get his hands in the clay. Donna said she almost said no to her son because she didn't want him to get messy. Luckily, she flashed back on what she had learned in our class and said, "So what if he gets messy?" and allowed her son to play in the clay. Donna struggled, however, with allowing herself to join him. She said she finally realized, "I was holding myself back for no good reason." That's when she said "YES" to being playful.

I told Donna all she had to do in that moment of turmoil was to turn to her inner child and give her permission to play, too. That would have ended the struggle. Tears streamed down Donna's face as I told her this, for she knew in that moment she had spent a lifetime being the good little girl, not having permission to be playful and creative.

Being an Enlightened Mom means that you have permission to be playful and have fun. Your example will bring so much love and light to your kids. They will grow up knowing that it is okay to be who they really are, not needing to be good, living by a set of rules that says you must be perfect to be loved. Instead, they will grow up following their hearts.

Margaret is the mom to young adults. I told her that in spite of the fact that her kids are already grown, she is giving them a tremendous gift by living with a playful heart. It's never too late to start. Not only will you give your children this gift, but you'll set an example for your spouse as well.

A lot of men stay boys forever, but some still tend to work too hard and are way too serious. If this is your situation, you may find that you don't allow yourself playfulness because your spouse doesn't. This is what some of the moms discovered in one of my Enlightened Mom classes as we looked at bringing more playfulness into their lives.

I guided the moms into a deep meditation, having them ask their loved ones how they might feel if they were more playful. When the moms asked their children's spirits, each of them was very excited. Every one of the moms got a clear message that their kids wanted to have more fun with them. Since Margaret's kids are grown, she visualized her husband and asked him what he thought. He said,

"You're being irresponsible." Of course, this isn't what Margaret wanted to hear. I reminded her that she was talking to the part of her husband that is buried in negative programming, the part that says you must be serious to be loved. I invited Margaret to go back into her meditation and look at her husband's inner child. This is the truth of who he is. The answer was different this time. Margaret's husband said, "Yes! I want you to play so I can learn from your example." By giving herself permission to release all of her "good girl" rules and play, Margaret would have an opportunity to set an example for her husband to do the same.

The Truth About Playfulness

1. It's time to release your guilt about being playful. Take yourself into a healing space once again, getting fully grounded, giving yourself permission to open up and receive God's love.

2. Visualize each of your children, one at a time, and ask them how they feel about you bringing more playfulness into your life. If your children are grown, that's okay. Ask each of them to bring forth their inner child. Ask each little kid how he or she feels about you bringing more playfulness into your life. If you get stuck and feel as if you can't trust yourself to get an answer, check in with the crown of your head and make sure it is open like a camera lens.

3. Do step number two again. Only this time, do it with an adult in your life with whom you feel you can't be playful around. If you're married, look at your hubby. If you're a single mom, look at your boss, your friend, your parent, you name the person. It doesn't matter. Choose the person who you feel reflects your negative belief that it isn't okay to be playful. Visualize the person in front of you and see that person's inner child. Ask the little kid what he or she will learn from you being playful.

4. Give thanks to each of the spirits you have just talked to, knowing that they are here to help you reconnect to your heart. Send them back to the beautiful white light of God.

5. Celebrate that you finally know the truth about playfulness.

∼ ∼ ∼ ∼ ∼

Go to The Enlightened Mom Meditation CD #3, Track 6, to learn the truth about playfulness!

∼ ∼ ∼ ∼ ∼

When you deny your creative, playful side, it's as if you are telling God that a mistake was made when you were created. God is the greatest creator of all. And since we are the children of God, we are here to create and have fun. This is putting God first. As moms, we tend to deny this truth due to guilt. We feel that if we give ourselves this kind of love, our families will resent us. That's a myth.

Stop the cycle! You can do it. Stand in this truth: when you allow yourself more play time, it will affect your whole family for the better. Release any and all guilt you have about being playful. The greatest gift you can give your family is to be an example of peace and joy. Playtime is the main thoroughfare to getting there.

What Makes You Feel Alive?

Having fun is a key component to being an Enlightened Mom. When you allow yourself to be playful and be fully present in the moment, you connect to your heart. You surrender to God. You move from your left brain of always thinking, controlling and being afraid, to the right brain of creativity and fun.

Playtime is essential for you to tap into the real you. After all, the little kid inside of you is the heart of who you are. And kids need to play. Imagine if you made your son or daughter work, work, work, never allowing him or her to take a rest. Your kid would hate you.

Well, this is what you do to the little girl inside of you when you don't allow her to play. She gets really mad and resentful. The problem is that we tend to blame others for our pain. They are not to blame. You have to give yourself permission to have fun and be playful. And when you do, you tap into the creative, unique being that God made you to be. This is where you discover the real you.

It's Time to Play!

1. Sit down with pen and paper and get grounded.

2. Ask the little girl inside of you, "What would really make you feel happy and alive? What do you feel passionate about? How would you like to spend your time playing?" Make a list of the items your inner child feels passionate about.

3. Look at the list and see which item really excites you.

4. Close your eyes and set an intention to bring this into your life. Visualize yourself having this kind of playtime. Feel it in your body as if you're doing it right now. See your surroundings and what you're wearing. Say, "God, I open myself up to your divine love and guidance. I give myself permission to have this kind of playfulness in my life. I thank you for showing me the way." Say, "Yes, yes, yes! Thank you, thank you, thank you, God, for this wonderful abundance. I give myself permission to have this in my life and to set this example for my family and the world around me. YES!"

5. Trust and rest in the knowingness that you deserve this kind of love. Ask God to reveal the time and place for you to create this playfulness. Then watch for the messages and take action.

~ ~ ~ ~ ~

**Go to The Enlightened Mom Meditation CD #3, Track 7,
to create some play time, Mom!**

~ ~ ~ ~ ~

After 20 years of living in Southern California, our family decided to make a move to a small town in Florida. I knew I wanted to add more color to my life and get back to tennis. I was ready to take action. I had played tennis once in 10 years and it wasn't very pretty. The balls went everywhere. I set an intention to find a class to take. I really didn't know where to go since we had just moved. When I asked people if they could suggest a class, no one seemed to have an answer. Or if they did, it meant I had to join a club or team. I had no desire to do either. I just wanted to hit balls. I also wanted to be with other women who wanted to be like kids and play. My first experience with tennis years ago had been very playful, until my group joined a team. The competitive nature in everyone took over, and the playfulness went away. I had no intention to create this again.

I said a prayer to God and set an intention, asking to bring tennis back into my life, not knowing how it would come about. Then I let it go. I surrendered, knowing that God would take care of the rest. And that's exactly what happened.

Kolbi's partner for her school science project was staying with her neighbor for the weekend. We had to coordinate the girls getting together in the morning to cover some last minute details. The plan was for the neighbor to drop off the little girl at our home on her way to work. When I asked the neighbor what she did, she said, "I'm a tennis pro."

"Yeah!" I thought. I knew this was no coincidence and it wasn't. This lady worked at a local athletic club that just happened to offer women's tennis clinics for the public, in spite of it being a membership club. I had no idea the club offered these kinds of classes. The pro insisted that I come to her clinic. I did. Not only did I go, but the clinic was exactly what I had imagined. It was fun! The women were relaxed, playful, and had no need to be competitive. Each one supported the other for their good shots and laughed with one another at the bad ones, especially when I hit a home run and knocked my ball over the back fence. I had so much fun and was thrilled with this wonderful gift. And it happened simply because I followed my heart, set an intention, and then ALLOWED myself to receive God's guidance about where to play tennis.

Mom, set an intention to have more playtime in your life and watch it unfold. When you add playfulness to your life, you can't help but smile again.

The Three Ps: Passion, Purpose and Play

Playfulness comes in many ways. Maybe you spend time playing outside with friends, but spend no time finding what makes you tick. I know lots of women who are like this. They are really good about playing on a physical level and, yet, they have sadness and pain surrounding their hearts. That's because they've denied themselves in some way. They aren't living their lives creatively, being full expressions of God's love.

If you could create anything in your life, what would that be? Would you like to create some work outside of the home that fulfills some hidden passion that you've always desired? Or would you like to stay at home with your kids all of the time, but want to be of service in your own unique way? Whatever way you choose to express yourself is an avenue to be playful. When you follow your heart, everything feels like playtime.

My work is my play. It is my passion. It is also how I am of service not only to my family, but to every person I come into contact with. I didn't know I had this passion until I decided to heal and get to know myself.

I had always been interested in developing my intuition, was intrigued by meditation and believed in the "other side." Ever since I was a little girl, I felt there was something more than the mere existence that we were each experiencing. I was right. God was talking to me that whole time and I didn't even know it. Then when my dad died, my therapist said I needed to get into meditation. I knew she was right. I was extremely uptight. As soon as I said I was ready to shift my life, God guided me to a healing school. My life became a magical adventure. Not only did I attend the school, but I also went to any seminar and spiritual class I could find. I devoured every book that came my way, seeing what rang true for me and what didn't. I got in touch with my heart. I was in play mode and found my passion. And in that passion, I found my purpose.

What would a life of passion, purpose, and play look like for you? What intrigues you the most? I had you do the prior exercise because I'm inviting you to get in touch with your heart and what it wants right now. Maybe you need to take time and be playful like a kid. Or, maybe you're ready to play by bringing your gifts out into the world. It doesn't matter where you are in your life, the key is that you allow yourself to bring passion, purpose and play in whatever way feels right to you.

I've mentioned my client Elaine several times in this book. She is the mother of three and has a Ph.D. She is one smart cookie and prior to kids had been a teacher. As I coached Elaine, she began to realize that she needed something more for her life and was struggling with the idea of going back to teaching. It was what she knew. But it no longer lit her fire. As she got in touch with little Elaine, she realized that travel was one of her real passions.

Elaine told me how much she loved to travel with her husband and three little girls, exposing her kids to Europe in a fun, informative way. Elaine said she loved research, too. When she looked at combining her two loves, she knew she wanted to eventually open a travel company focusing on the family, seeing the world from a child's perspective. Elaine gave herself permission to play and made a decision to explore her idea.

"Ecstatic" is how I would describe Elaine the day she came in with the most beautifully written intention for her business. She shared with me that it had come so easily for her once she had allowed herself to relax and had allowed her heart to talk to her. She was on fire! She was on a whole new adventure, allowing God to be the guide. Her old tears of sadness were replaced by the biggest, most brilliant smile. Little Elaine finally had permission to play and live a creative, fulfilling life.

Elaine's happiness at that time was short-lived. Her mom responsibilities quickly doused that flame. She had tasted the fires of passion, but once again, put them away. Her smile disappeared and the tears came back. Elaine felt there was no time for little Elaine to play.

I reminded Elaine that her tears were simply the little girl inside of her feeling shut down. We are children of God. We are meant to be creative, passionate beings. When we suppress that part of ourselves, we become sad, angry, and frustrated. When we, as moms, continually deny ourselves passion and play, we want to run away.

Elaine's sadness stayed with her for a period of time until she woke up to a message that God was sending her. "Terri," she said, "over the last six months two people have broken wine glasses in my home to the degree where they were cut badly and bleeding." This was unreal to Elaine since usually if you break a glass, it is due to someone dropping it or knocking it over. Most of the time you don't get cut when this happens. Elaine went on, "The first time was when a little boy was visiting and knocked over his dad's wine glass. The boy's arm was cut. The second time was when a friend of mine, who is a mom, came over this weekend and dropped her wine glass. She cut her middle finger so badly that she had to have stitches."

I agreed with Elaine that these incidents were a little bizarre and felt as she did that a message was being sent to her. I had no idea what the symbols meant, so I decided to look them up in *Mary Summer Rain's Guide to Dream Symbols*. I asked Elaine what parts of the two situations stood out to her. She gave me those items. Here are the definitions:

> "**Wineglass:** specific new idea that has full potential."
> "**Cut:** illustrates the act of severing something."
> "**Arm:** personal work/efforts applied to one's purpose."
> "**Middle finger:** centeredness; balancing element."

As we looked at these definitions, Elaine and I both knew that God was sending her a message about her work. Elaine felt the idea for her company was right on target with her heart. She had opened up to passion and the company had a wonderful chance of moving into full potential. However, the arm being cut meant that she wasn't putting enough effort into her purpose. The middle finger being sliced sent Elaine the message that she wasn't balancing her time. Her friend whose finger was sliced was a mom. This part of the message told Elaine that she was separating from her purpose due to the fact that she is a mother.

The message was clear: Elaine's lack of balance in her life was cutting her off from her purpose. That's what we tend to do as moms. We deny our playful, creative selves due to our mom duties, and cut ourselves off from our passion and purpose. We think this is the loving thing to do. But now we know that's not the truth.

God was really working on Elaine by sending her those messages over a six-month period. She wasn't spending enough time playing, being passionate and creative with her life. She spent all of her time on her family. As a result, Elaine became mired in work, trying to be a great mom. Thankfully, her vibration attracted these situations to show her where she was stuck.

I wasn't sure how to help Elaine get back to center, so I asked God for some help. That's when I was guided to have Elaine break down the hours of her week.

There are 168 hours in a week. I had Elaine subtract all of the hours she was committed to weekly. Those hours included sleeping, cooking, exercise, homework with the kids, and all of the other aspects we spend time on as mothers. Elaine was in shock! She was very thorough about how she spent her time and couldn't believe she had almost 20 hours a week left over! I'm not kidding when I say she was in shock. She had no idea that there was this much time left over to explore her life with passion and play.

We mommas tend to keep ourselves so focused on what we have to get done that the moments we do have to play and create are lost while we sit thinking and worrying. Life doesn't have to be this way.

Making Time for Passion, Purpose and Play

1. Take a pen and paper and get fully centered.

2. At the top of the page, write TIME FOR ME.

3. On the left-hand side write COMMITMENTS. On the right-hand side write HOURS IN THE WEEK: 168.

4. Go down the list of commitments and subtract how many hours you give each item. Take a look at this example:

COMMITMENTS	HOURS IN THE WEEK: 168
Sleep	-50
	Total 118
Cooking	-15
	Total 103
Cleaning/picking up	-8
	Total 95

Continue this exercise with any of the following items that pertain to your life: hours at work, exercise, shuttling kids, school commitments such as PTO, homework, miscellaneous items such as groceries, errands, bathing/preparing for day or bedtime, religious commitments, volunteer work and family time. Subtract the hours from each of these and add any other items that I haven't listed.

5. Take a look at your list. Are there any hours in the week left over? If there are, how do you want to spend those hours? Are you ready to spend some playtime tapping into your passion and purpose? Are you ready to explore and allow your life to be an adventure? Are you ready for some real fun, creating a continual connection to God, sharing your light with the world? If your answer is "YES" to any of these questions then look at your week and see where you want to make a commitment to yourself and God.

6. If after going through your week, you realize that there aren't enough hours in the day then see where your life is out of balance. If it's still all focused on the family then it's time to take a look back at your perfect mother pictures. Whose approval are you seeking? Allow this exercise to be another opportunity to heal any negative beliefs you are living by.

7. Ask the little girl inside of you what she wants to explore. Be the artist of your life! Give yourself permission to live creatively and take INSPIRED ACTION.

Elaine made a commitment to spend at least one day a week exploring her passion. In the beginning, she realized this was a little difficult. She got caught up in "perfect pictures" again of how much she was supposed to work and how much she "should" get done with creating her company. Eventually she realized that her battle within was that she really didn't want to go full blown with her company yet. Creating a company in Elaine's mind meant that she had to give it 150% effort. But this didn't ring true for her. Her heart said no. She wasn't ready to make this kind of commitment. Elaine's two older girls were in school, but she still had a little one at home.

I invited Elaine to explore, to allow the little girl inside of her to be creative and play, finding what really worked for her. I cannot begin to tell you how our sessions changed after she gave herself that kind of permission to play. Each time she walked into my office, she had something new and exciting to share. Don't get me wrong. There were struggles, too. Like the time she couldn't understand why she was more interested in writing than working on the travel company. I explained to Elaine that God was taking her on a wonderful, magical adventure. She just needed to take her blinders off and be in the flow of her heart.

I had a coaching session with Elaine after several months of not talking to her. The joy that emanated from her was absolutely breathtaking. Elaine finally realized that she loves being a mother and staying home. She has given her little girl within permission to play and create. She is building her company one step at a time, with no worry as to when the company will completely come to life. In the meantime, she is having a tremendous amount of fun, being a mom, taking her kids on trips, doing research for her future work.

"Elaine, why did you feel you needed time with me today?" I asked at the end of the session. "Am I missing something? Your life seems great!"

"It is, Terri. I wanted you to know how wonderful everything is and share with you all the miracles that are happening. I'm doing a lot of writing. I've always wanted to write and now I'm having fun, playing with it."

Elaine resisted writing at first. Her old way of being kept her blinders on and told her that if she was to spend time writing then she wasn't being focused on her goal. But once she gave herself permission to explore and be on a magical adventure, she found another gift to share. She writes beautiful, funny little stories that will be a part of her monthly newsletter when her company is ready to take off. Elaine is building the foundation of her company as she finds herself. She is cherishing her moments as a mother, but also allowing the little girl inside of her to play. Elaine is walking the path of The Enlightened Mom.

Living with Purpose

I used to write God regularly and ask, "What is my purpose, dear God?" I spent a lot of time on this question and didn't allow myself much playtime out of a fear that I was missing out on something I was "supposed" to be doing. But the answer was always the same. "Terri, there is no purpose other than following your heart, aligning yourself with love." Well, my heart wanted to play, to be passionate and to be alive. And it's still that way! This feeling deepens every day and the more I honor it and love it, the more joy I experience in my life.

Your purpose on this planet
is to be in alignment with God.
Your purpose is to be an expression of love.

This is an extremely important message when you look at how we live our lives. We want to experience abundance and unconditional love. We want this for our children. We want to know that we've done everything in our power to prepare them for the future. We want them to experience success in every aspect of their lives. The problem is that we live in a world that says success is when you work, work, work to achieve. We've bought into a notion that says success comes from the outside world. This is why I hear so many people say, "I don't know why I'm here." They've lived their lives always trying to please the outside world and lost their connection to their hearts.

I have a different definition of success. Success for me is when I allow myself to be in divine alignment with God and follow the passion in my heart. This is when I feel the most love and when I'm the best mom.

Love manifests in many different ways. God created you with distinct gifts. When you allow yourself to play and explore your passions and then express those gifts, you align yourself with love. This is why people confuse "purpose" with the idea that you have to be doing something. There is nothing you have to do. It's just that when you connect to your heart and embrace who you are, you discover your gifts and suddenly find yourself wanting to share them with the world. But remember, no matter how it manifests outwardly, it begins with love. It always starts with a connection to your heart. That is your purpose.

Isn't it a whole lot more fun to see life this way? The idea that you can follow your heart and play, discovering your passions and gifts to share with the world is so much better than working yourself to death. The beautiful thing about this is, due to the Law of Attraction, when you allow this kind of abundance into your life, not only do you experience love, you will raise your vibration and attract all different kinds of abundance and miracles. Be an example of this, Mom. Playtime allows you to add color to your life. It opens you up to the creative child within. We think that play is going to take us away from being responsible moms when, in fact, it takes us closer to love. It aligns your heart with God, the greatest creator of all.

~ ~ ~ ~ ~

CHAPTER 12

Surrender into Abundance

om, you are a beautiful gift. Just by being you, you bring peace, light and love into your home and to the world around you. As you own this truth and surrender to the messages that God sends you each and every day, you create a life of abundance. Surrendering is the key. It can be a little scary, however, when it means you must let go of your need to control and trust in the messages you receive.

"Okay, ladies, today we're going on an adventure!" I exclaimed to a small group of Enlightened Moms sitting in front of me on the patio of a local bookstore. For eight weeks, these women had been scraping away negative beliefs, learning the tools in this book, helping them to create a divine connection. Now it was time to put those tools to the test.

"Your adventure is to walk into the bookstore and be open to God's guidance. You're going to stay open and centered and allow God to show you something that you're ready to see. This is a message that will help put your life in the flow and be more at ease."

"So, ladies," I continued, "as you walk into the bookstore, you may feel an urge to walk to the left or walk to the right. You may even find yourself crawling on the floor. I've shared with you many times that I like to walk into a bookstore, asking for guidance, and the way I get the message is to watch for an arrow in my head. Do this if it works for you. It doesn't matter how you get your guidance. Just trust that it's there for you."

Eyes bulged and grins spread across each of the moms' faces. I'm not sure if at that moment they were grins of joy or grins masking the fear. I know some of the women were still not convinced that they would be able to do this assignment. They believed these kinds of miracles might happen for others, but not for them.

A few of the women had already experienced miracles from the first day of class, but there were others who were a little more skeptical. Cassie was one of them. Her life had been blanketed in negativity and judgment with constant complaining. During the Enlightened Mom course, she had begun to realize that she had to change her attitude about her life, her husband, and about money. Cassie lived with a sense of lack and wasn't sure she could receive the kind of guidance I had been talking about. Cassie doubted she was worthy. Ironically, she was the first mom to finish the assignment.

"I'm converted, I'm converted, I'm converted!" Cassie cried tears of joy as she came back to the patio. "I can't believe it! I walked into the store and felt a nudge to turn right. Then I felt I had to move down the aisle and turn right again. Directly in front of me was Joel Osteen's book, *Your Best Life Now*. It was staring me right in the face. I've seen him on TV or in ads every day for at least three weeks now and felt I was supposed to learn something from him, but I ignored it. So, I opened up his book and the first message I received was, 'God supplies all of your needs.' The next message was, 'Quit complaining that nothing good ever happens.' And, finally, 'Start declaring everything and command light to come in.' I can't believe I got these messages!"

Cassie's final thoughts said it best as she threw her hands up in the air, "I get it now! I used to ask God for guidance and would get so angry because I never got any answers. Now I realize the messages were always there. All I had to do was give myself permission to open up and receive them!"

Cassie was absolutely right. She opened her heart to receive God's messages that day. She released the need to control and allowed God to be the guide. Cassie had finally surrendered.

Surrendering is the greatest challenge you will ever encounter. Your ego, otherwise known as your humanness, wants to control you and tell you what to do or how to do it. It makes you question everything. Your ego takes you out of trust and moves you into darkness.

Sally is another Enlightened Mom and is also one of my coaching clients. She used to be on anti-depressants. But by walking this path, she made a decision, with her doctor's guidance, to get off of her medication. At first Sally felt exhilarated. She used the tools in this book and felt as if she were in control of her life for the first time in years. Then darkness set in again.

Sally came in for a coaching session during this difficult time, agonizing as to whether to get back on her anti-depressants. She said her mind wouldn't stop questioning everything. Sally said she continually used her tools but felt she wasn't getting anywhere. As she explained what was going on, I knew she was going through a tremendous growth period of healing. Instead of nurturing and loving herself, however, she judged herself for this dark time. As a result, her pain remained.

As our session came to a close, Sally's problem was revealed: she didn't trust the message that had been sent to her. Sally shared with me that God had told her during meditation that she was going through a growth period. She was releasing the old and making room for the new. Instead of honoring the message, however, she chose not to trust it. Her darkness grew and, as a result, she questioned herself as to whether to get back on her medication. If she had trusted herself and the messages she had received, her fear would have dissipated.

Throughout this book you have taken tiny steps of surrender by doing the exercises I've given you. Please know that it takes time to integrate everything you've learned. And just like Cassie and Sally, it will take some time to fully release the controls of your life and surrender them to God. It's okay. Give thanks and celebrate your humanness! That's why you're here: to have a human experience. You are a spirit first on a magnificent journey to reconnect to God. You do that by embracing your humanness and surrendering to the messages in your heart.

Surrendering doesn't happen overnight, and just when you think you've "gotten it," you feel as if you're starting all over again. There will be many times you feel as if you're walking in darkness. Celebrate these times, too. Know that while in the darkness you have many options. You get to choose how to create your life. Just by seeing life this way, you surrender into abundance.

Please don't judge yourself when you find darkness surrounding you. You will most likely be going through a huge growth period, like Sally did, letting go of the old way of being. I remember the first time I went through a big shift. I felt so tired and could barely move, but knew I wasn't sick. My gut told me a part of my ego was dying and that I needed to allow this process. So I did. I allowed myself to be in a healing space for three days, really honoring and nurturing myself. When I came out of it on the other end, I felt as if I had been reborn.

Trusting yourself and the answers you receive is imperative for you to step into abundance. So often people get answers like Sally did, but don't trust their knowingness.

Take a moment and reflect on what you've learned so far from reading and doing the exercises in this book. Has there been any one moment that stands out in your mind when you surrendered to the messages and were thrilled with the results? If there has been, anchor yourself in that feeling. Go back to it and know that the feeling will grow exponentially as you trust and follow your heart. The feeling you experienced was a little glimpse of what's in store for you as you travel the path of The Enlightened Mom. It only gets better! Know that you can have this feeling any time you want. All you have to do is surrender.

God is Limitless

God IS limitless. Sometimes in our quest to follow our hearts, we humans tend to forget this. To truly surrender into abundance, you must get your head out of the way and listen to the messages in your heart. And as you do, you will realize that you are a part of this beautiful loving energy that makes up the universe and is limitless. You will KNOW that everything in your life is happening for a reason and will soon trust that all is perfect. You'll release your need to control and find a peaceful flow. Your life will be filled with abundance.

Liz is an Enlightened Mom. She attended an eight-week course I offered. From the first session, her life started to shift. Liz immediately opened up to feel the presence of God and began experiencing peace for the first time in years.

It was the third week of class when Liz woke up in the morning to discover that her little boy was sick. She was very disappointed because she didn't have childcare and knew she would have to miss class. Liz had seen tremendous healing changes in her life and in her family dynamics and didn't want to miss out on any new tools that might create more healing for her family.

Well, guess what? Liz did come to class! She came after a wonderful miracle happened. She told us that when she didn't see any way for her to be able to attend the class, she sat down and prayed. Liz told God that she really wanted to come and loved what was happening in her life. She surrendered to the message in her heart and asked God for help. And then help arrived. Liz's husband, out of the blue, came to her and said he would miss work so that she could attend our session. She was absolutely blown away! He had never missed work before to help her out like this, and she didn't even have to ask him for help.

This is how God is limitless. We tend to think in terms of what we can do as humans. But when you finally surrender and release the beliefs in your mind that say you're not worthy of God's limitless abundance, miracles happen.

In *Ask and It Is Given: Learning to Manifest Your Desires*, Esther and Jerry Hicks explain that there are three steps to manifesting what you want in your life. The first step is for you to ask for what you want. It's that simple.

The second step is really interesting. It says you do nothing because this step is God's job. The second step is simply that your request is given. The Hicks explain, "Every question is answered.

Every desire is given. Every prayer is answered. Every wish is granted. But the reason that many would argue that truth, holding up examples of unfulfilled desires from their own life experiences, is because they have not yet understood and completed the very important Step 3~for without the completion of this step, the existence of Steps 1 and 2 could go unnoticed."

"Okay, okay, okay! So what's Step 3?" you ask.

The Hicks tell us that in Step 3, you must ALLOW yourself to receive what you've requested. That's it! The thing that gets in the way of ALLOWING, however, is that you have negative limiting beliefs that tell you that you're not worthy of God's unlimited abundance. When you ask for something and don't get it, it's because those limiting beliefs sit at a lower vibration and don't match the energy of what you're asking for. But as you walk the path of The Enlightened Mom and surrender your mind to the messages in your heart, you raise your vibration and match the energy of the things you want. That's when they show up and you begin to know that God is truly limitless.

As I started my healing journey, I believed in God's loving abundance and saw little miracles happen here and there, but when I truly KNEW that God was limitless was during my book tour for *Message Sent.*

The first day of my trip, I found myself facing a dreary two weeks of snow and rain alone in New York City. The timing of the tour just happened to land during the onset of the Iraq War, so several of my interviews were immediately cancelled due to the deluge of news coverage. I felt a battle within as to how to handle the changes in my plans. My heart wanted to hibernate and take a nap, but I thought I was "supposed" to be out in the city "making" life happen. I struggled with what I believed I had to do versus what my heart wanted. My manager also wanted me to get out and buy tickets for either *Hairspray* or *Thoroughly Modern Millie.* She said they were both great Broadway plays and wonderful metaphors for my work and that either one of them was a "must see" while in the city.

My heart wasn't into the theatre at that moment. I just wanted to curl up in a robe, sleep, and eat anything I wanted. As my struggle persisted, I decided to look up ticket prices and availability of the shows on the Internet. Oh, my gosh! I couldn't believe how expensive they were. I finally said, "Okay, God, this is the deal. I'm not going to spend that kind of money on something that I'm not sure I really want to see. Plus, I don't want to deal with anything today. I'm going to be a vegetable. Tomorrow I will get up, go to the gym, eat healthy and face the world. And if it is for the highest good that I see one of these plays then show me the way."

Thankfully, I honored my heart that day. I curled up in my robe and ate everything I wanted. I rested and gave myself time to be the vegetable I was craving to be. The following day I did as I promised myself and headed for a local gym. My intention was to take a Pilates mat class.

I stood outside of the classroom waiting for the prior class to end. I began chatting with this young, dynamic woman who was a regular at the gym. She promised me I would get an awesome workout. She was right. The class was great and upon finishing it, we found ourselves talking again.

"So how long are you in town for?" my new friend asked.

"Ten days."

"Are you going to see any plays while you're here?"

"Well, my manager wants me to see either *Hairspray* or *Thoroughly Modern Millie,* but I don't know if I will."

I was shocked with what my new little "earth angel friend" said next. "Well, I just happen to be in management at the Marriott Marquee and *Thoroughly Modern Millie* is playing at the theatre in our hotel. I'd love to take you as my guest."

Not only did my new friend take me to see the show, we had the best seats in the house! Plus, she took me to a beautiful dinner prior to the show in the Marriott Marquee's exquisite steakhouse.

I will never forget my trip to New York and the miracle I experienced. I followed my heart to stay in the hotel that first day and let go of the struggle and control I had begun to create within. I allowed myself to be in the flow and trusted that the highest good would be revealed.

The highest good is being in the flow with your heart, focusing on what you want. I used to believe that the highest good was to listen to this great big GOD outside of me and only if I listened to the guidance correctly would I then receive abundance.

You are the one who determines what you receive in life. No one does it for you. God is not going to strike you down if you follow your heart. Your heart IS God speaking to you. When you don't trust those messages, you shut yourself down to abundance. You are the one who does it, no one else. You always have a choice. You can keep knocking yourself up against the wall and do things that you feel you're "supposed" to be doing, which is what we tend to do as moms, or you can move into awareness and see when it's time to shift your thinking. It's up to you. When you trust in the flow and release your limiting beliefs, miracles happen. That's when you begin to KNOW that God is truly limitless.

Survival Issues Get in the Way

I see a lot of moms struggling with the idea of surrendering to their hearts and receiving God's limitless abundance due to survival issues. They don't trust that all is well and that they are taken care of. I used to be the same way. Instead of trusting God, our egos get in the way and tell us that we have to control our world to survive. Jesus told us the truth, however, when he said, "Therefore I tell you, do not worry about your life, what you will eat or drink; or about your body, what you will wear. Is not life more important than food, and the body more important than clothes? Look at the birds of the air; they do not sow or reap or store away in barns, and yet your heavenly Father feeds them. Are you not much more valuable than they?" *(Matthew 6:25-26)*

You are valuable. You are a child of God. Your true nature is one of abundance. If you're not feeling this in your life then it's because, once again, you have false beliefs ruling your subconscious mind. KNOW that God is limitless and that everything you need is there. You just have to allow it in.

For generations we have been programmed with the belief that the woman is the nurturer and the man is the provider. In spite of the fact that a lot of women now work outside of the home, this belief still affects many moms. As a result, women shut down their thoughts and feelings and won't say what they need so as not to be a burden to their hubbies. I was one of those women, but over time realized that my hubby wasn't the provider. God is the provider. Everything you need is sitting in the universe just waiting for you to allow yourself to receive it. It took me a long time to realize this.

During the early years of my marriage to Steve, we lived in a very affluent community with a giant 7,000-square-foot house. I could have had anything I wanted but never allowed myself that luxury unless Steve gave it to me. I was blessed to have so much wealth around me. However, when it came to asking for something I wanted or needed, I shut myself down. I wouldn't even go buy a new shirt. I didn't allow myself to follow my heart and say what I needed out of some belief that said if I did, I would cause Steve pain. This belief haunted me for a very long time. It began to change when I decided to create a healing weekend workshop with a friend.

I was just starting to put myself out in the world. My friend and I set up a retreat in Palm Springs called "Take Charge of Your Life." We put money down on the hotel to hold the rooms and sent e-mails to everyone we knew. Everything was falling into place. I was thrilled.

Not one person signed up. I was devastated. I couldn't believe what I was experiencing. I knew it was part of my mission to speak in front of people and share some of the tools I was learning, so why in the world was this happening? I got my answer by going within.

I asked little Terri what was the gift of the situation. She told me that she hadn't really wanted to create the event and had only done it to make Steve happy. He had been contributing a lot of money to my work efforts and I felt responsible for creating a burden on him. My heart wasn't committed to doing the workshop yet. I wanted to be in full surrender mode, allowing God to guide me and to be in charge of my life, but instead, due to my guilt, I went against my heart and followed my head, charging forward with gusto.

Not only did I NOT make any money to relieve Steve's burden, but I also put us almost $2,000 in debt! Boy, did I learn my lesson. In spite of being in debt, I received an amazing gift. From that point on, I knew I had to get in touch with what my spirit truly wanted and live from my heart, no longer living from guilt and my head.

When you live from a belief that your survival needs are met by something other than God, you revert back to codependency and perform for love. You shut yourself down to surrendering to your heart and, as a result, shut yourself down to abundance. That's what I did. I lived my life worrying about how Steve would feel when it came to money. This was one of the biggest issues that got in the way of our marriage. When I didn't listen to that little voice within, I closed myself off to Steve out of resentment. I blamed him. It wasn't until I started looking at why I wasn't receiving abundance that I realized I was doing this to myself.

One belief I discovered said that there is never enough. That belief gradually diminished as I took tiny steps to give myself what I needed and trusted that the universe would take care of it. Every time I followed my heart and honored my wants, miraculously money would appear. That was the Law of Attraction working at its finest.

A belief that I find rather interesting now is that as I began walking a spiritual path, I didn't want people thinking I was materialistic for wanting nice things in my life. I felt this went against the description of what a woman of God is. Baloney! I soon realized that if you need money to define you then you might want to look at your pride issues. These keep you in resistance from experiencing joy. That's because you're still concerned about what other people think. On the other hand, when you allow yourself to receive abundance and express yourself in creative ways with money then this is an expression of love. If you are bringing joy to your life, but not defining yourself by material abundance, you are bringing joy into the world.

As I went deeper and deeper into my issues about money and started questioning what seemed to be my overall inability to manifest financial rewards, I realized I was performing for God. I had no idea this was going on in my life. I came to this realization one day while taking a shower. As the water poured over my face, something told me to talk with little Terri. I envisioned her standing over in the corner dancing around. I asked her, "So who are you still performing for?" This is the response I saw: little Terri shaking her bottom and pointing up at the sky. I was in shock! That's when I knew I had to do some deep introspection.

I discovered a belief that said I had to get things done right or else God wouldn't reward me. Talk about a lack of trust in oneself and in God! Because I never trusted that I was doing it "right," I never allowed myself to receive rewards. I was the one shutting myself down to God's love. This was a part of my old "perfect pictures" again. There is no one you need to perform for to receive abundance in life.

Our basic instinct is to survive. This is why we don't trust and get so caught up in money issues, shutting down to our hearts and the miracles that exist. Instead of ALLOWING ourselves to receive, knowing that abundance is part of our natural birthright and that God is limitless, we go into fear. We live from false beliefs that tell us how we must be and what we have to do to survive.

Money is energy and is simply a reflection of the beliefs you hold onto. Just like every other issue you've already learned about in this book, money issues are a gift and an opportunity to create a greater connection to God.

My friend, Patty, is the mother of three kids. She went through a very tough divorce some years ago and, as a result, found herself dealing with survival issues. She had a tremendous fear of being unable to provide for her children. When I asked her how she got through this, she said, "I had to be still and consciously make that connection to feel the presence of God during those dark moments. Each time I connected, the experience was so peaceful that it allowed me to move forward with hope." Patty also said that the key was for her to trust that the universe is abundant and that God would provide. She said it was a constant exercise in surrendering. Patty released her fears and her lack of abundance one moment at a time.

I'll never forget the day I wrote to God and asked about money issues. The response I received when I put the pen in my non-dominant hand was, "Terri, I didn't put you on this planet to suffer. I put you on this planet to prosper." Wow! I could not believe that I got such a profound message. I knew right then that any issues I had with money were self-inflicted and not my truth.

If staying in survival mode is what keeps you from following your heart and allowing abundance into your life, go back and use any of the tools you've learned in this book. This is my greatest desire for you: that you will walk away with a storehouse of goodies creating a spiritual tool chest and that you'll trust yourself to use them whenever an issue comes up for you. This is what it's like to be an Enlightened Mom. You embrace your humanness, including survival issues, and allow them to take you to your heart, creating a life of peace, abundance and love.

Whether it's with negative thoughts about money and what you have to do to receive it, or any other false beliefs you hold onto, as you release lower vibrations by using the tools in this book and give yourself permission to follow your heart, miracles will happen. When you create a connection between your head and your heart, you raise your vibration. That's exactly what happened to Liz, the mom I wrote about earlier who needed childcare to attend my class. In just a few sessions of using The Enlightened Mom tools, Liz manifested a miracle in her life. She went from believing that she wasn't worthy of being loved to believing that she might be worthy of some help in her childcare situation. She asked, the universe provided, and then she allowed herself to receive a miracle.

Trust that God is the provider of your life. God is limitless. You will begin to truly KNOW this, not just believe this, as you surrender to the messages in your heart and create a connection to God.

Abundance Leads to Service

God is everywhere and is a part of you. As you own this truth and use the tools in this book to create a connection to God, you will begin to see the light emanating from you. The peace, love and abundance you discover will overflow to all those you love. Pretty soon, your family and friends will want what you have. They'll see the changes in you and want the changes for themselves, too. When you surrender to the messages in your heart and live your life as an expression of love, you will feel the joy emanating from you and become a gift to the world around you. This is your greatest act of service: to create a connection to God and live a life of abundance, sharing the love with everyone.

I went to the library some years ago and asked God to show me a message. Knowing that God's messages are everywhere, I began to wander around the library. I had no idea what I was looking for, but just allowed myself to be guided. I walked up to some books and knew in my gut that this wasn't what I was looking for. Then I found myself in front of some videos. I allowed myself to float along when suddenly a tape by Dr. Deepak Chopra caught my eye. It was called *The Way of the Wizard: A Guide to Re-awakening the Magic in Everyday Life.* I had never felt compelled to follow Dr. Chopra's work, but for some reason that day, was guided to take the tape.

I took the tape home and plugged it into my VCR. As soon as I heard the first word I knew it wasn't for me. The message was for Steve. I asked him to come to the room and watch the tape. God was working on Steve and was using me to get to him.

In *The Way of the Wizard,* Dr. Chopra discusses the different levels of consciousness that we humans go through in creating a connection to God. He tells us that we begin with innocence, moving on to ego, to achiever, to seeker, to different levels of union consciousness.

Steve watched the tape and, as it finished, began crying. "I don't want to be an achiever anymore, Terri. I want to be a seeker." I knew exactly what he meant and thanked God for this miraculous gift.

Until the day I decided to change my life and step onto a spiritual path, I had lived my life as an achiever, too. This was my need to survive in full action! I sought every achievement and award possible, believing that these things would make people love me. This intense drive made me tired and angry. I pushed this same attitude on A.J., my stepson. But over time, by creating a connection to God and opening up to receive love, I became a more loving wife and mom. I stopped focusing on achievement and turned my focus to healing and love. Steve had watched me shift my life and consciousness throughout the years. He saw how loving I had become and how I had surrendered my life to God. And in that surrendering, miracle after miracle revealed itself in my life. My light had overflowed to Steve and now God was calling him to open up his heart.

Steve had an amazing life. He was a captain in the Marines during Vietnam. He returned home and eventually became a highly successful owner of a women's clothing manufacturing company. His business was even listed as one of the top 100 fastest growing companies in

Los Angeles. Whether it was with cars, boats or homes he owned, Steve was always the epitome of success. He was also a gorgeous and charming man. However, none of these things ever brought Steve much inner abundance. He was tired of being an achiever. By watching me heal over the years, he knew it was time for him to heal as well.

Right after Steve said he wanted to be a "seeker," the next words he spoke were "I want to sell everything." So we did. We let everything go. Our house sold without ever going on the market and at full price! For the next year-and-a-half, Steve went within to find himself and to create a connection to God. I asked him one day what he wanted now. He said, "I want to do something bigger than myself. I want to do something for God and the planet."

By shifting my life and having the courage to go within to find myself and create a connection to God, I changed. But the greatest gift was when my life became an example for Steve to shift. Without even knowing it, my life became one of service to him.

Steve's decision to become a seeker was a wonderful blessing to our family. However, at times, it was quite scary. Right after we sold our home, our boat burned and sank to the bottom of the ocean and the stock market took a great hit. We lost a lot of our nest egg. Talk about survival issues! At times, Steve felt as if he was losing everything he had worked for. We both had to look at our beliefs about suffering to do God's work. The opportunity to shift that belief revealed itself when we sold our home.

Part of our deal when our home sold was that we would have a four-month escrow. That's because we had no idea where we were going! Our home sold so quickly that we didn't have time to think. We thought we were moving out of state but were uncertain where that might be. So we did some exploring. We were taking our time when all of the sudden I found myself talking to television producers. This simply happened. I didn't go searching for it. The producers were interested in me co-hosting a spiritual television show. My background was in television, but I had made a choice to leave it a long time ago. However, this had me intrigued. That's when I told Steve I wanted to stay in Southern California and explore this option.

"I'm not buying a house at the height of this market, Terri!" That was his response to me so we agreed that I would go in search of a rental. Talk about a chore! Ugh! We were moving from a large home with five bedrooms and all I could find were homes that were three bedrooms and maybe a total of 1600 square feet. Most of them were old, too, which didn't sit well with me since I had horrible allergies. I wanted to stay as far away from mold as I could. I finally found a home that was large enough to take care of our family and hold our furniture, but it was dark and depressing. The whole situation was depressing until I had had enough. That's when I took a stand and yelled out to the universe, "Okay, God. I don't believe I have to suffer to do your work. You find me a house!"

I made a decision right then not to settle for a home that wasn't what I wanted. I was taking a stand for abundance and following my heart. I took a stand in trust. I had no idea where we were going to live, but knew that something had to shift. And it did! Three days later a realtor called me out of the blue. I had met him once and really didn't know him. This was the message he left on our answering machine, "Mrs. Amos, I heard you've decided not to move out of state for now. I just sold a beautiful home down by the beach. It has four bedrooms and three-and-a-half baths and was built in 1995 (making it five years old at that time). My buyer has now decided he would like to go abroad to live and would like a family to rent his home. If you're interested, would you please give me a call?"

"WOW!" was all I could think. In that moment, I let go of the belief that I had to suffer to follow my heart. I also got extremely grounded in the belief that God is indeed limitless.

I'm so thankful I went to the library that day and trusted the message to pick up Dr. Chopra's tape, even though I wasn't quite sure what the message was in it. By handing it over to Steve, we stepped onto an incredible journey together. Miracle after miracle was revealed, one of the greatest being the creation of ConsciousOne.com. Steve's vision of doing something for God and the planet came true when he co-founded this Internet website. It is a storehouse of educational information, providing online courses based on many teachers' and healers' works, assisting people all over the world on their journeys to self-acceptance, empowerment and love.

My small act of service that day when I brought Steve the tape led him to a huge act of service for the world. I'm so grateful I listened and surrendered to my heart. And it all began when I made a choice to become an Enlightened Mom.

The path of The Enlightened Mom is one of service. We tend to think of honoring ourselves as selfish, but to truly be an example of unconditional love, you have to first find it within yourself. And as you do, you will become a healing light for everyone around you.

My daughter Kolbi struggled with a couple of friends when she was in the sixth grade. They both were controlling and she felt they were causing her a lot of pain. She blamed them for her unhappiness.

This drama with Kolbi and her friends went on for quite a while. I finally suggested that she see it from a different perspective. I invited her to see that she is the creator of her life and that she had brought these girls to her to learn about herself and heal. I asked her, "What bugs you the most about these girls?"

"I feel like they want to control me, Mom. They tell me what to do all of the time. I can't stand when they boss me around."

As you already know from reading this book, when you find fault with someone else, it is a reflection of something needing to be healed inside of you. I knew Kolbi came into this world to learn how to express herself. I had watched her for years struggling to speak her true feelings. This situation with her friends was a reflection of what was going on within her.

I walked Kolbi through a healing process and asked her what was hurting deep inside. She said, "I don't feel I can speak up to them." As a result, she, in her own way, became controlling by having emotional, angry outbursts. She would hold her voice in, over and over again, until she exploded. Her daddy and I continually urged her to speak up for herself, not only with her friends, but with us as well. We gave her full permission to speak her mind.

Kolbi finally shifted her consciousness when she got angry with her dad one day. In her mind, he was the epitome of the authority figure, which is what she had made these girls in her life. She had given them her power, believing they were taking it away from her. That all changed when Kolbi allowed herself to have an emotional outburst with her dad. It was filled with anger and tears. Instead of getting mad at her, however, we congratulated her. Steve had no need to get angry with her. He knew that this process really had nothing to do with him. He was neutral. Kolbi's outburst didn't cause him any pain. That's because he felt good about himself and knew that he didn't take away her power. She gave it away. By allowing Kolbi to get to the bottom of her pain, she healed that day. She gave herself permission to speak out and, as a result, took back her power.

When you shift your life into love, it overflows to everyone. By healing your pain, you won't get caught up in your kids' dramas. Instead of being like so many moms who get involved in a negative way, when you walk the path of The Enlightened Mom, you bring love and healing to the situation. This is true service.

Sharing the Gift of You

As I embarked onto the path of The Enlightened Mom, I simply wanted to heal and be a more loving person and mom. It was so much fun! I had a blast! Over time I began to feel a calling to share my work with others by going out and speaking to the world about this message. I was ready to step into a new level of service. This scared me a little as it went against the grain of what I believed a good mother should do. That's when I was guided during meditation to go within and ask my girls' spirits how they felt about this new aspect of my journey.

I got really grounded in God's light. I knew I needed clarity. Then I visualized Mackenzie's spirit in front of me. I asked her, "Kenz, I'm considering doing more public speaking which will mean I will be gone from home a lot more. How do you feel about this?"

Kenzie's spirit said, "Mom, I came into this lifetime to learn how to live powerfully. When you go out into the world and live powerfully, your example gives me permission to do the same."

Wow! I couldn't believe what I was hearing. This was the exact opposite of the belief I was raised with. I had always understood that to be a good mother meant to stay home and dote on your children.

I decided to ask Kolbi's spirit to come before me in this meditation to see what she had to say. Kolbi is a highly creative kid and is always flittering around. When I asked her what she felt about me going out into the world to share my work, she said, "Mom, I'm here to learn how to focus my creativity. When you write every day and go out and share your message, you show me how to focus my creativity, too."

This meditation absolutely blew me away. Thankfully, I trust myself and the messages I receive daily, so I knew these messages from my girls' spirits were right on.

Later that day after doing this meditation, I went to lunch with a publicist I had just met. She had attended one of my workshops over the weekend and wanted to learn more about my work. Our conversation turned to her relationship with her mother. I asked her, "So what was your biggest issue with your mother?"

She looked away for a moment, taking the question in, and then turned to me and said, "I wanted her to be more."

I felt as if a lightning bolt hit me with those words. God was really working on me. My mind swirled, "Of course, that's what my girls' spirits were telling me in meditation earlier this morning. They want me to be all that I can be so that my example will show them how to be all that they can be. Wow!"

That whole day was a miracle to me. The belief of what a good mother is supposed to be was blown right out of the window. I discovered in that moment that my life is truly an example for my kids. I was in fear to go out and follow my heart but that's exactly what their spirits said they wanted me to do. Their messages showed me that living from my heart is truly a gift to them.

Whatever makes you feel loving and helps you be of service is the right thing for you to do for your family. That's because it's the right thing for you to do for you. Surrender to the messages. When you live from your heart, you become an expression of love, and live a life of service.

We think to be of service means to give ourselves up. But to be of service is to open up to be a channel of love. And the only way you can be that channel of love is to get in touch with your heart. That means to get in touch with what you feel, what you think, what you need and want.

If you are a mom who enjoys working out in the world but feels guilty for not doing everything for your kids, take a look at this. Check into your beliefs and see what is right for you. If working outside of the home makes you more loving then you are doing the right thing for your family. If you question this, do as I did and go into a deep meditation and ask your children's spirits. They'll tell you what they need. You won't even have to question it. Remember, we're all here with spiritual agreements. Your kids want to learn from you just as you learn from them. Listening to your heart and trusting the messages will lead you to a life of service.

Surrender into a Magical Adventure

The more you surrender to your heart and trust the messages you receive, the more magical your life becomes. You will step into a miraculous adventure and become a messenger of God.

It was a beautiful day on the Gulf Coast and I was on a mission to get my printer fixed. Since the repair shop was over an hour away, the gentleman there suggested that I come early so they could fix the printer within the day and I could take it back home with me. I was thrilled, so I took my journal along and made plans to enjoy my day until the repairs were done.

My daughter's high school was about a third of the way between our home and the repair shop, so I suggested that I save her a trip on the bus that afternoon and pick her up on my way home. It was a wonderful plan for both of us until the gentleman at the repair shop told me my printer couldn't be fixed. "Great," I thought. "Now what am I going to do? Should I kill time waiting for Kenz to get out of school?"

My gut said, "Go on an adventure!" My family and I had just moved to the Gulf Coast from Los Angeles and I hadn't spent any time in the surrounding areas since we had moved. This was the perfect opportunity to explore. I pointed my car in the direction of home and allowed myself to wander.

Before I knew it I was near the high school and still had two hours to waste. I found a beautiful park and started to write my thoughts and feelings in my journal. However, little Terri, the five-year-old child within me, had a different idea. She said, "This isn't any fun. I want to be on an adventure!" So once again I started driving, having no idea where I was going.

One of the reasons we moved to the Gulf Coast is because some friends of ours in Los Angeles had property here and suggested that this area was a great place to live. Their family spent summers on the Gulf and had contemplated moving here for years but had never made the transition. However, upon seeing us move while they were here on vacation, they decided on a whim to purchase a house. This was a little scary for Patti. She is the mom of five kids and knew this kind of sudden upheaval could produce a lot of havoc. While they were waiting for their escrow to close, they stayed in their little vacation home in a town near Mackenzie's new high school.

As I continued my drive that day, I heard Patti's name in my head and realized that I was heading right for their summer home. This is the conversation that went on in my mind, "I'm not going out there. What if Patti and her hubby are having sex? Their kids are in school and they're probably alone. I'm not going to barge in on them!" But an urge inside of me kept telling me to drive. I knew Patti was still struggling with the move at that time and knew she would probably enjoy talking to a friend. I would have called her but didn't have her number. So the argument inside of me continued.

All of the sudden I felt a nudge to make a right turn into a furniture store parking lot. Actually, I saw an arrow in my mind's eye pointing that way. It just popped up. Now I was really confused. The argument in my head escalated. "I don't need to look at furniture. I have furniture. I'm not going there!" So, once again, I continued on my journey. However, the arrow wouldn't go away! As I passed the furniture store, the arrow in my mind turned into a big "U."

"That's it," I thought. "Okay, okay, okay. I'm turning around and going in." So I did.

I had no idea why I had entered the furniture store. I meandered from one display to the next wondering what in the heck I was doing there. That's when I turned around and got my answer. Patti was there.

Do you have chills right now? I did when this happened. I could not believe it! Patti and I stood in the middle of that store for over an hour. We talked and she vented, all the while I stood amazed at the gift of surrender.

I almost didn't surrender that day. I nearly talked myself out of the messages I received. I'm so glad I didn't. I got to experience firsthand God's limitless abundance and love. I surrendered my head, listened to my heart, and became a messenger of God. What a gift!

I've had a lot of people tell me, "Wow, Terri, I wish I could get guidance like that." You can! I never knew I could either. The reason I've shared all the tools in this book with you is because they are what gave me such clarity. By releasing limiting beliefs that disconnected me from my heart, I have connected to God. It simply takes a commitment to yourself, to love and honor the way you were created, and to trust and surrender to the messages you receive each day.

Liz, the student I mentioned earlier, saw tremendous changes in her life following her graduation from The Enlightened Mom course. She made a commitment to heal and to trust the messages that were revealed to her each day and, as a result, saw miracle after miracle show up in her life.

It was exactly one year after Liz's graduation from The Enlightened Mom course when she shared an inspiring story with some moms and me at a yoga gathering. As we sat around after class, Liz told us about a miraculous experience in one of her recent yoga sessions: she had seen angels come into the room and felt their loving presence. Every one of the moms was in awe of her story. But Liz's message said it best, "Anyone can do this!"

Liz was right. Anyone, including you, can have these kinds of miracles when you make a decision to open up your heart and trust the messages. Abundance is available to everyone. All it takes is a commitment to love and honor the way you were created, making a divine connection to God. And as you open up to this kind of love, and surrender to your heart, you step onto a miraculous adventure, becoming a messenger of God.

I sat with Mackenzie one night when she was little. As she dozed off, I saw a vision. I looked across the room and saw myself riding a sea turtle. I rode on its back as it dove into the depths of the ocean. At the bottom I saw a book. It looked to be very old and weathered, bound in leather. It was beautiful. As I opened the book I was surprised to see the title, "Finding the Love Within." I knew this was a message for me. God was telling me that I had to find love within myself. Later on I looked up what turtle meant. It means "the mother."

Some think taking the time to find the love within is selfish. Mom, it is the greatest act of service you will ever do for the world. By going within and loving and honoring the way God made you, you will create a divine connection and become a light for all those you love. You are not selfish for loving yourself this way. By healing the pain and living from your heart and what you believe, you set an example for others to do the same. As you stand in your truth and love and honor your uniqueness, you will release the anger, judgment, and blame that you've been holding onto for a lifetime. No longer will you feel the need to control everything. No longer will you judge others for being different than you. No longer will you feel judged by the people around you. Just by embracing the way God made you, you become an expression of unconditional love not only for yourself, but also for everyone else. You create a divine connection to God and become a messenger of love. I believe this is what Christ meant when he said that the kingdom of God is within you. This is abundance. Abundance doesn't come from the outside world. It comes when you surrender to your heart and find the love within.

Step into abundance, Mom. Get to know yourself and create a connection to God. Love and honor the pain that you've been holding onto throughout the years and move into compassion and joy. Allow yourself to receive God's miracles. Be a messenger of love. As you do, your light will spread to the world around you. This is the greatest gift you will ever give your family, loved ones and friends. Give the world the gift of you. This is the path of The Enlightened Mom. The world deserves this kind of love. It wants to experience the real you.

~ ~ ~ ~ ~

EPILOGUE

The Next Chapter

"**Mom**, have you talked to Dad lately?" Mackenzie asked me this question over the phone. It was a beautiful day in late February. Kolbi, her friend Riley, plus Riley's grandma, and I were exhausted after a weekend dance competition in New Orleans. We had been gone since Friday and it was now Sunday afternoon as we made our way home. We were about three hours out when Mackenzie called.

"Yes. I talked to him about an hour ago. Why?"

"He was supposed to pick me up thirty minutes ago and he's still not here. Mikey and I are at Jordan's house and her whole family had to leave and couldn't give us a ride home. We're stuck here and I really want to go home."

"Baby, when did you last talk to Dad?" I asked.

"About 30 minutes ago. He said he was on his way, but he's still not here. I've called and called but he's not picking up." Mackenzie explained. "Will you see if you can reach him?"

I figured Mackenzie was simply being impatient, as so many teenagers tend to be, but said I would try to reach Steve. I called and called, but continually failed to connect to him. So I made a decision to call my neighbor, Jen, to see if she or her hubby, Dave, would go and check on Steve. I did and Jen said she would get back to me.

Normally I wouldn't have worried, figuring Steve had gotten sidetracked; however, he had complained all weekend about throwing his neck out of whack after cleaning all of our cars that past Friday. When I talked to Steve over the phone while on our way home, he shared how much pain he had been in during the last 24 hours. He added that the pain had spread and was so intense that he had slept sitting upright in the chair the night before. Steve frequently dealt with neck and back pain. Due to his immense size, he often threw down three or four aspirins to relieve some of it. I knew he had been hurting over the last few days and was concerned that he might have taken too many aspirin and had knocked himself out. That's when I made the decision to call Jen. I never imagined the answer she would give me when she got back to me.

"Terri. He's gone."

"What? What do you mean? Where is he?" My brain wasn't connecting the words Jen was saying.

"Terri, I don't know how to tell you this. He's gone. I'm so sorry. Steve is dead."

"Oh, God! Noooooooooo!" I sobbed into my cell phone. "No!!!!! Not Steve!"

"Daaaddddyyyy!" Kolbi's screams pierced me from the backseat.

I can't begin to explain the fear, the sadness, and the rage we all felt after Steve passed. He was so young. A heart attack took his life that day at the age of 56. My kids lost their daddy and I lost my best friend and husband of almost 17 years. As I write this, the tears begin to flow. Just thinking of my kids and the idea of them losing their daddy still makes me want to protect them from all of life's pain and sorrow. But I know I can't. All I can do is live as an example of surrender and trust.

Surrendering to my heart and trusting that the universe will provide, support and protect us.

Right before Steve left us, I thought I had finished this book. I celebrated the whole month of December and planned on finding a publisher after the holidays. But the book wasn't finished. When Steve passed, my heart said I needed to take the year off. At first I struggled with this. In spite of the fact that Steve left us with a nice life insurance policy, I still had many moments of fear where my head said I must be in survival mode and get working. Several times I thought it was time to pick up this book and move forward with it, but each time I meditated on this, I was told to "sit on it." Luckily, my heart won out, so I did. This time was an exercise in following my heart and standing in my truth in every area of my life. And now, as my heart tells me it's time to finish this book, I am told to share with you some of the gifts of these past several years.

Steve's death was the hardest challenge I've ever faced, and, at the same time, one of the greatest gifts God has ever given me. Because I practice all of the tools in this book, as I sat at Jen and Dave's home the night of Steve's death waiting on the police to finish their investigation in my home, I decided to ask his spirit to speak to me. As I sat on my neighbors' toilet, I got fully grounded in spite of my fear and churning stomach, and imagined Steve before me. I asked, "Why now? Why did you need to leave us now?"

"I finally let go of the controls," is the answer I heard from the voice in my head. There was a peace about me in that moment for I knew this was the truth. Steve had beaten advanced prostate cancer a few years prior to his heart attack, but he lived in fear of it coming back. Thoughts of his cancer haunted him due to intermittent bleeding and pain in his bladder, both a result of radiation damage. I truly believe he willed himself to live. Steve's greatest desire was to see our girls grow up and to make sure we were taken care of. He believed it was his job to provide for all of us. But in those last few months prior to his death, Steve saw me growing deeper in my faith and knowingness that God is the provider, not him. By seeing me stand in this truth and by owning this for himself, I believe Steve was able to release the controls of his life and move to the other side.

When I say that Steve moved to the other side, I'm not kidding. What I know for sure is that he is still watching over us. The day after he passed, I took a walk. I knew I had to stay grounded and centered. I also knew that this was a part of my divine path and that the more I could release resistance and embrace the situation, the easier I would get through this period of grief. As I walked, I once again invited Steve's spirit in. I felt his presence with me so completely. I knew he was walking with me. But as I continued my walk, I realized his spirit wasn't limping. A botched back surgery had left him with a slight limp some years ago, but it was no longer there. When I asked his spirit what the deal was, he said, "There's no pain over here."

I was thrilled to know that Steve's pain was gone. He had suffered for way too long. I was so thankful that he had finally let go.

I continued with my walk and my talk to Steve's spirit. I asked him, "What is the gift I am to learn from your passing? I know there is a gift here and I want to embrace it rather than resist it. I have no intention of looking back 10 years from now, trying to figure it out. I want to walk through this time with as much grace and ease as I can, so please tell me what I am to learn from this situation."

"You're going to become a better business woman, Terri," is one of the things I heard in my head.

Steve's spirit was right. He was an entrepreneur and had his fingers in many financial pots. When he passed, I found myself wading through the rat's nest of all of his investments. Probate was dragging me there. For months, my days were filled with weeding through the quagmire of contracts and talking with men about business deals I really knew very little about. In the beginning I found myself pushing, trying to get it all done, but only found myself butting up against walls. I heard a tape playing over and over in my head, "These men are driving me crazy. All of their egos are trying to control my life! God, why are they doing this to me?"

Luckily, my tools kicked in. Playing the victim was not who I am. I forgot for a moment that I am the creator of my life and, as a spirit, had chosen to have this experience. That was my spiritual agreement with Steve. So I had to change my attitude. I had to ask, "God, what's going on here? I feel as if all these men I'm dealing with are trying to control my life. What is the reflection here?"

The answer I received hit me in the head. "Terri, these men are simply reflecting what you're creating. You're running the male energy of 'doing' and making things happen, rather than allowing life to unfold around you. Let it all go. Slow down and allow God to take over." So I did.

In spite of the rat's nest Steve left, my lawyer told me that this probate ran smoother than most he'd ever experienced. By allowing myself to receive messages on how to deal with each business investment and by following that guidance, I not only walked through the probate with grace, I learned a lot about business and the ins and outs of working with lawyers and contracts. And as a result, I am more comfortable in my skin than I've ever been. And now know that I can follow my heart and still be a good businesswoman.

Miracle upon miracle showed up in my life as I listened for God's messages. Sometimes they came from going within. And other times the world presented me beautiful gifts.

Shortly after Steve passed away, I had lunch with a friend. As I sat there, I felt the need to get my tires fixed. This thought had been running through my head ever since Steve had passed. Prior to his death, he had mentioned that my tires were worn and that they were no longer safe. I had neglected them due to having too much on my plate. But on this day as I sat with my friend, I knew it was time to listen.

I said my good-byes to my friend and got in the car with the intention of heading to the tire store a few blocks down. As I turned on my car, the radio blared, "TIRE SALE…TODAY ONLY!" It just happened to be at the tire store where I was heading.

I breathed a sigh of relief knowing that God was guiding me. I got my tires fixed and not a minute too soon. The gentleman there who helped me said that the tread on two of the tires was completely bare. I had visions of what might have happened if I had not listened to my guidance.

"Now my family is safe," is what I felt as I got in my car and drove away. That feeling quickly disappeared the next day, however, as I drove down the street and suddenly heard a thump, thump, thumping coming from my rear tire. I pulled over into a parking lot only to discover that my brand new tire had a bolt sticking out of it! Oh, my gosh! I could not believe what was happening. I had a moment of darkness, but thankfully, my thoughts shifted and I began to breathe. I knew I needed help.

The parking lot I had pulled into was quiet, so I drove slowly to the one at the next building. Just as I arrived and got out of my car, a man walked out into the parking lot. He asked if everything was okay. I told him my story and the next thing I knew, he and his friend were changing my tire.

I thanked the men and told them that they were my earth angels. They just laughed at me. But as I got into my car, I knew this was the truth. They were messengers of God sent here to help me.

This whole incident was a reflection of a false belief in my mind. I had thought that I could control my world to make it safe for my family. But that belief went away when my tire was blown. What a gift! I heard clearly in my mind that I couldn't control life this way. Life has all kinds of ups and downs. All I can do is travel this journey and trust that God will ALWAYS protect me and provide the help that I need. I just have to be open to receive it!

Who would have ever thought that blowing a tire could be such a wonderful gift? But it was exactly what I needed to experience as I walked through this time of Steve's passing.

One of the most profound miracles that occurred after Steve's death was in April, about six weeks after he left us. I was in my bedroom, playing tug-of-war with my little Maltese, Squirt. I threw her toy down the hall to my bathroom. She went to get it and came back to tug some more. We did this several times. Only the third time into the bathroom, she stopped. Squirt stared into the open space and sat down as if someone were talking to her. She was so still. Her ears were pulled back. I asked her, "What are you doing, you silly girl? Come on."

Slowly, Squirt walked towards me with her ears still back. Something was going on. I wasn't sure in that moment what it was. Squirt sat down in front of me and got very still again. That's when I heard in my head, "Steve is here. He's talking to Squirt."

I wasn't sure what to believe. I was confused as to whether my grief was playing tricks on me, so I blew it off...until the next day. I took Squirt out in the backyard. Once again, she stopped in her tracks and got very still. When I checked in with myself, I knew Steve was trying to connect with me. It became a running joke that week. My late husband was trying to talk to me and he was using my dog to get to me!

A few days later I walked towards my car in the driveway. Squirt followed me. She loves to ride in the car and whenever I take her somewhere, all I have to do is say, "Squirt, do you want to go bye-bye?" That's when she heads straight to my driver's side door and hops around until I let her in the car.

I parked in the driveway that day because we had two classic cars in our garage and there was nowhere for me to park. Those oldies were Steve's babies. What brought him joy, however, only gave me fear when he passed. I had no idea what to do with them. Our plans had been to sell the cars and have our kids' college tuition in hand. My head kept telling me to start pushing to get rid of them. I knew that one of the cars was starting to rust and needed some work. I believed the longer I held onto them, the harder it would be to find someone who wanted the cars. But that day as Squirt and I made our way to my car in the driveway, I got a message that relieved my worries.

Squirt stopped as she ran by the oldies. Instead of running straight to my car as usual, she went dead still, pulling her ears back again. I had never seen her act like this. "What?" I asked. "Steve, are you here? What are you trying to tell me?"

That's when I heard in my head so clearly, "Don't worry about the cars, Terri. They're going to sell in the next six months." I was thrilled! But I have to admit, I still wasn't sure I could believe what I was hearing. I made a decision to let it go and see what would happen. All I could talk about that evening was how Steve was haunting me, giving me messages through our little dog, Squirt.

The next morning, I went to the store for a quick errand. As I stood at the cashier and pulled out my wallet, something shiny and gold dropped into my purse. I knew it wasn't a coin. I looked down and realized that Squirt's dog tag was sitting there. This wasn't just a dog tag. This was a tag that I had bought prior to moving to Florida. I had purchased the tag so that when we arrived here, I could put it on Squirt. However, I thought the tag never made it to Florida. For days I looked for it. I knew I had put it in the change portion of my wallet. But when I searched for it, it was gone. I opened every pocket and fold of my wallet, and I looked through my purse and never had any luck. So I finally gave up and bought a new tag for Squirt. For almost two years I carried that same wallet and often that purse. I cleaned out both fairly regularly and never once did I see that tag. So you can only imagine my shock that day as I stood at the cashier, looking at this shiny gold dog tag…in the shape of a heart.

My face flushed and the cashier asked me what was going on. I said, "Today would have been my 17th wedding anniversary. My husband passed away almost two months ago. He's been sending me messages all week through my little dog, Squirt. And look at this dog tag. It's in the shape of a heart. It's been lost for almost two years and now it drops into my purse. I know my husband just sent this to me. He's telling me he loves me."

With tears in both of our eyes, I thanked the cashier and said good-bye. I sat stunned in my car for a while, staring at the golden heart in my hand. I knew that it was a symbol of Steve's love for me. Once again, he was using my dog to get to me. That's when I felt his presence. "I love you, Terri," he said. "Happy Anniversary."

God's messages to help us heal and grow come in so many ways. I would never have believed years ago that my little dog Squirt could be a messenger of God. And how about that dog tag showing up after being gone for two years? God is truly limitless. And that message I heard in the garage that day about giving the cars six months to sell? Well, that's exactly what happened! Almost six months to the day of receiving the message, I sold both cars. Two different men from two states contacted me and said they were interested in Steve's oldies. These were acquaintances of Steve's. But I didn't call them, nor did I run an ad. They simply showed up right when I was ready to receive them.

Being open and willing to receive is what allowed me to experience so many miracles after Steve's passing. God IS limitless. As you trust and listen to the messages around you and in your heart, God guides you through life's darkness.

There was one more message I received from Steve during our walk together the day following his death. After he told me that I was going to be a better businesswoman, he said, "You're going to surround yourself with women." I had no idea what that meant until I got to know my new husband, Charlie Britt.

Charlie and I were acquaintances through our daughters' high school dance team. We didn't know each other well. All I knew about him was that he was a nice man, raising his daughter as a single father. His wife of 17 years had committed suicide five years prior. When Steve passed, Charlie extended his hand as a support and a friend. As we spent more and more time together, however, I saw the amazing gift God had sent.

I'll never forget the day Charlie and I drove up to his farm in Alabama. As we shared our philosophies about life, he began to talk about childhood programming and how it affects people's relationships. All I could think was, "Has this man been taking my classes?" Needless to say, I was intrigued.

What looked to be a friendship with a little intrigue rapidly grew into a realization that this man was my soulmate. Charlie has a heart as big as the universe, makes me laugh until I cry, and sends tingles down my spine when he touches and kisses me.

When I say our relationship moved "rapidly," I mean like the speed of light. We began dating three months after Steve's death.

You may be wondering, "How in the world could Terri move so quickly? What about her kids? Didn't she feel the need to grieve? What about giving herself some time?" All of these questions are valid and, let me tell you, I asked them myself. However, the answer I continually received was, "Follow your heart, Terri. Let God be the guide."

What I knew for sure is that I grieved for almost three years prior to Steve's death. When we found out that he had advanced prostate cancer, our whole family grieved, especially me. Our relationship changed as a result of his sickness. We became better friends and companions, but due to his intense radiation damage, I had settled into acceptance that many aspects of our relationship would never be the same, especially our physical relationship. The parts that were missing, and what I soon realized had been all along, were passion and romance.

One of the ways I spent my time after Steve left us was to read. But instead of focusing on heavy messages, I gave myself permission to enjoy romance novels. With each story I read, I got clear about what I wanted in my next relationship. I wanted everything Steve and I had together, plus a lot more passion and romance. I remember claiming this for myself one evening while taking a walk in my neighborhood. This was still at the stage when Charlie and I were getting to know each other. He drove by and as we talked on the side of the road, I asked him to drive me home. Once in my driveway we talked some more. That's when Charlie asked, "Steve was a lot older than you. Was he like a father to you?"

"No," was my reply. "He was older than me but we met equally on an emotional level. I do realize now that when I married him I was in survival mode. My next marriage will be about passion."

I had finally spoken it out loud! I already had passion in my life with my work and the way I lived my life. Now I was claiming a passionate romantic relationship as well.

A few weeks later, Charlie drove up on his Harley Davidson motorcycle. He looked so darn cute! He bought his Harley right before Steve died. He told me that he almost bought a single seat for the bike, but had a thought that maybe, just maybe, someone would show up in his life that would like to ride on the back. He took a stand for what he really wanted when he bought a bike with a double seat. He said "YES!" to himself and the universe sent him me.

Not only did God answer Charlie's request for a passionate relationship, but for a dynamic, intimate one as well. Charlie later shared with me that he had denied himself in his marriage to the point of giving himself up, believing it was the loving thing to do. He said he had lived from the false belief that said, "You must deny yourself to make others happy." But Charlie now knew this was a lie. In spite of all of his self-denial, his wife committed suicide. I'll never forget the night he told me, "I can only be myself in this relationship, Terri." Yeah! I thanked God for this wonderful gift. Not only is the passion and romance in our relationship amazing, but the freedom we have to be ourselves and the intimacy we share on all levels is fantastic!

People constantly ask me how I brought such a wonderful man into my life so quickly after Steve's death. My answer is: The Law of Attraction. I've spent years healing negative beliefs, giving myself permission to honor and love the way I was created. When I finally gave myself permission to have passion in all areas of my life, Charlie arrived.

It has been quite a ride with my new hubby. I have to admit there were days early on where I wanted to run for the hills. My head had me truly scared. I was afraid of being a new stepmom to Charlie's daughter, Haylee. I was terrified of blending a family. And most of all, I was concerned for my girls. I didn't want them to hurt anymore. Their hearts had already been broken with the loss of their daddy. But no matter what I did to pull away, my heart always guided me back to Charlie.

For years I've seen parents think they are protecting their kids by not remarrying after a divorce or a death. That so-called protection is called codependence. It sends a message to that child that the only way you will ever be happy is when others fill you up. Well, we know that's a lie! That's what I had to remind myself every time I considered pulling away from this new relationship. I didn't want to be an example of codependence. I knew the most loving act would be for me to follow my heart, instead of my head, so that my kids could grow up to live abundantly as well. I know true protection is when we listen to God's guidance in our hearts. By standing in this truth, I made a choice to marry Charlie. We got married 17 months after Steve passed.

It wasn't an easy ride to the wedding altar. Our girls all had moments of anger. In the beginning of my relationship with Charlie, Haylee opened up to me beautifully. But as soon as she saw an article about blending families on Charlie's computer, she shut down. She wouldn't speak to me. Even when I walked right next to her, she would turn and avoid me.

The wise woman inside of me knew Haylee was hurting. She wasn't mad at me; she was scared of losing her daddy and scared of facing the changes that were about to take place in her life. I knew this was the truth. On the other hand, the little girl inside of me was terrified. Old feelings of blame and punishment surfaced. Little Terri wanted to believe that she had done something wrong to Haylee and felt that's why Haylee shut me out. Little Terri's fears said, "This is too hard. Run for the hills!" Thankfully, my tools kicked in once again and I thanked God for the gift.

As I went within to talk with little Terri, I realized that Haylee's actions were a reflection of something much deeper: I had to truly forgive myself for the mistakes I had made with my stepson, A.J., early in my marriage to Steve. At that time, there was no forgiveness in my heart and I certainly didn't embrace mistakes as gifts. Instead, I punished myself. Little Terri did not want to go through that again and that's why I feared being a stepmom again. But by walking this path of The Enlightened Mom, I know that everything, mistakes and all, are wonderful gifts to connect to our hearts. And in that knowingness, I released the pain of the past and moved lovingly into the present.

I finally cleared the chaos in my mind about A.J. and opened my heart to being a stepmom again. As soon as I did, Haylee shifted.

The hardest part of following my heart and marrying Charlie was the fear of hurting my girls. I knew their hearts were still in horrible pain due to their dad's passing. Of course I didn't want to add to their pain. I also knew that it could take years for them to heal. That's when I decided it was time to do some deep introspection.

My greatest fear was revealed: I was afraid of losing my girls' love. Little Terri still had a lingering belief that said, "If you follow your heart, you will be abandoned and rejected."

Little Terri didn't want to be alone. So I made a decision to allow my girls' anger to be an opportunity to heal, and to release shame and guilt for following my heart. I made a choice to see every difficult situation with them as an opportunity to love, nurture and accept the child within me, creating a greater connection to God.

Kolbi's anger erupted first. But she loved Charlie and was developing a playful, dynamic friendship with him. I knew that her pain wasn't so much about my relationship with Charlie, but about losing her daddy and about the changes in her life that were happening. As soon as Kolbi realized this, she shifted. She became more supportive in spite of her fears and pain.

Mackenzie was my greatest test. She had been what seemed to be completely supportive of my new relationship with Charlie from the beginning. When Kolbi and Haylee shut down and expressed their anger, Mackenzie would always say, "Mom, they have a right to be mad. But you have to follow your heart. We want you to be happy." At times, Kolbi shared this sentiment, but it was Mackenzie who voiced it the loudest. I was so proud of both of them and knew that by living from my heart all of these years and encouraging them to do the same, they knew this as truth, too. However, as we grew closer to the wedding, Mackenzie's anger was revealed and she shut down.

With each day that passed, I prayed for healing. I wanted my wedding to be a happy, joyous occasion for everyone, and for my family to be whole. But what I soon realized was that I could not make this happen. I had to surrender it to God. I had to get out of the way and send love to the pain. Instead of being in guilt and trying to make things okay for Mackenzie, I had to move forward in my life and know that it was God who had guided me here, and it was God who could take the pain away.

Amazingly, the night of our wedding reception, Mackenzie shifted. She had played her part perfectly and now was done. Her spirit helped me get completely grounded in my truth, honoring the messages that God gave me. And in my surrender, a miracle occurred. Mackenzie not only shifted from pain to love, I did, too.

Following my heart to that wedding altar was one of the hardest things I've ever done. I knew my girls were hurting. I knew that they might never forgive me. But I also knew that it was God who had guided me and that I had to listen. Thankfully, I communicated this to my girls throughout the whole process. Every time one of them got mad and vented about their pain, my response was, "I am so sorry you're hurting. The last thing I would ever do is intentionally hurt you. However, I have to put God first in my life. And God tells me that this relationship with Charlie is the loving thing to do."

I'm so glad I communicated my heart with Mackenzie and Kolbi! My girls and I have never been closer. The love, respect and communication between us is greater than we have ever known.

Charlie and I blended our families and have created a warm and loving home. It's not perfect by any means. We have our ups and downs like any family. We have three teenage girls, two female dogs, Erly (the lady I mentioned earlier who lives with us), and Charlie and me. I believe that's what Steve's spirit meant when he said I was going to surround myself with women. He was right. What a blessing! There are so many gifts with these teenage girls. Charlie and I both know that whatever comes our way, it's a chance for healing our hearts. And as we do, we deepen our connections to God, becoming examples of kindness, compassion, forgiveness and love.

That's the gift of your children. That's the blessing of every relationship and every situation. No matter what is happening in your life, whether good or bad, it is an opportunity to create a connection to God. That's why you're here. To remember who you are. You are a child of God. And in this truth, you have the ability to create a life of peace, abundance and love as you walk the path of The Enlightened Mom.

~ ~ ~ ~ ~

ACKNOWLEDGMENTS

I am in deep gratitude for this journey that I have taken, and for the family and friends who have played their parts to support me with my life's mission. This book wouldn't exist if it were not for them.

To my daughters Mackenzie and Kolbi Amos, you two have been the most precious gifts a mom could ask for. You are not only my children, but are also my teachers and friends.

Mackenzie, thank you for being my firstborn. From the moment I laid eyes on you, my life changed for the better. You opened my heart to "mom love," a special and unique bond that only a mother can share with her kids. Thank you for being you and for allowing me to share our story. I love you!

Kolbi, I never thought I could love another child as much after having your big sister. But I knew I was wrong when you came into the world. Through you, I learned how big my heart could grow. You are truly a blessing and a gift! Thank you for being all that you are. I love you, Bears!

To my mom Lee Utley, thank you for being my mom. I value your constant support, friendship, and unconditional love. Thank you for allowing me to share our story. You are a woman of courage and I am eternally grateful!

I am a very blessed girl when it comes to the men in my life. To my dad Keith Utley, you set the tone of what a woman deserves when it comes to having a loving husband. Thanks Daddy! I miss you!

To the father of my children and my late husband Steve Amos, thank you for allowing me time to expand and grow throughout our 19 years together. Your love and support touched me at the core.

I never knew that love could get any better until my new hubby, Charlie Britt, came into my life. After Steve passed, I asked for unconditional love, passion, romance, support, compassion, authenticity, friendship and playfulness, and then Charlie arrived. Thank you Charlie for being you and for being my partner in this new chapter of my life. Your constant love and support are valued gifts, allowing me to bring this book out into the world. I love you!

I am very blessed to have two wonderful stepchildren. To my stepson A.J. Amos, you were the original catalyst for me to change my life. I only hope you know how much I appreciate you and love you. Thank you for being you and for allowing me to share our story.

To my new stepdaughter Haylee Britt, thank you for working so diligently to keep your heart open and allowing me into your life. I love you and will be forever grateful.

I have three very dear friends who are like sisters to me. Not only have they supported me throughout the years, they've also allowed me to include pieces of their lives in this book. Thank you Barb Watts, Linda Cote, and Patty Kamson. I love you all and feel so very blessed to call you my friends.

And to Erly Cruz, thank you for all that you do and for being another source of love for our family.

Thank you to my extended family and friends who graciously said yes when I asked to write about them. Reneé Ball, Robin Dyer, and

Patti Brown-Troop…thank you. And thank you to those whose names I did not mention.

To Debbie Brill, thank you for being a friend and for allowing me to share your story at the beginning of this book. Your courage to face life's daily challenges continues to inspire me.

Many years ago I had a calling to share the tools that healed my life and thought the way to do that was to write a book and THEN go out and teach the message. My mind said, "Write. Then teach." However, my heart had another idea. It said, "Flip the switch on that mindset, Terri. Get out there now!" Thankfully, I listened to my heart and some amazing women showed up for my classes. Their stories are many of the ones you've read in this book. Even though their names have been changed, their stories are real. To all of you, you know who you are, thank you from the bottom of my heart for allowing me to tell your stories.

I have been blessed with some wonderful clients over the years. Their stories are here, too. Before I knew I had a calling to share this message with moms, these men and women felt guided to work with me. Thanks to all of you for listening to your hearts, and thank you for allowing me to share your stories! You have been such a gift in helping me find my life's calling.

When I made a decision to step out into the world with this message, I knew I needed to surround myself with love and support. I set an intention and, almost immediately, my Enlightened Mom team showed up! Mary Kay Morgan of www.AffiliateWealthPartners.com, you're not only a creative genius and a valued partner, but you're also a great friend. Thank you!

Jennifer Tingle, what would I do without you? You are my right arm and such a gift. It doesn't matter what I ask you to do, I can always count on you. Thank you for being you!

John Nicoll of www.InnerLightDesign.com, thank you for this beautiful front book cover and for creating www.TheEnlightenedMom. com. You captured my heart's desire and made it a reality.

Debbie Ally, thank you for always being there to lend your hand and support our team!

I am in deep gratitude to Marci Shimoff. Marci, you are such an inspiration! Thank you for writing the Foreword to this book, and thank you for your wonderful support and guidance.

To Cindy Tyler of www.Vervante.com, thank you for walking me through this publishing process and making this book a reality.

And to Blaine Lee, thank you so much for doing such a wonderful job designing the interior of this book and the back cover. I am grateful and thrilled for your beautiful creation!

I am truly blessed to have such wonderful people in my life, and I know none of this would exist if it weren't for the all-loving presence of God. Thank you, thank you, thank you, God, from the bottom of my heart!

BIBLIOGRAPHY

Books

Andrews, Ted. *Animal Speak: The Spiritual & Magical Powers of Creatures Great and Small*. Woodbury, MN. Llewellyn Worldwide, Ltd. 2002.

Beattie, Melody. *Beyond Co-dependency: And Getting Better All the Time*. Center City, MN. Hazelden Foundation. 1989.

Capacchione, Ph.D., Lucia. *The Power of Your Other Hand: A Course in Channeling the Inner Wisdom of the Right Brain*. Franklin Lakes, NJ. The Career Press, Inc. 2001.

Ferrini, Paul. *Love Without Conditions: Reflections of the Christ Mind*. Greenfield, MA. Heartways Press, Inc. 1995. www.paulferrini.com

Gawain, Shakti. *Creating True Prosperity*. Novato, CA. New World Library. 1997

Gray, Ph.D, John. *Children Are From Heaven: Positive Parenting Skills for Raising Cooperative, Confident, and Compassionate Children*. NY, NY. Harper Collins Publishers, Inc. Mars Productions, Inc. 1999.

Harris, Bill. *Thresholds of the Mind: Your Personal Roadmap to Success, Happiness and Contentment*. Centerpointe Research Institute: www.centerpointe.com. 2002.

Hawkins, Dr. David R. *Power vs. Force: The Hidden Determinants of Human Behavior*. Carlsbad, CA. Hay House Inc. 2002.

Hay, Louise L. *You Can Heal Your Life (Gift Edition)*. Carlsbad, CA. Hay House, Inc. 1999.

Hickey, Isabel M. *Astrology: A Cosmic Science*. U.S. CRCS Publications. 1992.

Hicks, Esther and Jerry. *Ask and It Is Given: Learning to Manifest Your Desires (The Teachings of Abraham)*. Carlsbad, CA. Hay House Inc. 2004.

Joseph, Arthur Samuel. *Vocal Power: Harnessing the Power Within*. San Diego, CA. Jodere Group, Inc. 2001.

Medhus, Dr. Elisa. *Raising Everyday Heroes*: *Parenting Children to be Self-Reliant*. Hillsboro, OR. Beyond Words Publishing, Inc. 2004.

Millman, Dan. *The Life You Were Born to Live: A Guide to Finding Your Life Purpose*. Novato, CA. An H.J. Kramer Book published in a joint venture with New World Library. 1993.

Orloff, Dr. Judith. *Positive Energy: 10 Extraordinary Prescriptions for Transforming Fatigue, Stress, and Fear into Vibrance, Strength & Love*. NY, NY. Three Rivers Press, an imprint of The Crown Publishing Group, a division of Random House. 2004.

Osteen, Joel. *Your Best Life Now: 7 Steps to Living at Your Full Potential*. NY, NY. Faith Words. Hachette Book Group USA. 2004.

Paul, Margaret and Erika J. Chopich. *Healing Your Aloneness: Finding Love and Wholeness Through Your Inner Child*. NY, NY. Harper Collins Publishers, Inc. 1990.

Rain, Mary Summer and Alex Greystone. *Mary Summer Rain's Guide to Dream Symbols*. Charlottesville, VA. Hampton Roads Publishing Company, Inc. 1996.

Richardson, Cheryl. *Take Time for Your Life: A Personal Coach's 7 Step Program for Creating the Life You Want*. NY, NY. Broadway Books, a division of Random House. 1999.

Taylor, Steven Lane. *Row, Row, Row Your Boat: A Guide for Living Life in the Divine Flow*. Dallas, TX. Brown Books Publishing Group. 2004.

Miscellaneous

Ashley-Pitt, Alan. *On Creativity*. n.p.

Chopra, Dr. Deepak. *The Way of the Wizard: A Guide to Re-awakening the Magic in Everyday Life*. VHS. 1996.

Harman, Jeff. Astrological Consultant. www.JeffHarman.com.

Kamson, Patty. Intuitive Astrologer and Spiritual Consultant. www.PattyKamson.com.

"enlightened." WordNet 3.0, Farlex clipart collection. 2003-2008. Princeton University, Clipart.com, Farlex Inc. 13 Jan. 2011 http://www.thefreedictionary.com/enlightened

"unconditional love." *Dictionary.com's 21st Century Lexicon*. Dictionary.com, LLC. Retrieved from Dictionary.com website: http://dictionary.reference.com/browse/unconditional love. 2003-2010.

Virtue, Doreen. *Healing with the Angels Oracle Cards (Large Card Decks)*. Carlsbad, CA. Hay House Inc. 1999.

ABOUT THE AUTHOR

Terri Amos-Britt is on a mission to unite moms from around the globe to take a stand for healing our world. She is the founder of www.TheEnlightenedMom.com, a community created to celebrate and support moms, and is the co-founder of its parent company, Enlightened Family Institute, Inc., with her husband Charlie Britt. Terri is the author of *Message Sent: Retrieving the Gift of Love* and co-author of *A Juicy, Joyful Life* and *Wake Up Women.*

As a spiritual coach and motivational speaker, Terri shares her experiences as a wife, mom, stepmom, widow, former Miss USA and television host, inspiring moms to create lives of peace, abundance and joy, setting the tone for their families to heal. When mom heals, the family heals…the world heals!

To learn more about Terri's work or to contact her for speaking engagements, go to www.TheEnlightenedMom.com.

Be a Part of
The Enlightened Mom
Movement!

Mom, YOU have the power to create change not only in your life and home, but also in the world. As we mommas stand together for healing anger, frustration and blame within ourselves, and move into peace, acceptance and love, we set the tone for the world to heal. Yes, together, we have that kind of power!

Please join us in The Enlightened Mom community today and be a part of this global movement.

When mom heals, the family heals... the world heals!

www.TheEnlightenedMom.com
Moms uniting to heal the world!